Home Automation with Raspberry, Google & Python

(English Edition)

–

TABLE OF CONTENTS

Home Automation with Raspberry, Google & Python

⊝⊝⊝

Dedicated to my wife

to you, gorgeous,
thank you for your love,
thank you for your patience,
thank you for your company,
thank you for your collaboration,
please never change.

–

1.-INTRODUCTION

With the massive incorporation, in the last decades, of the great majority of the components of the family unit, to the work life and the culture of the leisure, the houses have undergone a desertification process that extends to the majority of the working day and which generates the need for automatic multiple control and more and more parameters that affect the comfort of the home.

Among the many activities of home comfort control, the following stand out: the switch on, off and control of the operating temperature of the heater, the actual temperature indicated on the thermostat, the control of the heating or air machine itself conditioning, energy saving monitoring, smoke alarm, fire, flood, presence detection, intrusion alarms, opening windows and doors, garage gate status, doorbell status, connectivity status of the home, availability of power supply, the switching on and off of the lights and other home automation devices, the movement of blinds, opening and closing of water or gas valves, the activation of various scenes, activation or deactivation in a "holidays mode", etc.

On the other hand, in the same last decades, the development of consumer electronics systems, many of them associated with the home, the ease in access to new technologies by all members of the same (mobile, tablets, computers, etc.), the proliferation of home automation devices (sensors, actuators, applications, integrators, voice assistants, etc.), cost reduction of such systems, the democratisation in the use of Artificial Intelligence (software and devices specific, personal assistants, etc.), the great ease of access to the information provided by the Internet (search engines, training content, free dissemination of information, explanatory videos, manuals, discussion forums, download of information by manufacturers and users, tutorials, etc.), action integration software, etc., has been drastically promoted.

With all this, the emergence of electronic and computer systems has been enhanced, at a very low cost or even free of charge, associated with the needs of digitalisation of activities in homes and which, in most cases, aim to facilitate the lives of users just at that time in the absence of housing, automating some tasks (heating control, blind movement, alarms control, reporting, etc.) and also when any or all family members are present in the home (bidirectional voice control from the use of home multimedia, TV, lighting, blinds, alarms, thermostat control, creation and application of scenes, guard dog simulator, etc.).

In this book, in addition to the implementation of new systems, the update of the home automation systems of the 90s, based on individual alarms, decentralised, supported on multiple incompatible platforms, with complex software, unfriendly, without access from the exterior of the house, without close support and with very little configuration capacity, to a 21st Century system, which integrates these functionalities in the use of current communication, also adding integration with personal communication systems (e-mail, messaging, social networks, etc.), based on multiple devices (mobiles, tablets, laptops, etc.) and interacting bidirectionally with the voice of household components, using Artificial Intelligence devices (personal assistants, specific devices, etc.).

In this approach the use of micro-electronic and computer systems of easy availability, simple and at a very affordable price plays a fundamental role, which have allowed us to act on one side of the interface with the systems of the last decades and on the other side, bring the state of the home to the user in the distance, knowing and being able to act with the old alarms and new ones arising from the new environment, making the relationship with home technology much easier, fun and above all really an useful task.

In this sense, the development of the project described in this book is concrete for the home in question, but its components: sensors, actuators, control hardware, display hardware, software, assistants with Artificial Intelligence, home automation structure, decision making, project organisation, information structure, home automation activities, interfaces, algorithms, configurations, training applications, information applications, etc., are common, extrapolables and useful for other environments, other homes and especially other home automation enthusiasts who wish to implement similar solutions to those proposed here or simply want to enter to this exciting world of modern digital home automation. A scaling of minimum solutions that could be implemented using the complete project described in this book is proposed below.

Specifically, the system is based on an analog-digital interface between the old alarms (water, smoke, gas sensors, etc.), the new alarms (Internet connectivity, power supply, garage gate status, doorbell status of the main door, etc.), actuators that carry out the appropriate procedures (intelligent thermostats with proximity detection of users to their home, water and gas shut-off and opening valves, interface with **KNX*** lights and window blinds, actuators on traditional systems with infrared controls such as TV, audio system, decoder or access to **Netflix***, etc.), a friendly, simple, cheap, universal and fun computer system **(Raspberry***), a modern, continuous programming language growth, multi platform, with free support on the web, with millions of users, with all kinds of information (**Python***) and a modern Artificial Intelligence device, easy to use, cheap, fun and valid p For the whole family (**Google Home*** or **Alexa***).

14

Finally, in this second edition, new graphics, variable calculations, hardware schemas, software and functional blocks, improvements in sensors, **Python*** scripts, proposals for minimal and solutions and escalations, etc. have been added.

For the ebook edition:

<u>Other titles</u>:   Author's library.
<u>Blog</u>:   Author's blog.
<u>Profile</u>:   Author's profile

⊖⊖⊖

2.-COPYRIGHT

The author of this book is Gregorio Chenlo Romero, who reserves the rights granted by Law in each region where this book is published.

This book, in its 2nd and English edition, was published in January of 2020 and the copyrights that the Spanish Law grants it from the moment of its publication apply. All rights reserved. The total or partial reproduction of this work is not allowed.

With the symbol (*) next to each product, logo, idea, etc., it wants to indicate respect for the brands, owners and suppliers of hardware, software, etc., described here, so it could be recognised that all of them are possibly registered trademarks and possibly have the rights that the law can grant them.

The author is not an expert on this subject and doesn't have or doesn't know if any of them are subject to any type of copyright, which prevents him from using them as a reference in this book. All of them are extracted from the **Google Browser***, so it is understood that their use is public, at least as a reference, in works similar to this one.

On the other hand, it is affirmed that the system detailed here is used only for the particular environment of the home, without any commercial claim, without any guarantee and declining all the responsibility that the readers, other people, third parties, companies, etc., could perform on their own by using the information described here.

Although everything described in this book has been implemented and tested, any responsibility for the incorrect operation or not exactly identical to that indicated by the various components, both hardware and software, is also declined.

Finally, indicate that the various public sources used, web, etc. are attached, reaffirming the rights that correspond to them and declining any responsibility, guarantee, etc., consequence of the variation or disappearance of these sources of information.

3.-GENERAL DESCRIPTION

The general structure of the home automation project described in this book is extremely simple and only consists of three basic pillars:

- Hardware.
- Software.
- Automatic actions.

This three pillars add value to the system, downloading the user of repetitive tasks that the system can perform itself in the absence or presence of the user at home.

Both the hardware and software described here correspond to modern solutions, documented on the web, easy to get, at reduced prices and easy to implement, following this or other guides and aimed at users with basic knowledge of analog electronics, digital electronics and **Python*** programming.

*Hardware Elements

1. A series of **sensors** that detect various alarms (power failure, Internet connectivity failure, gas leak, fire, smoke, flood, air toxicity, garage gate status, light switches, control buttons, presence sensors, twilight sensor, LCD control centre, etc.) and variables to be treated (humidity, temperature, opening and closing, etc.).

2. A series of **actuators** that operate according to the state of the sensors and the variables (switches, electro valves of water or gas, window blinds, lighting, infrared emitter, etc.).

3. A **centralised system** in a control hardware, based on **Raspberry* Pi 3 B+,** hereinafter **Raspberry*_home automation.**

4. A n **access, visualisation,** entertainment and control system with touch screen, based on another **Raspberry* Pi 3 B+,** hereinafter **Raspberry*_ screen.** This second **Raspberry*** is not essential.

5. A home **connectivity structure** that allows linking and supporting all the previous elements (Fiber Optic, Main Router, Bridges, interfaces, LAN, WIFI, etc.). The Fiber Optic is not essential and can be replaced by another type of connectivity: **DSL*,** cable, **3G/4G*,** etc. but it is the better solution.

6. A n **Artificial Intelligence system,** that allows the user to interact in a friendly and fun bidirectionally way with the system, adding value to the project, **Google Home*** (**Alexa***** is also valid).

This system is not essential but it is highly recommended.

7. A customised **electronic interface,** which allows the current system described previously to be linked to the old home automation system, based on a **KNX*** bus, with decentralised and poorly configurable devices.

8. A very simple system **power supply** with several voltages: **+3.3v** and **+5v.**

9. An external **"watchdog"** type circuit that resets and restarts the **Raspberry*_home automation** if it exits the program, due to some action not contemplated, an unexpected error in the system, etc.

10. An **UPS** (the **CoolBox*** **SCUDO-600B**) has been used to guarantee the electrical supply to the system (**Raspberry*_home automation,** main Router, Bridge, etc.), for enough time to send the power failure alarm and make a security copy of important files.

11. An additional **screen,** in this case an old tablet (**ZTE***), that allows to easily act with the system event viewer. This item is expendable.

*Software Elements

1. A custom control software, **p_global.py**, developed in a friendly programming language, **Python*** and supported by a simple and easy operating system, **Raspbian***. This language and operating system is used in both **Raspberry***.

2. Other additional **software packages** that improve the interface of **p_global.py** with the user (**Colorama***, **Tkinter***, **Apache***, **Samba***, **LXTerminal***, **NO-IP DUC***, etc.).

3. A totally free action **integrator** (**IFTTT***), which facilitates the interaction between sensors, actuators, variables and **p_global.py**, through very simple rules to create and maintain, of the type **"if this then that"**, easy to implement in a simple web or APP environments and with extensive documentation and examples on the web.

4. A **personal messaging** product with the system, very simple and free (**Telegram***), based on a **BOT*** written in **Python*** too, that runs on the **Raspberry***_**home automation**.

5. A **tele-system management software**, also free (**VNC***), which allows remote access to the **Raspbian*** operating system of both **Raspberry***.

6. Other **software and APP**, that help the configuration of the whole system (**iCircuit***, **Pycharm***, **VirtualBox***, **IPScanner***, **Eagle***, **Etcher***, **Home***, **Kasa***, **EdiLife***, **Tadoº***, **Speedtest***, **Ihc***, etc.).

*Automatic Actions

It has already described the hardware and software necessary for the system to function properly, but something really important and that, in my opinion, provides the greatest added value to the project, is to provide it with certain intelligence and autonomy, to make decisions and actions according to the status of variables, sensors, actuators, time, date, etc. and that allows the user to download repetitive tasks, security actions, absent actions, holiday tasks, scenario management, etc.

Let's see some examples:

Situation (if...)	Action (then...)
1.Real temperature > 26°C (78,8°F)	Closes window blinds of the living room to 50%
2.Actual temperature: 20-23°C (68-73,4°F)	Opens living room window blinds
3.It is day: (11:00-21:00/22:00)	Opens living room and bedrooms window blinds. Turns off ambient light in the living room and bedrooms lights
4.It is night: (21:00/22:00-11:00)	Closes window blinds of the house (winter/summer)
5.Power supply returns	Turns off lights if supply restoration turned them on
6.Close garage gate	Turns off garage and laundry lights
7.Turn on sofa light	Turns off movie status and room ambient light

Situation (if...)	Action (then...)
8. Close/open living room windows blinds	Disables movie status
9. "Holidays mode" is on	Turns off ambient lights, TV, decoder, set thermostat to absence, turns off the heater, closes the gas & water valves, turns off the screen
10. "Holidays mode" is off	Turns on the control screen, if it is daylight, sets the thermostat in automatic mode, opens the gas & water valves
11. Turn off the lights	Turns off all lights, ambient & other home automation lights, except hall.
12. Active movie status	*If it is night: turns off living room lights, turns on ambient light, TV & decoder. *If it is day: in addition to night: closes the window blinds of the room
13. Open all or living room window blinds	Turns off living room lights and ambient lamp
14. Close water/gas valves	Turns off the heater, set the thermostat on absent mode
15. Gas/smoke alarm	Closes the gas valve, turns off the TV & sets the thermostat in absent mode
16. Any alarm	An e-mail is sent to each defined user, coloured lamp is lit en red until the end of the alarm & a

Situation (if...)	Action (then...)
	warning is issued by **Google Home***
17.Open water/gas valves	Sets **Tadoº*** in auto mode
18.Flood alarm	Closes the water valve, turns off the TV

As seen in the previous examples, the automatic actions can be infinite and can be simple or as complex as desired.

When one of these automatic actions is activated, **Google Home*** announces a brief message on its speaker, indicating the end of such automatic action.

In this way, the user has an adequate visual and auditory feedback of the execution of the direct commands or of the automatic actions that the system is executing.

The volume of the message (do not disturb), is automatically adapted according to the schedule defined in the **APP Home***. This option is also used to verbally check the status of certain system states.

These functions could be deactivated automatically when the house is empty, using the "away" and "home" geolocation functions of the **Tadoº*** thermostat and that we will see later.

To complement the previous option, the feedback with the user has been implemented with a coloured LED lamp configurable from an **RM mini Broadlink*** interface, so that the user has additional information, for example: when the garage gate is opening or closing, coloured LED lights in red, when the daily activity reporting is sent by e-mail, lamp turns on briefly in green, when window blinds are automatically lowered or raised, etc.

Below are the most important parts of each of the components of the project and sure can help other users, so the title of this book (**Raspberry***, **Google*** **and Python***), both to develop similar solutions or facilitate their ideas to improve, expand or propose other solutions, etc.

Finally, this book also describes how to interact with an existing **KNX*** home automation installation, however this functionality is not essential for the heart of the project.

For any query it can uses the author's blog:

gregochenlo.blogspot.com

Which includes operating diagrams, circuits, comments, recommendations, explanations, etc. and it can also makes any kind of queries

⊖⊖⊖

4.-SENSORS

The are many sensors on the market that could be used for this or other similar projects. The choice of sensors used is a personal matter and will depend on the objectives of each project

Here, the sensors described in detail below have been used for several reasons: either because they are already integrated into the current project housing, or because they are very easy to obtain in the market and add, either because of their economic facilities of acquisition, because they have been prescribed by other home automation enthusiasts, there's extensive information about them on the web, they're tested and they work reliably, because they are easily manageable from the **Raspberry*_home automation**, because the corresponding **Python*** modules exist, etc.

To each description is added the part of the global home automation circuit (which is included at the end of this book) in which the device in question is included.

Temperature and Humidity Sensor: DHT22

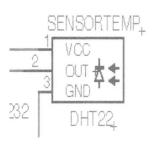

Temperature and humidity sensor is located, in this project, next to a **Western Digital NAS***, to ensure its correct environment but it could control another device (kitchen, laundry, bedrooms, living room, etc. but always indoor places).

In this sense, in the home automation program, adequate temperature and adequate humidity limits have been established that, if exceeded, generate the corresponding actions, alarms by e-mail and bidirectional voice on **Google Home***.

This sensor could be located anywhere else to monitor, for example, the temperature and humidity of a room, the garage, the laundry area, the heater or water storage area, operation of dehumidifiers, etc. (In this case we must take into account the distance between this sensor and the **Raspberry***_home automation that controls it, with a maximum of 30 meters or 98 feet).

Air Quality Alarm: MQ135

Electrochemical sensor that measures air quality by varying its internal resistance depending on the concentration of the gas to which it is exposed.

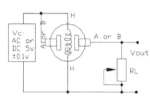

It is located in the garage of the house and detects excessive concentrations of harmful gases (Co2, Nh3, Nox, etc.), produced by the accumulation of vehicle exhaust gases in a closed environment such as a garage.

This sensor has a potentiometer that allows to regulate its sensitivity, avoiding false alarms.

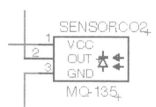

We will see later the interface it needs to connect to the **Raspberry*_ home automation.** It could also be installed in other rooms such as the kitchen, fireplace area in the living room, etc.

*Gas Leaks Alarm:
AE09/GM*

Sensor of natural gas leaks, located on the roof of the kitchen, next to the heater of the heating of the house. There are similar sensors on the market to detect leaks of propane, butane, methane, etc.

This device has, in the same box: natural gas sensor, alarm and power LED, acoustic buzzer,

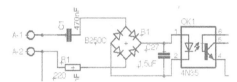

sensitivity adjustment potentiometer, relay with voltage-free output and 220v power supply, also the version with power supply at +12v. It also has a disconnectable fuse. Its consumption is 5w.

It is integrated in **KNX***, through a module of binary inputs type ON/OFF with 220v and the **Raspberry***_**home automation** through another interface of 220v, specific, which we will see later.

Flood Alarm: AE98/iN220

Flood sensor, one for each of the bathrooms of the house, kitchen and laundry. Are located in all wet areas that can cause flooding in the house. The probes of these elements (maximum 3), are connected in series (maximum 50 meters or 164 feet) and actually constitute a single sensor distributed by the units susceptible to flood alarms (laundry, kitchen and bathrooms).

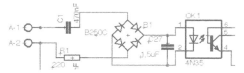

It is composed of a probe and a detector that has power and alarm light indicators, acoustic alarm, relay with voltage-free contacts and integrated power supply.

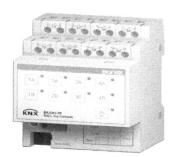

Like the previous case, this sensor is connected to the **KNX*** bus, through a binary input module and to the **Raspberry*_home automation** through a specific 220v interface.

Smoke and Fire Alarm: AE085/R220B

Smoke and fire sensor, one for each floor that it wants to control and is activated when a fire produces enough toxic combustion products (whether visible or not), especially those that are in their initial phase.

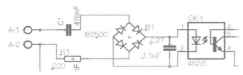

This sensor has an ionic camera detector, power LED and alarm LED, acoustic buzzer, dual 220v power supply, a rechargeable +9v battery and a potential free relay. At rest, the LED launches small green flashes that confirm its correct operation.

Like the previous ones, it is connected to the **KNX*** bus through a binary input module that translates the 220v ON/OFF input into a specific **KNX*** telegram and can be captured by the bus and to the **Raspberry***_ **home automation.**

*Electric Supply Alarm

Sensor based on its own interface (hereinafter it calls it the "**220v Interface**"), which detects the

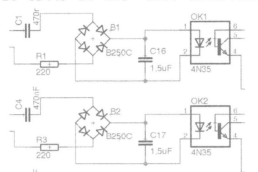

presence of the 220v power supply in the general electric distribution panel of the house and translates it into a signal that attacks the appropriate **GPIO*** of the **Raspberry***_ **home automation.**

This circuit has an interface that adapts the 220v level to the +3.3v levels of the **GPIO*** of the **Raspberry***_**home automation** system, using a R1+C1 pair, adjusted to the input of a rectifier bridge, B1 and capacitor, C16, which generates a positive and suitable signal for an optocoupler, OK1, which allows electrically isolating the 220v Interface from the **Raspberry***.

At the exit of the optocoupler there're filters and voltage adapters so that it can connect without problems to the **GPIO*** of the **Raspberry***_**home automation.**

Later we will see, in more detail, all these elements and the mathematic calculation of their optimal values.

*Garage Gate Alarm

Based on an interface of its own that detects the +24v of the LED lamp of the garage gate machine

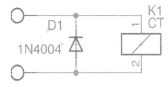 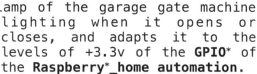

lighting when it opens or closes, and adapts it to the levels of +3.3v of the **GPIO*** of the **Raspberry*_home automation**.

To do this, it uses a +24v 1–contact **Finder* relay**, whose output attacks the 220v

Interface.

This system is only thinking to detect the situation of opened or closed state of the garage gate but, for security reasons, neither opens nor closes it, although technically it was feasible using the necessary adapter. For this reason this system is treated in the section of the sensors and not of the actuators.

Later we will see all the elements that make up this sensor, the calculation of the optimal values of its components, the states, their transitions and the timing of operation between these states.

*Doorbell Alarm

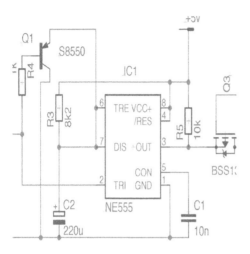

Sensor based on an interface, also its own, that detects the +18v generated by the interface bus that feeds the doorbell to access the general entrance of the house, attacks a retriggerable monostable adjusted to a pulse of a certain duration and that finally adapts to the necessary +3.3v levels of the **GPIO*** of the **Raspberry*_home automation.**

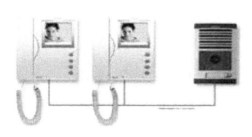

As we will see later, this sensor detects each press of the bell, as long as it is done in a certain time and filters noises, electrical parasites, bounces, etc.

We will also see the components, the mathematical calculation of their optimal values, the states, the transitions and the timing of each of them.

*Reset and Alarm Simulation Buttons

The Reset Button resets the main screen and certain variables of the home automation software **p_global.py** or forces the general reset of the **Raspberry*_home automation** (short or long press). Via software, the bounce time is controlled and via hardware, with pull-ups, false unwanted pulsations are avoided in the operation of the button.

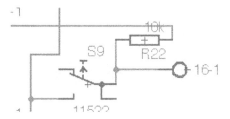

On the other hand, the alarm simulation push-buttons, also with their bounce times and pull-ups, allow the fictional activation of flood, fire, gas, supply cut-off, toxic air, etc. alarms that help create the project and perform tests with these alarms, especially in the development phase of home automation control software, without the need to force the real activation of each alarm.

*Internet Connectivity

This "virtual sensor" allows software detection of connectivity with the **Gmail*** mail server, by performing a ping to the **Gmail*** server on each loop of the main body of the **p_global.py Python*** module and checking its access availability.

This function is useful, for example, when it needs to automatically reset the main Router, if it is suspected that the connectivity cut is repaired with that reset and communicate to the user, via e-mail, when the Internet connection is restored and how much that cut has lasted.

This operation can be extended to other elements of the network: Switches, Fiber Optic Interface (**ONT***), Bridges, etc., and even have a record of Internet outages in case they have to be claimed to the telecommunications operator.

⊖⊖⊖

5.-DETAIL OF SOME SENSORS

We have already briefly described the sensors used in this project, some of them can be easily acquired in the market (electronics stores or specialised websites) and others have had to be created, or at least build the electronic interfaces, both analog and digital corresponding to adapt its electrical output signals to the electrical signals required by the centralised control system located in the **Raspberry***_ **home automation.**

Next we will see in detail the electrical circuits that make up these interfaces.

DHT22: Temperature and Humidity Sensor

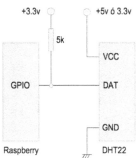

1. Power at +3.3v directly from the **Raspberry*_ home automation.** If it is fed at +5v it is necessary to use a logical level converter (for example a **SODIAL***), between the **DHT22*** and the **Raspberry*_home automation.** The **DHT22*** internally includes 3–6kΩ pull-up.

2. The sensor samples must be spaced in periods longer than 2 seconds to avoid reading errors.

3. Use the software-managed bidirectional serial **DAT*** protocol via pin **1-Wire*** (must be enabled in the ip-config of the **Raspberry*_home automation**) and with the following structure:

[Start] [Response Bus] [Humidity High] [Humidity Low] [Temperature High] [Temperature Low] [Parity]

Total 40 bit.

For example:

Binary Code	Observation
HH=0000–0010	
HL=1001–0010	Total: 0292hex=65.8% RH

Binary Code	Observation
TH=0000-0001	
TL=0000-1101	Total: 010Dhex=26.9 °C
1010-0010	parity

4. Operating temperature: −40 to 80°C (−40 to 176 °F) with 0.1°C (0.18°F) resolution.

5. Operating humidity: 0–99% with 0.1% resolution. Maximum length of the **1-Wire*** bus of 30 meters or 98 feet.

MQ135: Air Quality Sensor

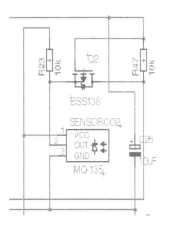

1. Powered at +5v and 140mA of consumption for preheating the sensor. Take this consumption into account to connect it to a suitable power supply.

2. Specific power supply (+5v and 500mA).

3. Pin AO: analog output (not used in this project, it needs an analog-digital converter, for example connect it to an **Arduino***).

4. DO pin: digital output.

5. Reverse logic operation: DO=L implies toxic gas alarm, DO=H there isn't toxic gas alarm.

6. Green LED ON: the sensor is powered.

7. Red LED ON: there is an alarm due to poor air quality.

8. It has an adjustable trimmer to regulate the sensitivity of the sensor and avoid false alarms.

9. Due to the sensor consumption (140mA), this sensor is connected to a specific switch 220v and 1A located in a general electric distribution panel that allows it to be easily disconnected if necessary.

10. This sensor must be connected to a logic level converter, for example a **SODIAL*** or equivalent, which uses several **Mosfet BSS138*** and 10kΩ resistors to adapt the +5v output to the +3,3v needed for the **Raspberry***_ **home automatio**n.

I will not tire of commenting that it should not connect +5v signals to the **Raspberry*** inputs or outputs. Any input signal in the **GPIO*** that exceeds +3.3v will burn the circuit board.

*220v Interface for Old Alarms

1. All the old alarms, generate a digital signal type on/off, via relay, of 220v that is integrated in the binary input **KNX***. This binary input, when it detects 220v in one of its input ports, generates a **KNX*** telegram that automatically acts with the corresponding actuator: gas, fire, smoke → that close the gas electronic valve, flood → that closes the water electronic valve.

2. The output of each of these alarms, connected to the **KNX*** binary module, is also connected to the circuit we have called the "220v Interface" and since we are going to connect 220v outputs with +3.3v inputs of the **Raspberry*_home automation**, it is highly recommended, as we will see, to isolate the two circuits with optical couplers.

3. At each output of 220v, connect a resistance vs capacitor pair of type 220Ω+470nF, with a total impedance Z=220+6k8jΩ, to reduce the input current of the optical coupler to less than 30mA.

   To calculate these values use: $P=i^2R=1/4w$ (power of an ordinary resistance) and with i=30mA maximum, so we have R=220Ω.

   On the other hand:

   $$C=I/(2\pi FV)=(30*10^{-3})/(2\pi*50*220)=470\text{nF}$$

(choose a capacitor for more than 500v and change 50Hz to 60Hz in America).

Finally, the total impedance is:

$$\boldsymbol{Z = R + Ic} = R + (1/(2\pi fC)) = 220 + (1/(2\pi * 50 * 470 * 10^{-9}))\Omega$$

With it Z=220+6k8jΩ (change 50Hz to 60Hz in America).

4.   Bridge rectifier **B250C/1000v***, which achieves the continuous voltage for the optical coupler in each alarm.

5.   1.5uF/35v capacitor (e.g. from tantalum) to avoid random jumps of the optical coupler.

6. Optical coupler **4N35*** coupler that is activated with each alarm zeroing its output.

7.   10MΩ resistance based on the photo transistor at the input of the optical coupler to avoid noise and set its sensitivity.

8.   Stabilisers in pairs of 1uF, 100nF capacitors and 10kΩ pull-up attack on each **GPIO*** of the **Raspberry*_home automation.**

9. The **Raspberry*** inputs are +3.3v, with output current limited to 7mA by internal resistance of 470Ω. Do not exceed this current to protect **Raspberry***. This input is stabilised with a pull-up of 470Ω at +3.3v, that is, a maximum input current of 7mA (maximum 16mA).

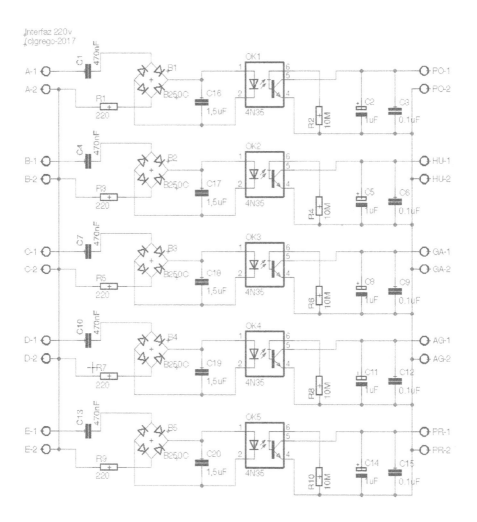

*Reset and Simulation of Alarm Buttons

1. To generate the "short reset" (erases screen and starts certain variables) or "long reset" (total system reset) or simulates alarms.

2. For the reset button and for each alarm, it uses a push-button block S1, type **11522***, 10kΩ as pull-up, with 3mm red LED, 470Ω resistor and 1uF capacitor to test each alarm and adapt to +3.3v of each **Raspberry*_home automation** input pin.

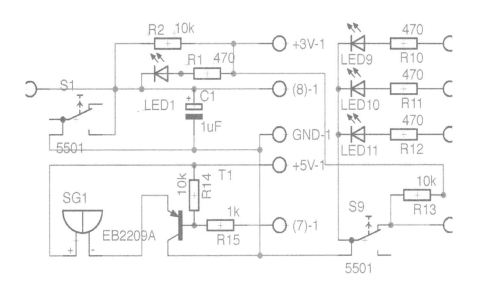

45

*Garage Gate Status

For security, the garage gate is only used as a system sensor, to know if it is open or closed. To detect the opening or closing signal of this garage gate, the connection to the +24v LED lamp integrated in the gate machine is used.

It could has installed some end of career switches and directly detect when the gate is open or when it is closed. This solution is more reliable but requires the installation of much more wiring.

The configuration used here is as follows:

1. When the gate opens, the +24v of the ON state of the gate machine lamp are converted to 220v through the **Finder24v*** relay, located in the general electric panel of the house and protected , before reverse induced currents, by diode **1N4004***. It is advisable to place this relay in a **DIN*** rail socket for easy installation, removal and maintenance. The trigger current of the relay is low, so it can be fed directly from such lamp.

2. This 220v signal, generated by the relay contacts, is processed in the 220v Interface in a similar way to the rest of the alarms and thus attacks the **SODIAL*** logic level converter in order to adapt it to a **GPIO*** pin of the **Raspberry***_home automation.

3. In the garage gate 3 states have been defined: [open], [still_open] and [close] to be able to know at any time if the gate is really closed or has been left open and if necessary send by e-mail the corresponding alarm.

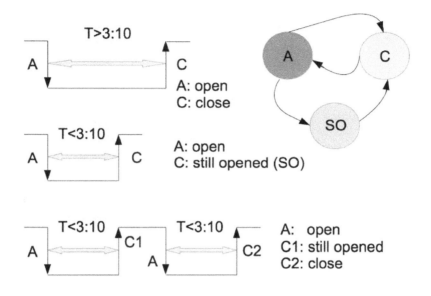

4. The lamp turns on for a maximum of 3:10 minutes from opening or closing until it turns off freely without user action and this time is what it will controls in **p_global.py** to know the status of the garage gate.

5. The [close] state is detected by the lit lamp time exceeding 3:10 minutes (a certain time to open, plus a certain time to close, which is greater than just opening or just closing). Perhaps, because of this software complexity, it would be easier to have the limit switches detected, but by software it is also possible to contemplate it.

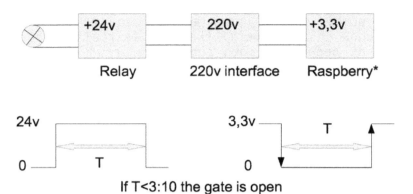

If T<3:10 the gate is open

6. The transitions between states can only be the following and are all controlled by software using several flags:

- ◦ [open] to: [still_open] (t<3:10)
- ◦ [open] to: [close]   (t>=3:10)
- ◦ [still_open] to: [close]
- ◦ [close] to: [open]

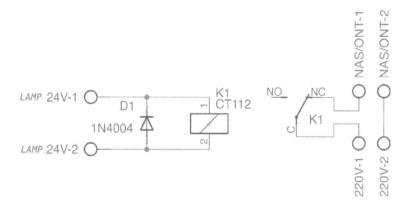

*Doorbell Interface

The doorbell signal is picked up on terminals
[_&L] of the ADS* bus (Audio Digital System currently
replaced by the VDS*) of the Fermax City Line 106C107H*
intercom with the following information:

1. The Fermax ADS* system is supported on a Fermax*
   bus [_&L] with 3 lines at +18v.

2. The bus is accessible at the terminals of the
   Fermax 1088* Telephone Interface existing in the
   housing panel (used to integrate the bell signal
   into the telephone system of the house), but
   could be taken directly from the ADS* system in
   any point on the bus [_&L].

3. When the bell rings, the signal (L) coded
   between 0 and +18v is produced on terminals
   [_&L] of the ADS*.

4. The +18v are converted to +5v, signal (1), with
   a voltage divider with the pair R1+R2:
   56kΩ+22kΩ.

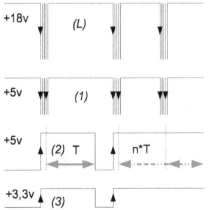

5. The +5v signal attacks
   an integrated circuit
   NE555*, configured in
   a monostable
   retriggerable mode,
   set to a pulse of 2
   seconds, which jumps
   in falling edge n*T
   pulses.

The value of the pulse T, signal (2), is achieved with the pair: R3+C2 = 8k2Ω+220uF. T is calculated as: T = 1.1*R3*C2= 1.1*8k2Ω*220uF = 1.98 seconds.

6. The monostable **NE555*** MUST be configured in retriggerable mode (n*T pulses), using a **PNP S8550*** transistor and 1kΩ resistor.

7. The output pulse is converted to +3.3v, signal (3), with the **SODIAL*** level converter that features the **Mosfet BSS138*** and two 10kΩ resistors.

8. This pulse goes directly to the **Raspberry***_home **automation** bell alarm pin.

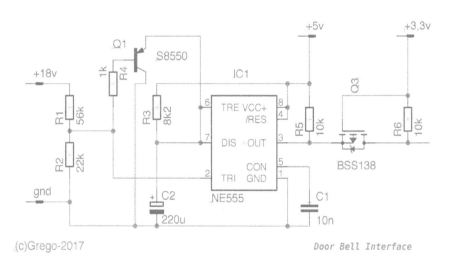

(c)Grego-2017   *Door Bell Interface*

⊖⊖⊖

6.-ACTUATORS

This section describes in detail the mission, the performance, construction and operation of all actuators (control, special, etc.) used in this project.

We have various families of actuators:

✔ **Control actuators**: which have been used to know the states of the system, such as the main LED and audio zoom.

✔ **Actuators with other systems**: such as relays or the infrared WIFI converter.

✔ **Actuators to control the stability of the set**: such as the watchdog, the automatic reset differential, etc.

✔ **Final actuators**: lighting, window blinds, thermostat (activate presence or absence), water and gas valves, etc.

✔ **Special actuators**: they provide additional and friendly information about the situation of the system such as **Google Home*** or **Alexa***.

*LED

The home automation interface has three **LED** (red, yellow and green), which indicate the status of the system in "traffic light" mode.

These 5mm LED are directly connected to the **GPIO*** of the **Raspberry*_home automation** through a 470Ω resistor for each state:

Red   (important alarm)
Yellow   (slight alarm or warning)
Green   (normal operation).

This resistance adjusts the consumption of the LED to the output power level of the **GPIO*** protecting the **Raspberry***.

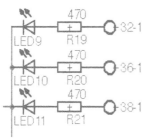

As these LED are connected to the **GPIO*** of the **Raspberry*_home automation**, they are fully configurable, being able to assign, by software, various functions.

The function of each LED *(red:* smoke alarm, water, gas, etc., *yellow:* gate, doorbell, online, etc., *green:* reset, keys, thermostat, **IFTTT***, voice, **BOT***, CK, etc.), inputs vs outputs are assigned in the table that we will see in a later chapter.

*Audio Buzz

To know, in a very simple way and even a few meters away, if the system is working correctly and within what is established by the **p_global.py** program, an **NPN S8050*** transistor set, 10kΩ resistor and active piezoelectric buzz are available for generate an acoustic trace of the state of the system and that also acts as a watchdog clock (CK) and we will see later.

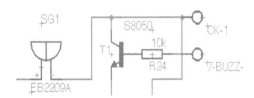

This buzzer can be any of the market, piezo type, with built-in oscillator and activated, for example with +5v.

Here, the piezoelectric buzzer **EB2209A*** from **Digisound*** has been used, which admits voltages from +3v to +20v, with continuous sound, frequency 3.8kHz, maximum intensity 12mA and acoustic level +90dB to 10cm.

*Relays Module

For the performance in the high energy outputs (devices connected to the 220v network), we have a block of 8 isolated from **Raspberry*_home automation** relays by optical coupler.

Each relay disconnects from the power supply, when a certain alarm occurs, to a certain device: NAS, ONT, ROUTER, etc. (for example if it is suspected that it is essential to restart the main Router and it is not accessible).

The relay module used is the known **KKMOON*** of 8 independent relays. In this project we have 5 free relays for future actions.

In addition, the relays have the following additional circuit to ensure their correct operation, especially when the system is restarted, so that no relay is activated in an uncontrolled manner due to the **GPIO*** unknown status.

1. **74ls14*** inverter chip (Schmitt trigger), powered at +5v and with 1kΩ pull-down at each input, to avoid unwanted starts of the relays when the **Raspberry*_home automation** system is started due to its unknown status of the **GPIO***.

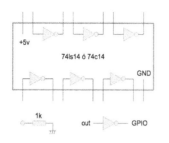

2. A **74c14*** powered at +3.3v could also be used. Thus the electrical signals will be the following:

In	Out	GPIO*
H 220v	0,3v L	3,5v H
L 0v	3,4v H	0,1v L
P_on	0v L	3,5v H

3. Optical integrated couplers to electrically isolate the external devices of the **Raspberry*_ home automation**.

4. Each device is connected to the **C—NC** terminals of the corresponding relay, in order to be normally powered at the rest of the relay, so that when acting on it, it disconnects the power from the device.

5. The block of the 8 relays is powered by an external power supply (filtered and stabilised) at +5v to have enough power in each coil. 90mA are required per relay, an average of 360mA for the total, but if they are connected more and will work regularly, a higher power supply is necessary.

6. In our case, on the relay interface, the VCC + JD_VCC pins are bridged as an additional external power supply is not necessary.

7. Next it can see the electrical scheme:

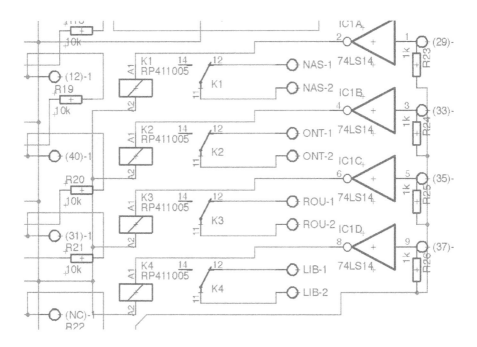

*Window blinds, Lighting, Thermostat, Valves & LCD Control Display

For operation with window blinds, house lighting, **KNX*** thermostat (absence or presence activation), valve opening or closing and so on, the **KNX*** bus interface, **5wg1-117-2AB12*** from **Siemens*** is available connected to the **UART*** (serial communication) of the **Raspberry***_**home automation**, by the RxD, TxD and GND pins, through the **PEI-10*** connector of this interface. The details are:

1. The **BTI*** (Bus Transceiver Interface) bus that owns the **KNX*** standard is accessible on the **PEI-10***.

2. Since the electronic circuits of the **Raspberry***_**home automation** and the **KNX*** bus have power supplies with different voltages and earths, a total electrical isolation must be used between both circuits. This is achieved with the **ADUM_1201*** logic level isolator and adapter interface.

3. The **BTI*** bus also has an internal power supply of +5v/10mA and +20v/25mA supplied by the power supply of the **KNX*** bus of the house, with enough power to handle the signals and interface power

ADUM_1201*.

4. The communication parameters of the **BTI*** bus reach up 19.200 baud, asynchronous, 2-wire (TxD and RxD) and with handshake software.

5. The **BTI*** bus access protocol is produced by the **CSMA/CA*** protocol.

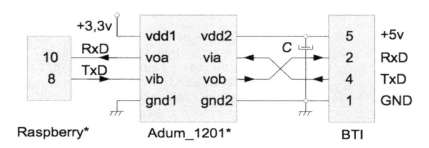

| Raspberry* | Adum_1201* | BTI |

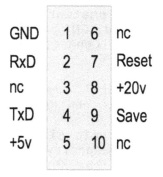

GND	1	6	nc
RxD	2	7	Reset
nc	3	8	+20v
TxD	4	9	Save
+5v	5	10	nc

6. To suppress noise induced on the **KNX*** bus, a pair of capacitors, C=1uF+10uF, is connected between +5v and GND of the **BTI*** bus directly to the input of the **PEI-10*** port. The **BTI*** bus pins are as follows:

7. The RESET and SAVE pins of the **BTI*** bus are not used.

8. The **ADUM_1201*** isolator and level converter is powered on the one hand with +3.3v of the **Raspberry*_home automation** and on the other with +5v of the **BTI*** bus.

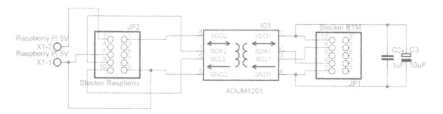

The water valve used is the **CEME 688***, which is usually open and closes when it receives 220v power from the **KNX*** relay when it is activated with the corresponding **KNX*** telegram, consuming 17w.

When the 220v supply disappears, the valve goes back to open and the consumption of its coil is zero.

The city gas valve used is **Watts MP16/RM*** which is also activated at 220v supplied by a **KNX*** relay when the corresponding telegram is received. This valve is normally open and when closed, its reset must be manual for safety reasons.

An interesting **KNX*** device, although not essential, is the LCD control display.

Here it can centralise various tasks, for example: turn on or off all the lights in the house, raise or lower all window blinds, adjust the thermostat, activate the barking of the guard dog, etc.

*Watchdog

The following external watchdog powered by a clock signal, CK, generated by the system software **p_global.py** is used to control the flow of the program, avoiding unexpected stops and software crashes. If the CK signal disappears, because the program does not run properly, the watchdog circuit automatically resets the **Raspberry*_home automation.**

The internal watchdog of the **Raspberry*_home automation** (implemented by software on a hardware timer) was discarded because it was not reliable.

1. The watchdog CK clock signal comes directly from pin 7 of the **Raspberry*_home automation**, which is also used to generate the acoustic trace that attacks the Buzz, it is a square signal, +3.3v amplitude and between 1 & 5Hz frequency controlled by software.

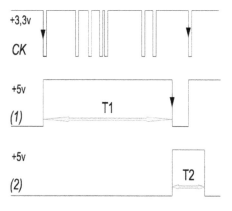

2. This CK signal attacks an integrated **NE555***, in monostable configuration, adjusted by the R+C= 39kΩ+220uF pair at a pulse activation, T1, of 10 seconds, calculated as: T1=1.1*39k*220u = 9.5 seconds, see (1).

3. The 10-second T1 pulse signal is continuously regenerated (monostable retriggerable) by the **NPN S8050*** transistor and the 10kΩ resistor.

4. If the pulse signal T1, of 10 seconds, disappears, a pulse, T2, of +5v is generated by the second **NE555***, adjusted by the pair R+C= 8k2Ω+220uF at 2 seconds, calculated as: T2 = 1.1 *8k2*220u = 2 seconds, see (2).

5. The second signal, T2, of 2 seconds and +5v, activates the reed relay **G—3570***.

6. The **G—3570*** reed relay temporarily joins, during those 2 seconds, the reset pins of **Raspberry***_ **home automation** (RUN **Raspberry*_home automation**) producing the corresponding total system reset. These pins do not come factory soldiers, we must carefully install them on the **Raspberry*** board.

7. The relay also serves to electrically isolate t h e **Raspberry*_home automation** from watchdog electronics.

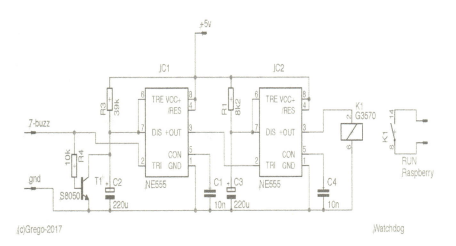

*Other Actuators

Other actuators, such as WIFI or **KNX*** switches, to turn off or on 220v powered devices (ambient lamps, hard-to-reach devices, etc.), infrared WIFI signal converting devices (to operate with the TV, decoder, coloured LED lights, sound amplifier, **Apple*** **TV**, **KNX*** switch with infrared control, **KNX*** relays, etc.), are described in the software section.

All of them require a specific software configuration, pairing with WIFI, registering in the manufacturer-defined APP, integration with **IFTTT***, availability of the corresponding **Python*** module, creation of the voice command in **Google Assistant***, assignment of group addresses, etc.

⊖⊖⊖

7.-SUMMARY
INPUTS vs OUTPUTS

In summary: so far we have described most of the hardware of the inputs and outputs of the system, being the **p_global.py** software in charge of relating them according to various situations, variables, functions and algorithms that we will go describing.

If this information is classified in this way, it is proposed to use a two-state and multi-status logic table, where the actions and the order in the outputs status are specified for each state of the inputs.

In this way we can clearly define how each input interacts with one or more outputs, prioritising the different actions and finally defining the home automation algorithm that is the heart of the system.

*Inputs

1. Temperature and humidity near de NAS system or in other places.
2. Garage gate (open state, still open or closed)
3. Smoke alarm in the kitchen and house roof.
4. Flood alarm in the kitchen, bathrooms, laundry or other wet places.
5. Gas alarm in the kitchen near de heater.
6. Reset button in the home automation interface.
7. Electric supply connected to general electric panel of the house.
8. Doorbell of the main door.
9. CO2 sensor in the garage.
10. **KNX*** devices: switches, relays, presence sensors, thermostat, twilight, LCD control centre, etc.
11. Internet connectivity.
12. Keys accessible by screen via **VNC*** or wireless keyboard directly connected to the **Raspberry*_ home automation.**
13. Status of the thermostat (absence, presence and actual temperature).
14. Actions from **IFTTT***.
15. Voice commands captured by **Google Home***.
16. Messages captured by **Telegram BOT***.
17. Commands captured by the **Raspberry*_screen** input window.

*Outputs

1. Reset relays of connected equipment: NAS, Router, etc.
2. Several general purpose relays.
3. Red Led (serious alarm).
4. Yellow Led (slight alarm).
5. Green Led (visual trace of correct operation).
6. Buzz (operating acoustic trace and CK for the watchdog).
7. Acting on **KNX*** bus: lights, window blinds, thermostat, valves, etc.
8. Actuation switches (ambient, bridge, etc.), and WIFI lamps.
9. Infrared converter performance (TV, decoder, **Apple*** TV, etc.).
10. Messages sent by **Gmail***.
11. Messages sent to **Google Home*** or **Alexa***.

With the inputs and outputs so defined it could define a logical action table, distribute the inputs in rows and the outputs in columns, so that for each input the affected outputs are specified.

In each intersection row vs column, the actions to be carried out can be specified and even in each action we could define the priorities between actions.

This table is essential to build the home automation algorithm of automatic actions, which in the background, together with voice-directed actions, are the soul of this project.

For example, in the following table we can see that if there is a gas leak alarm, the general relay is activated (it could disconnect the heater, close the gas valve, turn off any home appliance, etc.), the red LED turns on, the audio is activated on the buzz, a telegram is sent by the **KNX*** bus (we will see it later), an e-mail is sent to the addresses designated in **p_global.py** (we will also see it) and a voice message is sent to play on **Google Home***.

In addition to this algorithm we have assigned, for example, level 1 to be executed as a priority in the home automation control over other actions (send summary of daily activity, execute automatic actions, etc.).

	Reset relay	General relay	Red LED	Yellow LED	Green LED	Audio Buzz	KNX* bus	WIFI device	RM device	E-mail Gmail*
Temperature	X		X				X			
Garage gate				X		X		X	X	X
Smoke		X	X			X	X		X	(*)
Flood			X			X	X			(*)
Leak	X		X			X	X			(*)
Presence							X			X
Twilight				X		X	X		X	X
Reset					X	X				X
Power			X					X		X
Doorbell				X			X	X		X
CO₂		X	X			X	X			(*)
Online				X			X			
KNX*		X					X	X		X
Keyboard					X	X				
Thermostat					X				X	X
IFTTT*					X		X	X	X	X
Voice					X		X	X	X	
BOT*					X		X	X	X	X
LCD display							X		X	
Screen					X		X	X	X	X

(*) priority 1

☺☺☺

8.-POWER SUPPLY

In the system there are components that need +5v and others +3.3v, so a dual power supply is needed as indicated below. This power supply is very easy to build because the system consumption is very low and therefore many electronic components are not necessary.

This source is stabilised, regulated and with protection against electrical shortcuts.

There are multiple types of power supplies already built on the market, but here a custom one has been built, because it is very basic, easy to install and cheap.

The elements are as follows:

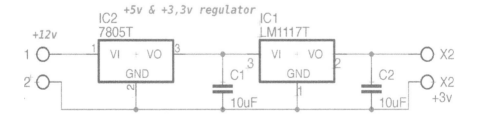

1. Voltage regulator **7805T*** and 10uF capacitor, which supplies +5v and up to 1A (limited by the AC/DC converter). This device needs an aluminium refrigerator.

2. **LM1117T*** voltage regulator and 10uF capacitor, which supplies +3.3v and up to 1A (also limited by the AC/DC converter and the **7805T*** regulator). This device needs an aluminium refrigerator.

3. The system is powered by a generic AC/DC converter of +12v and 300mA that provides sufficient power (for example a mobile phone charger or a small transformer type: 220v/12v and 4w minimum).

Next we will see in detail the mathematical calculations necessary to size these elements.

*Systems that need +5v

1. Acoustic buzz, to have sufficient audible power. If necessary, this buzzer could be fed up to +20v. It needs a minimum current of 12mA.

2. Air quality and CO_2 sensor **MQ–135***. It needs 140mA maximum.

3. **NE555*** doorbell interface. It needs about 10mA.

4. The two **NE555*** external watchdog interface, with a consumption of 20mA.

5. Inverter **74ls14*** in each relay input. 10mA of consumption.

6. **ADUM_1201*** logic level converter and isolator. 10mA of consumption.

7. Logic level converter **SODIAL*** 20mA of consumption.

8. Module of 8 **KKMOON*** relays. With an average point consumption of 90mA per relay. (**Important:** calculate this average based on the number of relays used and the activation time of each of them).

9. **Total consumption +5v**: 200–300mA and 1.5w

*Systems that need +3.3v

1. Pull-up for **Raspberry*_home automation** inputs to prevent correct data. Minimum consumption.

2. Temperature and humidity sensor **DHT22***. 2.5mA average consumption.

3. **ADUM_ 1201*** logic level converter and isolator. It needs 10mA.

4. **SODIAL*** logic level converter. 20mA consumption.

   Total Consumption +3.3v: 20–30mA and 0.1w

   TOTAL Consumption Interface: 200–330mA and 1.6w

   Source used: +12v 300mA and 3.6w

*Other power supply systems

In addition to the previous power supplies, this home automation system has a small UPS, in this case the **CoolBox SCUDO-600B***, of 600VA that allows to briefly power the system (ONT, Router, HUB, Bridge, **Raspberry*_home automation**, interface 220v, NAS , **ZTE*** tablet, additional HD, **KNX*** interfaces, etc.) and ensure the sending of the supply interrupt email and close the system in an orderly manner.

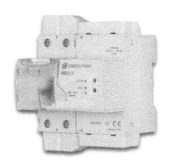

On the other hand, an optional but very interesting element to contemplate, especially in installations with habitual jumps of the home protection differential, is a self-resettable differential.

This element makes several rearmament attempts and this guarantees the electricity supply especially in the absence of the inhabitants of the home.

An example of this type of devices is the **Circutor REC3*** (40A load and 30mA sensitivity), which is super immunised against electrical parasites and makes 3 attempts to reset: at 3, 20 and 180 seconds.

It has two modes of operation: by isolation and by time.

In those installations in which the system does not automatically reset due to some small electrical leakage (greater than 15mA and less than 30mA) it is recommended to use the time mode.

To switch between the two modes (isolation & time), peel off the right side sticker of the **Circutor REC3*** and carefully change the position of the white switch that can be seen in one of the slots under that sticker, close the sticker and try again.

This differential can be tested by pressing the "**Test**" key, being able to observe how it jumps to the OFF position and in 3 seconds it automatically resets again and turns ON again.

The device has 2 LED: green indicates ok operation and red flashes when reset timing is activated, remaining fixed in red if resetting is not possible.

☉☉☉

9.-HOME CONNECTIVITY STRUCTURE

In order to communicate the different elements of the system: central control with **Raspberry*_home automation**, screen access control to the system, with **Raspberry*_screen**, sensors, actuators, etc., a series of elements are needed interconnected with each other, either by physical LAN (**Gigabit*** type 100/1000Mbs or 10/100Mbs), or by WIFI, as well as an external connection by Fiber Optic (it can also be by **DSL*** or even by mobile data type **3G/4G***).

The house of this example project has several floors and a garage, so the distribution of connectivity is done with a main router (the Fiber Router) in one floor, which distributes, via **Gigabit*** LAN, connectivity to the rest of the floors.

On each floor, a Router in Bridge LAN vs WIFI mode, generates the necessary communication both to devices with LAN connectivity (TV, decoder, **Apple*** TV, etc.), and to devices with WIFI connectivity (mobile, tablet, WIFI interface to infrared, etc.).

This distribution includes, in each of the floors, LAN coverage for fixed equipment (Bridges, HUB, **Raspberry***, **iMac***, TV, Decoders, **PS4***, **BlueRay***, **Apple*** TV, NAS, etc.) and WIFI for non-fixed equipment (mobile terminals, tablets, small switches, WIFI bulbs, digital WIFI radio, thermostat, IR-WIFI converter, other devices, etc.). Let's see the detail below:

*Main Router Configuration

1. Through the configuration web of each Router or of each Bridge, accessing its IP (see the table of IP that we have built later), make a backup of all the original configuration parameters, of each device in a file type : router_[router name]_original.cfg.

2. Connect a LAN port of the Router to the LAN of the **iMac*** (on a **Windows*** PC it would be very similar) and configure the network of the **iMac*** as follows:

<configure network> <manually> <ip / mask / router>
        <advancing> <hardware> <automatically>

   After the test, leave the **iMac*** again configured with:

        <hardware> <manually> <1000baseT> <duplex>

3. If the Router is not accessed with the factory username and password or those defined correctly later, try to erase the history of the browser used and try again.

4. On the main router (usually with default IP gateway **192.168.1.1**), ensure the correct configuration in the following sections:

Service	Configuration
WAN	Internet IP, etc.
Administration	User, pass (customise recommended)
WIRELESS	SSID, wap2-psk and custom password
LAN	Gateway, IGMP enabled, static DHCP
NAT*/portforwarding	TCP/UDP accessible from outside

74

*Bridges Configuration

To correctly configure the Routers that act as Bridge type LAN vs WIFI, with their corresponding IP, user defined WIFI SSID, user access and custom password, etc., the following tasks must be performed:

1. Directly connect the LAN of the main Router with the LAN of the Router that acts as Bridge, and in the Bridge perform the following operations:

2. Reset the Bridge by pressing the reset button, back, more than 10 seconds. There are tutorials on the web to reset all types of Routers and Bridges.

3. Connect a LAN port of the Bridge to the **iMac*** and configure the IP to, for example, **192.168.1. [IP], [IP]** being the IP address we assign to the Bridge.

4. Customise the user and password of the Router that acts as Bridge. Take good note of this configuration, if it forgets, it has to return to point 2 and reset the Router or the Bridge.

5. In LAN disable DHCP and **IGMP*** Snooping.

6. Change the name of the WIFI in the SSID section to [WIFI_name] and customise your password. It is recommended that the Router and Bridge password are all the same so that roaming between several WIFI in the home is easier.

7. Keep the WAN section as it is, (even in many Routers or Bridge, it is not necessary to put it in Bridge mode).

8. Keep the rest of the Bridge configuration as is, **do not change anything.**

9. On the Bridge configuration website, in the maintenance section, make a backup of the file **router_[router_name]_final.cfg**, so it has the original [*].cfg and the newly configured end.

10. To optimise WIFI roaming between the different Bridges, which ensure total WIFI coverage in the house, distribute the 2.4Ghz WIFI signal peaks in the available spectrum.

    Use, for example, the **Android** * **WIFI Analyzer** * APP for displaying the frequency distribution and reducing the channel width to 20Mhz (to have more space in the spectrum), for example:

WIFI	FLOOR	CHANNEL
WIFI_low	Low level	6
WIFI_first	1st level	2
WIFI_second	2nd level	13

11. The operation can be repeated in 5Ghz WIFI, although its frequency range is usually less sensitive to noise and interference between this type of WIFI.

HGU Router
Configuration

If the **HGU*** (Home Gateway Unit) Router, that is going to act as a Bridge, includes the Fiber Optic interface (some operators call it **ONT***), the following operations must be performed:

1. Connect the Router, which contains the **ONT***, to LAN, accessible from **iMac***, and enter the configuration web of this Router, usually 192.168.1.1.

   If the default IP was not the previous one, see what is in your manual or on the manufacturer's website.

2. Register the integrated **ONT*** code (Fiber to WAN interface) that is supplied by the Operator.

   This point is critical, without this operation the Router will not work.

3. Enter the configuration and disable **DHCP**.

4. Change the factory password for your own.

5. Change the IP to 192.168.1.[Custom IP].

6. Ensure that 2.4GHz and 5GHz WIFI are activated and with the appropriate password.

*Network Topology:
Router, Switches & Bridges

There are multiple options to perform this operation, here the following has been proven as optimal:

1. Connect each Bridge of each floor to the main Fiber Router via 1GB LAN. It is essential to ensure that this connection is as fast as possible, later we will see how the LAN is reviewed to guarantee this point.

2. Connect the low-speed networks: **Raspberry*_ screen, Raspberry*_home automation** (currently 300Mb maximum) to a high-speed 1Gbs switch or hub, they could also be connected to a 10/100MHz low-speed switch, if they are also connected by 5Ghz WIFI.

3. Connect the rest of the high speed devices: NAS, multimedia, entertainment equipment, etc., to the 1Gb high speed switch.

4. Ensure that devices that support 5GHz WIFI have physical access to the routers that generate this type of WIFI.

5. It is always recommended that the best router (advanced configuration, speed, etc.) be used as the main router.

*Protection of the Router & Bridges

To avoid unwanted access to the main Router and the Bridges, it is advisable to apply the following recommendations:

1. Customise usernames and passwords, adding letters (upper & lower case), numbers and special symbols.

2. Hide the SSID of the most sensitive WIFI, for example, the main router.

   It is important to preserve and know the name of the SSID for future access.

3. See the possibility of implementing a filtering table by MAC address of the devices connected to this equipment on each Router and Bridge.

   This option is tedious but it is the most reliable to guarantee a high level of access security to routers.

*Assignment of
IP Addresses

Nowadays there's a very high proliferation of devices connected to the WIFI and LAN networks of the home: TV, computers, tablets, mobiles, routers, bridges, home automation devices of all kinds (from light bulbs to humidifiers with essential oils selection and with different smells and colours, tooth brushes, smart watches, etc.), decoders TV, **Raspberry***, computers, NAS, WIFI sockets and switches, thermostats, video game consoles, multimedia equipment, ebooks, digital radios, infrared converters, weather stations, speakers with Artificial Intelligence assistants (**Alexa***, **Google Home***, **Homekit***), etc.

For this reason it is essential to apply a certain order in the assignment of the IP of these devices, for example those that have a fixed IP assigned in the Router, those that have a variable assigned by DHCP, classification by floors, by rooms, by type of device , etc.

To ensure that the devices have a stable fixed IP in the internal network, configure in the main Router (in general 192.168.1.1), the allocation table between IP and MAC address as follows:

<network configuration> <LAN> <Static DHCP>
<add new static lease>

And add the necessary IP from, for example, the following table, where MAC are fictitious and IP vs MAC can be easily obtained by scanning the internal network with apps similar to **Fing*** or **IP Scanner***.

Device	IP 192.168.1.x	Obs	MAC	Maker
Main Router	1	(1)	mac1	MitraStar*
Bridge living room	2	(1)	mac2	Askey*
Bridge 1st floor	3	(1)	mac3	AsusTek*
Router 2nd floor	4	(1)	mac4	Cisco-Linksys*
Decoder 4K	100	(1)	mac5	Arris*
Decoder HD	**101**	**(3)**	**mac6**	**Arris***
Raspberry*_home automation LAN	**62**	**(3)**	**mac7**	**Raspberry***
Raspberry*_home automation WIFI	63	(1)	mac8	Raspberry*
NAS	68	(1)	mac9	Wester Digital*
Tablet ZTE*	Dynamic	(4)	mac0	Samsung*
iMac* LAN	**70**	**(3)**	**maca**	**Apple***
iMac* WIFI	71	(1)	macb	Apple*
Raspberry*_screen LAN	**72**	**(3)**	**macc**	**Raspberry***
Raspberry*_scr_WIFI	73	(1)	macd	Raspberry*
TV living room LAN	74	(1)	mace	Samsung*
TV living room WIFI	75	(1)	macf	Samsung*
Apple* TV living room LAN	76	(1)	macg	Apple*
Ediplug*	**77**	**(3)**	**mach**	**Edimax***
WIFI bulb	**78**	**(3)**	**maci**	**TP-Link***
RM Mini*	**79**	**(3)**	**macj**	**HangZhou***
Google Chrome*	Dynamic	(4)	mack	Google*
Google Mini*	Dynamic	(4)	macl	Google*
Switch_1	Dynamic	(4)	macm	Expressif*
Switch_2	Dynamic	(4)	macn	Expressif*
Tadoº thermostat	Dynamic	(4)	maco	Tadoº*

Device	IP 192.168.1.x	Obs	MAC	Maker
WIFI extender	Dynamic	(4)	macp	TP-Link*
PC LAN	82	(1)	macq	Surecom*
Tadoº bridge (∗)	**90**	**(3)**	**macr**	**Tadoº***
TV room_1 LAN	94	(1)	macs	Samsung*
TV room_1 WIFI	99	(1)	mact	Samsung*
TV room_2 WIFI	95	(1)	macu	Samsung*
PS4* LAN	Dynamic	(2)	macv	Sony*
PS4* WIFI	96	(1)	macw	AzureWave*
Apple* TV living room LAN	97	(1)	macx	Apple*
BlueRay*	98	(1)	macy	Samsung*
Fire TV*	Dynamic	(4)	macz	Amazon*
Alexa*	Dynamic	(4)	macA	Amazon*
iPad* person_1	Dynamic	(4)	macB	Apple*
iPad* person_2	Dynamic	(4)	macC	Apple*
iPhone* person_1	Dynamic	(4)	macD	Apple*
Android* person_2	Dynamic	(4)	macE	Samsung*
Kindle∗	Dynamic	(4)	macF	Amazon*
Digital radio	Dynamic	(2)	macG	Sangean*

(∗) The **Tadoº Bridge*** is a wireless extension of the **Tadoº*** thermostat, connected wirelessly by a proprietary connection, in this case with a frequency of 868MHz **Mesh*** type (**6LoWPAN***) and with the same MAC address in both the Bridge and in the **Tadoº*** thermostat.

As an example, the following general IP assignment rules can be applied (this issue is not essential, it is about ordering the IP space):

1. IP type 192.168.1.x with x in the range [30:110] except Router and bridges.

2. Reserve the IP in the range [30:59] for dynamic IP assigned by the Router.

3. Routers, in general, only allow a maximum of 8 fixed IP to be reserved in their internal table. In the table above are those indicated **in bold**.

Notes about IP assignment rules:

(1)   IP set on the device.
(2)   IP not set but can be set on the device.
(3)   IP set on the Router as static IP.
(4)   Dynamic IP, assigned by DHCP.

*Important Issues

To ensure the correct assignment of IP addresses, so that remote access applications work properly, so that disks (physical or virtual) boot properly, etc., it is recommended to review the following aspects:

1. Turn OFF & ON the power supply of each device, so that it obtains its assigned IP according to the previous table.

2. Check the IP on the **VNC*** connections (described below).

3. Review the IP in **NAT*** of the main router (described below).

4. Update the IP on virtual disks declared in **/etc/fstab** of the **Raspberry***.

5. Check the IP in **Raspbian*** in both **Raspberry***, in the top bar:

   <wireless & wired network settings>

6. Review the IP in **Raspberry***, that the system file: **/etc/dhcpcd.conf,** include at the end of this file the following information:

   ```
   interface wlan0
   inform 192.168.1.[IP WIFI]
   interface eth0
   inform 192.178.1.[IP LAN]
   ```

An example of static IP allocation criteria could be the following:

According to floor, applies to the first digit of the IP:

6x	garage
7x	main floor
8x	1st floor
9x	2nd floor

According to device, applies to the second digit of the IP:

x0	**iMac***-LAN
x1	**iMac***-WIFI
x2	**Raspberry***-LAN
x3	**Raspberry***-WIFI
x4	TV_a
x5	TV_b
x6	**PS4***
x7	**Edimax***
x8	WIFI bulb
x9	**TP-Link*** WIFI extender

Notes about MAC:

They are sequences of hexadecimal numbers, of the type: **aa:aa:aa:bb:bb:bb,** where the first three blocks **aa** usually represent the brand and the last three blocks **bb** usually represent the type of device.

In the following web it can sees detailed information of a MAC:

https://www.adminsub.net/mac-address-finder

☺☺☺

10.–OTHER ASPECTS OF THE HARDWARE

Next we will see other hardware issues (HDMI, decoders, **Ethernet***, **Tadoº***, etc.), they are not essential but they are interesting. For example:

HDMI connection between the **Raspberry*** and the TV and that we will use in its initial configuration or when we cannot use **VNC***.

How we make our network compatible with the installation of two decoders (not essential for the project) and set up our 4K or UHD TV in the living room to take advantage of the benefits of a decoder type UHD (not essential).

Check **Ethernet*** cables for communication speed to reach 1Gbs. This issue is very important for the system to work smoothly and to realise the full potential of Routers, Bridges and Hubs. In most cases it is about installing the **Ethernet*** of the appropriate category cable and especially that the terminals of such cable are connected properly (we will see all this in detail).

Set up the network properly so that the **Tadoº*** thermostat works correctly. Remember that this element is not only a thermostat, it also controls the geolocation of users that is the basis for acting on devices to turn on/off.

Let's go into detail:

HDMI–CEC Activation

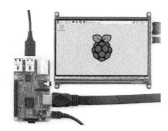

If the **Raspberry*** is connected to a TV directly via HDMI and the **Raspbian*** operating system screen is to be operated with the TV infrared remote control and no video signal is detected, the following sequence must be performed in this order:

1. Physically disconnect the entire HDMI cable at both ends.
2. Turn off the TV with the infrared remote.
3. Disconnect the TV from the power supply, more than 1 minute.
4. Turn on the **Raspberry***.
5. Connect one HDMI cable extreme end to the **Raspberry***.
6. Connect the other HDMI cable extreme to the TV.
7. Turn on the TV.

However, it is more practical to access the **Raspberry*** via **VNC*** (we will see it later), thus freeing an HDMI port from the TV and being able to access the **Raspberry***, both from home and outside it and with any device connected to the Internet: mobile, tablet, PC, **iMac***, etc.

*Connection of two decoders

Although this situation is not included in the home automation project, this interesting option can be found to extend the performance of the project and be able to handle such decoders with home automation orders. To do this:

1. Assign fixed IP in the DHCP table of both decoders.

2. Assign the previous static IP in the Router table (see previous sections).

3. To assign IP to the decoders, do the following:

4. Unplug and plug the power cable into the decoder.

5. When the 5 verified starting points (blank fill-in) appear, press the key on the assigned remote control with a face or stick.

6. Indicate the IP as static and assign that IP (for example 4K=100 and HD=101)

7. If the image remains locked in some decoder, assign the variable IP in that decoder and keep the static in the other.

*TV Living Room and UHD Decoder

The example discussed here is for a 4K TV of the **Samsung*** brand,but it is feasible for any other TV with HDMI, with 4K capability and analysing in its manual the type of HDMI and its location.

For example:

HDMI Location	Type	Connection
1 Upper right side	**STB***	**iMac***
2 Middle right side	**DVI***	**Chromecast***
3 Lower right side	**MHL*** (4K)	Decoder UHD (*)
4 Rear	**ARC***	**Apple*** TV

Later we will see how we can act, from the home automation program, with this decoder with a WIFI to Infrared converter.

(*) If the TV does not detect the UHD decoder, set it to UHD mode 2.160p 25 fps (50fps configuration may not be supported). If configured with 50fps, the HDMI must be plugged in/unplugged for proper synchronisation or switched to 50fps, to watch the TV in that resolution and revert to 25fps before turning off the TV.

*Gigabit Ethernet
1Gb connection

To obtain a stable Ethernet connection of 1Gbs (100/1.000baseT) the following instructions must be followed:

1. Use category **5e** or higher cable (category 5 cable is not valid).

2. Choose compatible **RJ45*** connectors, of high quality, with the correct closure clip and in good condition, so that they do not come loose and produce false unwanted disconnections.

3. The category 5e cable must have the 8 twisted wires in pairs 2 to 2 and with the following configuration:

4. The connection of the pairs: **1–2, 3–6, 4–5** and **7–8**, must be in this order at both ends, see the attached photo, **IT IS NOT VALID** that they are in another order, even while in parallel.

   For example with the following coloured wires: White Orange–Orange, White Green–Blue, White Blue–Green, White Brown–Brown.

   It is not necessary to connect the metal mesh to the **RJ45*** connector at either end. If this order is not respected in the connection of twisted pairs, a maximum speed of 10/100Mbs will be obtained instead of the 100 /1.000Mbs (**Gigabit*** or 1Gbs).

5. In the **Ethernet*** wall plugs, respect the colours indicated inside each plug, they are not necessarily in the same order as in the external pins of the plug.

6. Check end-to-end connectivity with an RJ45/RJ11 tester, for example the **TL-468*** tester can be useful for us. **IMPORTANT:** these testers only detect copper continuity and wiring parallelism, but not the order of the internal braid described above, nor the speed.

7. If 1Gbs is reached, on the **Ethernet*** port the 2 status LED located outside will flash in green (or will flash in orange), otherwise only one LED will flash green.

8. If the pairs are not braided and properly grimpated, the Bridge does not properly recognise the signal, the Router may be, but 1Gbs will not be achieved. If the port is not **Gigabit***, the switch or the Bridge, they do not show communication on the green LED but the 10/100Mbs communication, or the 300Mbs of the **Raspberry***, will work equally well.

*Troubleshooting
of Tadoº Thermostat

The Bridge of the **Tadoº** * smart thermostat acts as an interface between the **Ehternet** * or WIFI (high power consumption) signal of the Router or Bridge to which it is connected and the **868** * (low power consumption) signal that connects it with the **Tadoº** * thermostat.

This thermostat, in addition to its natural temperature control functions, is also very useful for generating routines that need to detect the presence of a household member. For this purpose, as we shall see, the **"away"** and **"home"** states that will act with **IFTTT** * are used.

Sometimes the **Tadoº** * Bridge is randomly disconnected from the network (punctual Internet cutting, interference with the multicasting of decoders, punctual power cuts, cuts in communication with the **Tadoº** * server, Router problems, etc.) & it doesn't work.

If it's no solved, do the following:

1. If the **Tadoº** * bridge is accessible locally, turn off/on the Router to which it is connected and if necessary disconnect/connect the **Tadoº** * Bridge from the Router port and if necessary disconnect/connect the **Tadoº** * Bridge from the power supply.

2. In this project, the power of the Bridge **Tadoº*** has been connected to an **eWelink*∗** switch, **Sonoff*** Basic model, whose configuration is described in the software section, this allows the disconnection/connection of the **Tadoº*** Bridge to the power supply of a comfortable and remote way.

3. If the Bridge **Tadoº***, it is only remotely accessible to do:

4. Turn off/on the **eWelink*** switch that powers the Bridge and wait for connection, if it is not solved:

5. Remotely enter the **Raspberry*_home automation** with **VNC*** and **NO-IP*** (both tools are detailed below).

6. Open, via **VNC***, a **Chromium*** session (**Raspbian* Chrome***) on the **Raspberry*_home automation** and enter the Router or Bridge to which the **Tadoº*** Bridge is connected, in general 192.168.1.[IP], accessing the username and password defined in the configuration of such Bridge.

7. Go to <maintenance> <reboot> and restart the previous Router or Bridge and wait for connection.

8. If it is not resolved with this procedure, everything points to a hardware failure of any of the system components or a fall in the **Tadoº*** server, in this case it is necessary to contact the **Tadoº*** company help desk.

*Osoyoo touch screen

Although this project uses a touch screen with HDMI connection connected to the **Raspberry*_screen** to be able to act on home automation, it is possible, but not recommended, to use other types of screens.

For example the **Osoyoo*** screen (www.osoyoo.com), although it is not recommended because it has little definition in both display and touch, but especially because it requires a special system version **Raspbian*** very difficult to configure and update.

However, if it wants to use the **Osoyoo*** screen, it is very cheap, do the following:

1. Download the latest version of the software suitable for the screen from the **Osoyoo*** website (see the version of the screen on the back of the same).

2. Unzip software with: **tar xzufLCD*.tar.gz**

3. Change directory with: **cd LCD_show_v6_1_3**

4. Run: **./LCD35_v**

5. Restart **Raspberry*_screen** with: **sudo reboot**

6. Finally, to pass the display of the **Osoyoo*** screen to HDMI:

   cd LCD_show_v6_1_3

7. Run: **./LCD_hdmi**

8. This screen has the great advantage of connecting to the **Raspberry*** via the **GPIO*** pins that are not commonly used (**SPI*** interface on pins 19 to 26) and also has the "exact" dimensions of the **Raspberry*** original board, which allows us to have a small screen, attached to the **Raspberry*** board, of low consumption, low price, touch and that allows us to quickly visualise and manage what happens in the **Raspberry***, but cannot compete with an HDMI screen.

⊖⊖⊖

11.-RASPBERRY*_HOME AUTOMATION CENTRALISED SYSTEM

For the centralised control of the system, a **Raspberry*** Pi 3, model B+, is used with the following functionalities and parameters:

1. **Raspbian* Stretch** operating system over **Linux9***.

2. Personal user and password customised.

3. Direct boot from the 32GB uSD memory card (may be smaller, but recommended this minimum size and fast, class 3).

4. Simulated HD on a 32GB uSB (not essential).

5. Fixed IP address: 192.168.1.x (see IP assignment table).

6. Private and public key generation with command:

ssh-keygen -R [Fixed IP] of the **Raspberry*_home automation.**

7. Access by **VNC*** server at 2.560x1.600 pixels resolution.

8. Support **HDMI-CEC*** for backup of **VNC*** use.

9. **Python* 2.7.** operating system

10. Graphic functions supported on **Colorama*** and **Tkinter***.

11. **GPIO*** 40-pin to control home automation systems.

12. WIFI connection 5GHz and LAN at 300Mbs.

13. We will see in detail the configuration of this **Raspberry*** and that constitutes the heart of this home automation system.

Assignment of the GPIO on the Raspberry*

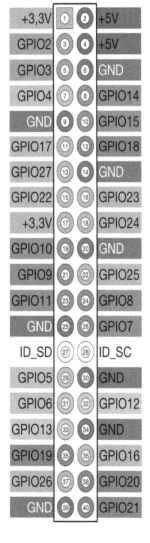

Given the large volume of **GPIO*** pins used in this **Raspberry***, (the reference of the pins is according t o **GPIO*** configured by software), practically all except those of the **SPI*** interface, it is necessary to perform the following operations:

1. To use pin 7 for Buzz audio, disable the **1-Wire*** interface on the **Raspbian*** raspi-config tool.

2. To use pins 8 and 10 for the UART (TxD and RxD), activate **Serial*** in raspi-config.

3. To use pin 3 for the **DHT22*** temperature and humidity sensor, deactivate **I2C*** in raspi-config.

4. To use pin 5 for yellow LED, which identifies a slight alarm, deactivate **I2C*** in raspi-config.

5. If necessary, activate pins 11 and 36 as RTS and CTS for use with **KNX*** or with an **RS232*** interface (in this project is not necessary as they are not used), activate **ALT3*** mode with:

```
git clone git://github.com/mholling/rpirtscts.git
cd rpirtscts
make
sudo ./rpirtscts on [off]
```

6. Pins 19 to 26 are reserved for the external LCD screen, although it is proposed not to use screens connected to these pins, it is much more advisable to use screens connected directly to the HDMI port.

7. Remember that all pins of the **Raspberry*** withstand voltages at +3.3v and 16mA maximum output current.

   Exceeding these limits involves the risk of permanent deterioration in the **Raspberry*** circuits.

8. For more information about **Raspberry*** hardware and software, check the official product page at:

https://raspberrypi.org

*Installation
from Zero

Below are all recommended operations to configure this **Raspberry***, most are common with the configuration of the **Raspberry*_screen**, although some specific to the latter are described below.

The main steps to follow are:

1. Format a uSD card, with a recommended capacity of 16 or 32GB, in **FAT32***.

2. Obtain the ISO or ZIP of the operating system, here **Raspbian* Strech**, from the main page of the **Raspberry*** organisation.

3. Add in the uSD, in folder **/boot**, a file named SSH, which is empty and without any extension. To create this file use, for example, the **Texedit*** and **Finger*** software and to record the ISO or ZIP on the uSD card it can use the **Etcher*** or similar software.

4. Insert the uSD card into the **Raspberry*** and boot it.

5. See the IP that the router has assigned to the **Raspberry***, for example, with the **IPScanner*** or **Fing*** software and use **SSH*** with **Terminal*** to connect to it as:

   ssh pi@192.168.1.[IP], where [IP] is the IP of the **Raspberry***.

6. By default the username and password are:

   username=pi password=raspberry

It is highly recommended to customise both parameters.

7. From **Raspbian Terminal***, **LXTerminal***, use:

sudo raspi-config

8. Configure the basic parameters of the **Raspberry***: language, keyboard, time, etc.

9. Activate **VNC*** (in some versions of **Raspbian***, this software is factory activated), serial (shell no, interface yes), **GPIO*** and resolution mode 82.

10. Configure the fixed IP to be used by the **Raspberry***, on the top bar of the **Raspbian*** panel (WIFI/LAN), for example as:

Raspberry*_home automation:
192.168.1.a0 for LAN and 192.168.1.a1 for WIFI

Raspberry*_screen:
192.168.1.b0 for LAN and 192.168.1.b1 for WIFI

```
Sudo crontab -e
@reboot /usr/local/bin/pigpiod
```

*Use of External Disks

Although it is not essential for this project, it is always convenient to have an external disk (HD or USB), connected to a USB port of the **Raspberry*** in which to backup or store heavy multimedia files.

To configure an external disk, perform the following operations:

Command	Description
sudo fdisk -l	lists the partitions
sudo mkfs.ext3	formats partition in ext3
sudo mkdir /media/[disk]	creates [disk] in directory: /media/
sudo nano /etc/fstab	edits initial configuration and add:
/dev/sdb/media/[disk] ext3 defaults 0	
sudo chown pi /media/[disk]	gives permissions and owner
sudo mount -a	mounts [disk]
df -h	sees size disk installed

*Upgrading the System

Updating and upgrading the **Raspberry*** operating system and firmware is essential to maximise security, have the latest version of information, correct errors that occur as a project develops, especially due to the instabilities of a phase of design, etc.

Command	Description
hostnamectl	knows the installed version
sudo apt-get update	downloads the software to update
sudo apt-get upgrade	upgrades to the downloaded version
sudo apt-get dis-upgrade	updates the firmware
sudo apt-get autoclean	deletes temporary files
sudo apt-get autoremove	deletes unnecessary packages

*Bluetooth settings

In the **Raspberry*** pi 3 B+, used as **Raspberry***_ **home automation,** it is necessary to disable **Bluetooth*** (BT) communications, so that the UART is compatible with the **KNX*** home automation.

To do this, do the following instructions:

sudo nano /boot/config.txt	and add:
dtoverlay=pi3—disable—bt	and also:
sudo systemctl disable hciuart	

With these instructions, it must uses **/dev/ttyAMA0** in the configuration instead of **/dev/serial=0,** so that in **Python*** the libraries operating the **KNX*** of the home automation program **p_global.py** work.

*Package Installation

On multiple occasions we will need to install additional software packages and we must know how to manage them: install, uninstall, delete, view, copy, etc.

For this there are multiple instructions that we can execute directly in **LXTerminal*** of **Raspbian***.

Some of the most important are the following commands:

Command	Description
sudo dpkg-get-selections	sees which packages are installed
sudo apt-get remove [package]	uninstalls the desired [packaged]
sudo apt-get purge [package]	deletes the uninstalled [package]
sudo apt-get autoclean	deletes orphaned packages
sudo apt-get autoremove	deletes unnecessary packages

Assign Fixed IP to Raspberry

To easily access the both **Raspberry***, for example by **VNC*** or by **SSH***, or to access from outside the installation, the **Raspberry*** IP must be fixed and static. Maintaining **Raspberry*** with fixed and known IP saves a lot of search time and prevents multiple errors in access. To do this:

1. Press the right mouse button on the top bar: <status monitor>

2. Wireless and Wired Networks Settings.

3. Configure Interface (for example):

   192.168.1.b2   LAN IP eth0
   192.168.1.b3   WIFI IP wlan0

4. It can also be done by accessing the configuration files such as:

```
ifconfig          see current configuration
sudo cp /etc/network/interfaces interfaces.old
sudo nano -w /etc/network/interfaces   and add:
    auto eth0
    iface lo inet loopback
    iface eth0 inet static
    address 192.168.1.b2
    network 255.255.255.0
    gateway 192.168.1.1
sudo reboot
```

5. Finally check that we access the **Raspberry*** properly, with this fixed IP, either by **SSH*** or by **VNC***.

*Startup Configuration

It wants that when it starts our **Raspberry***, for example after a drop in the power supply or a Reboot for an update, etc., automatically start the configurations (for example mount the disks in a network), home automation software (for example **p_global.py, Telegram*** **BOT***, event viewer, etc.), browsers (**Chromium*** for example), etc.

For this there are several options that should be tested depending on the updates, versions of **Raspbian***, etc.

Let's look at one of these options:

✓ For the **Raspberry***_**home automation** the following solution works well:

1. Create a program [*].sh for each program [*].py that it wants to start.

2. Make the [*].sh executable with:
   sudo chmod +x [*].sh

3. Test them, executing them with:
   bash [*].sh

4. **sudo nano ~/.config/lxsession/LXDE-pi/autostart**
   and add:
   @/home/pi/home_auto/[*].sh

5. Add the necessary @ ... for each [*].sh

In our case, for example, the following programs [*].sh have been created in:

/home/pi/home_auto/[*].sh:

p_starts_global.sh   starts **p_global.py**
p_starts_telegram.sh   starts **p_telegram.py**
p_starts_logfile.sh   starts **p_logfile.py**

The structure of the [*].sh are as follows, where **echo** displays a text, **cd** changes to the folder where the [*].py is located that we are going to execute and **Lxterminal*** starts a terminal window (**Lxterminal*** in **Raspbian***) of dimensions indicated in: **—geometry=CxR**, where **C** are columns and **R** rows and finally in **–title** the window title is specified.

```
#! /bin/bash
echo 'Booting p_logfile.py...'
cd /home/pi/home_auto
lxterminal --command='sudo python p_logfile.py'
--geometry=105x25 -title = 'Logfile'
```

✓ For the **Raspberry***_screen the following solution works:

sudo nano ~/.config/lxsession/LXDE-pi/autostart

And add:

```
@lxpanel --profile LXDE-pi
@pcmanfm --desktop --profile LXDE-pi
@Xscreensaver -no-splash
@point-rpi
@sudo python /home/pi/home_auto/p_screen.py
@sudo mount -a
```

✓ Other possible options are:

sudo crontab -e   and add:
@reboot sudo python /home/pi/home_auto/**p_global.py**
@reboot sudo python/home/pi/home_auto/**p_telegram.py**

To check if it works:

sudo service crond status   or:
/etc/init.d/cron status

*Boot from Disks
by FSTAB

To ensure the correct installation of the storage units defined in the configuration file **/etc/fstab,** add the following in **/etc/rc.local,** before exit0:

```
sleep 30            #wait 30 seconds to allow time
                    #to boot the discs
mount -a            #move the disks, no need to
                    #put sudo
exit 0
```

This solves the initial loading problems, sudo mount -a, defined in:

~/.config/lxsession/LXDE-pi/autostart

Raspberry
HDMI Resolution

The resolution defined in the **Raspberry***
configuration affects, on the one hand, the resolution
applied to its HDMI output, but also the resolution
displayed in remote mode from **VNC***.

To change this setting, do the following:

1. <Raspbian menu *>
2. <Raspberry Pi configuration *>
3. <Set Resolution>
4. <DMT mode 82 1920*1080 60Hz 16:9>

**RESOLUTION ERRORS: "Failed to add edge detection"
(interruptions):**

This error sometimes occurs with the upgrade to
Raspbian* Stretch and the solution is:

sudo pip install Rpi.GPIO==0.6.3   or also:
reboot every time that error appears.

It is convenient to review this situation every
time the system is updated with sudo apt-get upgrade,
however this error is likely to disappear with any of
the upcoming **Raspbian* Stretch** updates.

*Main Screen Settings

Although it is not essential, to make the startup of home automation applications more convenient (**p_global.py**, **p_telegram.py** and **p_logfile.py**), or others, it is highly recommended to add icons of such applications in the main **Raspbian*** bar that allow access agilely to each one, to do the following:

<toolbar> <add/remove items> <application bar> <other> <*. py>

Add in the **Raspbian*** folder <other>, the necessary [*].py applications as:

<preferences> <main editor menu> <applications> <other> <new item>

Finally we have to add the commands to start each of the scripts [*].py with the following lines:

```
lxterminal —command=
'sudo python /home/pi/home_auto/p_global.py'
—geometry=60x25 —title='Global'

lxterminal --command=
'sudo python /home/pi/home_auto/p_telegram.py'
—geometry=30x3 —title='Telegram'

lxterminal --command=
'sudo python /home/pi/home_auto/p_logfile.py'
—geometry=105x25 —title='Logfile'
```

And we would add all the scripts we need.

⊖⊖⊖

12.-MANAGEMENT SYSTEM RASPBERRY*_SCREEN

This second **Raspberry*** is not essential but has been added to the project to see how management and information can be shared between two **Raspberry*** and have more and better control over home automation.

This device performs three basic functions that are interrelated by a transition algorithm described below and that adds value to this equipment.

The equipment has a 7-inch touch screen, connected by HDMI to the **Raspberry*_screen,** very easy to get, at a very competitive price and very easy to configure, without the need to install any proprietary software of such a screen.

In addition, the on and off of this system (which in the case described is embedded in the wall and difficult to access), is controlled by an **eWelink*** switch, with a certain programming, which guarantees its adjustment to the schedule of more presence in the home and by an **IFTTT*** applet that turns off the screen when it is detected that there is no one in the house or holiday mode is activated, etc.

Let's look at the three functions of this screen:

Home automation command management screen.

From this option it can manages the most used or most interesting home automation commands: lights, window blinds, valves, devices, scenes, holidays mode, etc.

Support of a PLEX Server.*

With this server it has access to the multimedia content of the home, both from the home itself and from the outside (if configured) and with a friendly, easy-to-use multimedia manager, accessible from the TV, mobile, etc. and with additional information: order, classification, actors, directors, summary, etc.

Simulation of a Photo Frame.

This option allows it to take advantage of the multimedia capability of this screen using it as a photo frame when the access system to home automation commands is idle.

*Home Automation
Command Management Screen

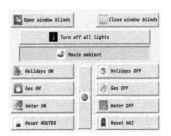

From here it has access to basic and usual functions in home automation or functions that make access to some devices more comfortable.

Let's see the implanted ones:

- Opens or close all the window blinds of the house.

- Turns off all lights: **KNX***, WIFI and **Sonoff*** devices.

- Activates movie scene (closes some predefined window blinds and turns off some predefined lights).

- Activates or deactivates the holidays mode (certain automatic procedures that simulate the presence of inhabitants in the home).

- Opens or closes the electro gas valve.

- Opens or closes the water electro valve. Reset the Router or NAS.

Support of a PLEX Server

This function, supported on a multimedia server, is very useful for the management and viewing of movies, series, etc., available on the NAS of the home and accessible from the TV, tablets and mobile phones of the home.

This function adds value to the traditional use from a TV with the **DLNA*** protocol: movie information (director, actors, summary, etc.), topics already seen, resume viewing, general sorting, sorting by themes, covers, trailers etc.

In addition, with this function it is no longer necessary to have a computer on to act as a server and, if necessary, the service is accessible from outside the home.

See the following website for more detail:

https://www.plex.tv/

This support for **PLEX*** is done in the background of the **Raspberry*_screen**, transparently, without interfering with the main management of home automation commands or the photo frame function.

*Simulation of a Photo Frame

View photos located on the NAS of the home, which is activated after a period of inactivity of this home automation management screen.

The transition algorithm between these three functions (home automation commands, photo viewing and screen protection) is as follows:

1. When the **Raspberry*_screen** is started, the **PLEX*** server starts over **Chromium*** in the background.

2. Start the **Python*** module for managing home automation commands **p_screen.py.** And the usual way of working is:

3. After 1 minute of inactivity, the photo frame mode is activated and photos of the NAS are displayed randomly. This option is configurable: disk, folder containing photos, transitions, times, etc.

4. After 10 minutes of presenting the photos of the NAS, the screen turns off and turns black to reduce consumption and extend the life of the screen.

5. If at any time it press on the screen, the process is restarted from point 2 and the cycle is repeated.

*Various

In the installation of the elements that make up the **Raspberry*_screen** system, or in maintenance tasks, the following order must be used in the connection to guarantee its correct operation.

1. See http://www.waveshare.com/wiki/

2. Start the **Raspberry*_screen.**

3. Connect the USB socket of the backlight or touch screen power.

4. Connect the USB power cable to the **Raspberry*_screen.**

5. Connect the HDMI cable to the touch screen.

6. Use a quality USB cable, so that it feeds the touch screen correctly and has all the internal cables, not just the charging cables, so that the data collected by the touch screen is transmitted.

*Network and Boot Disks

For the correct integration of the manager (**p_screen.py**) of the screen managed by the **Raspberry*_screen** in the home automation system (**p_global.py**), managed by the **Raspberry*_home automation**, it is essential to share information.

This is done through shared information files located on virtual disks that are started when booting the **Raspberry*** and must be configured as, for example, indicated below:

sudo nano /etc/fstab   and add:

```
# Network disks
//192.168.1.[IP]/public/home/pi/disks/public
                    cifs username=1,password=1 0 0

//192.168.1.[IP]/pi_home_auto/home_auto/home/
          pi/DISKS/home_auto cifs file_mode=0777,
          dir_mode=0777, username=1,password=1 0 0

//192.168.1.[IP]/sirio/home/pi/disks/sirio
                    cifs username=1,password=1,vers=1.0 0 0
```

In this example, both **public** (here reside for example, the photos of the frame), and **sirio** are physical disks in network and **DISKS** is a virtual disk, located in **Raspberry*_home automation** and that hosts the shared information files that are will describe later.

*Startup Configuration

As described to configure the start of the **Raspberry*_home automation,** it is necessary to configure the automatic start of the **Raspberry*_screen,** for this it is necessary to configure the following instructions:

sudo nano ~/.config/lxsession/LXDE-pi/autostart

and add:

```
@lxpanel --profile LXDE-pi
@pcmanfm --desktop --profile LXDE-pi
@xscreensaver -no-splash
@point-rpi
@chromium-browser
         http://192.168.1.[IP]:[port]/web/index.html
@sudosu
@sudo python /home/pi/home_auto/p_screen.py
@sudo mount -a
```

Here it configures the **Raspbian* Lxterminal*** screen that supports the execution of the **Python* p_screen.py** script that manages the command buttons home automation, the screen saver **Xscreensaver*,** also from **Raspbian*** and that performs the control of the transitions between the three functionalities of this **Raspberry*** and the **Chromium*** browser, starting the main page of the multimedia server **PLEX*** (explained below) and pointing to the IP of the **Raspberry*_screen,** accessible from the outside by the port **[port].**

For the option of remote use of the **PLEX*** server to work smoothly, low-weight multimedia files, optimisation of **Raspberry*** resources (a good memory card, few simultaneous programs, good cooling, etc.)

and internal network communications are needed. housing with minimum **Gigabit*** speed.

If all this is ok, we will have a **PLEX*** multimedia server with low cost and low consumption (less than 2w), with local and remote maintenance and that we can have on 24 hours, 365 days a year.

The remote access option to this server is configurable and can be activated or deactivated from the main menu of the **PLEX*** server manager.

In the configuration of the **Chromium***, do not add any startup web and use "open everything as it was before", so that in case of power cuts or reboot of the system, the **PLEX*** server is started properly.

*Screen Saver Settings

The transition algorithm between the **p_screen.py** application, the photo frame and the screen turned off, is based on the **Xscreensaver*** screen saver, to configure it to do the following:

sudo apt-get install xscreensaver

And configure:

1. Use the save **RIPPLES*** screens.
2. Activate after 1 minute.
3. Set photos to <advancing>
4. Remove effects in the **RIPPLES*** configuration.
5. Add the screen off after 10 minutes.

Any other screensaver and any mode other than **RIPPLES*** can be used, although this is recommended because of its ease of configuration and because it allows the integration of the photo frame and the screen off.

Gregorio Chenlo Romero (gregochenlo.blogspot.com)

*Configure the Touch Screen

The HDMI output of the **Raspberry*_screen** must also be configured for the correct operation of the **Waveshare*** display (7-inch model, 1.024*600 Capacitive LCD and HDMI) connected.

To do this, do the following:

sudo nano /boot/config.txt   and add:

```
# 7" screen configuration
     max_usb_current    =1
     hdmi_group         =2
     hdmi_mode          =1
     hdmi_mode          =87
     hdmi_cvt 1024 600 60 6 0 0 0
     hdmi_drive         =1
```

Important: remember the connection order explained above, this is:

Raspberry*_screen → backlight → USB → HDMI

See:

http://www.waveshare.com/wiki/

PLEX Server Installation

As previously mentioned, the **Raspberry*_screen** supports a **PLEX*** server to manage comfortably (with titles, actors, movie information, content viewed, classification by topics, etc.) multimedia content (movies, series, photos, music) located on the NAS or any other multimedia support existing in the home.

This information is accessible from any TV, (it is also accessible from the native **SmartTV*** service, called **DLNA***, but does not provide any detailed information), tablet, mobile, etc., and as we have seen, the system can be also configure to access all this information from outside the home.

Due to its low power consumption (less than 2w), the **Raspberry*** with the **PLEX*** server can be on for a long time during the day, without the need to locate the **PLEX*** server on a PC or on the **iMac*** with much higher consumption (more of 100w).

To manage the power off/on of this **Raspberry***, due to its difficult access, it has been connected to a WIFI **eWelink*** switch, of the **Sonoff*** Basic type, which allows it to programs the default start and end times of the **PLEX*** server activity and be able to access it from the outside, via WIFI, to its management.

123

The operation of this WIFI switch is described, in detail, below.

On the other hand, this switch is integrable in **IFTTT***, so it has been configured to turn off automatically when no one is in the house or the holiday mode is activated, using the geolocation service of the **Tadoº*** thermostat.

For the **PLEX*** server installation, do the following:

1. See: https://www.codedonut.com/raspberry-pi/
raspberry-pi-plex-media-server/

2. In **Terminal***, execute the following instructions:

```
sudo apt-get update          update the Raspberry*
sudo apt-get upgrade

sudo apt-get install apt-transport-https
wget -O -https://dev2day.de /pms/dev2day-pms.gpg.key

sudo apt-key add -

echo "deb https://dev2day.de/pms/ jessie main"

sudo tee /etc/apt/sources.list.d/pms.list
sudo apt-get update

sudo apt-get install plexmediaserver-installer
sudo nano /etc/default/plexmediaserver.prev

    And change:

PLEX_MEDIA_SERVER_USER=pi

sudo service plexmediaserver restart
sudo reboot
```

*Home Automation
Action Buttons

Another feature of the **Raspberry*_screen** is to manage some basic home automation actions that will be executed from the **Raspberry*_home automation.**

For this, the following buttons are built with **Python*** and the **Tkinter*** software:

Button	Description
Open window blinds	Opens all window blinds
Close window blinds	Closes all window blinds
Turn off all lights	Turns off all lights (both **KNX*** and WIFI)
Movie ambient	Activates MOVIE=ON (closes some window blinds, turns off some lights & turns on others)
Holidays ON	Activates HOLIDAYS=ON (performs some automatic procedures with some window blinds & lights at certain times)
Holidays OFF	Activates HOLIDAYS=OFF
Gas ON	Opens the gas solenoid valve
Gas OFF	Closes the gas solenoid valve
Water ON	Opens the water electro valve
Water OFF	Closes the water electro valve
Reset ROUTER	Resets Router 192.168.1.[IP]
Reset NAS	Resets NAS 192.168.1.[IP]

For the flow of information between both **Raspberry***, an exchange file is used, for example: /home/pi/home_auto/actuators.txt located in **Raspberry*_home automation**, later described in detail.

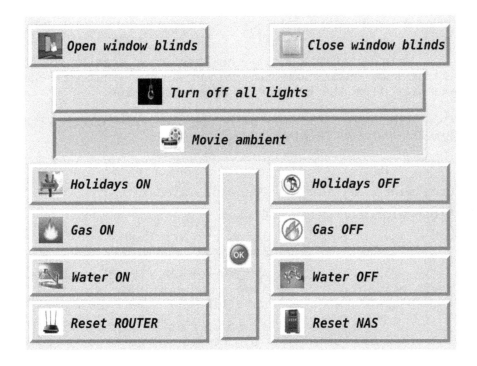

In order for both **Raspberry*** to access the information exchange files, it is necessary to enable full control permissions on them, by running:

sudo chmod 777 [*].txt

☺☺☺

13.-ADDITIONAL DEVICE SOFTWARE

In addition to containing the necessary and specified hardware, it is necessary to configure the software that is needed for each of the devices that complement the set of sensors and actuators.

Currently, home automation device providers are working together to have common communication and operating standards, but nowadays each device needs its specific software to function properly. To help with this integration process, **IFTTT*** is used that allows it to easily associates actions and devices.

The software configurations of some of the previously defined hardware elements and some other components that make up the sensors and actuators of the home system and which must be included in the **p_global.py** module and the **IFTTT*** integrator are detailed below.

NOTE: The MAC addresses used as an example include the manufacturer's identification in their first three blocks but may also vary

*Temperature and Humidity Sensor

To implement the necessary software to manage the **DHT22*** temperature and humidity sensor in **Python***, it is necessary to do the following:

1. Locate the **DHT22_py.zip*** file on the manufacturer's website.

2. Unzip **DHT22_py.zip*** in the same directory where the main **Python*** **p_global.py** program is located with:

   wget abyz.co.uk/rpi/pigpio/code/DHT22_py.zip

3. **sudo pigpiod** must be started with the daemon automatically with:

   sudo crontab -e   and add the line:

   @reboot /usr/local/bin/pigpiod

Edimax

For the activation or deactivation of the heater, the **Edimax*** **SP-1101W** WIFI plug has been used, which is easily configurable through the **Edilife*** APP and easy to manage directly from **Python***.

To configure this plug, perform the following steps:

1. Install the **EdiLife*** APP, as the previous **Ediplug*** does not work with the FW 2.04 version of the **SP-1101W***. Configure the **EdiLife*** APP on your mobile (supports **IOS*** and **Android*** operative systems), use the WIFI closest to the plug, of the 2.4GHz type (does not support 5GHz) and with sufficient signal strength.

2. At the time of configuring the **EdiLife*** APP, it is recommended to activate the airplane mode on the mobile, to ensure that the initial communication is carried out by the WIFI generated by the **Edimax*** (**Edilife55***) and not by the 3G/4G network of the mobile.

3. Edit the heater on and off programming in the **EdiLife*** APP of the **Edimax*** and change the password with a personal password.

Download the **Python*** module:

smartplug_digest_auth.py

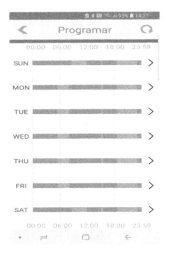

This version is valid for version **SP-1101W***, FW 2.04 of **Edimax***.

Rename the downloaded file to **p_smartplug.py** and copy it to /home/pi/home_auto (it must be in the same storage folder as our home automation project).

To configure the **Edimax*** again from the beginning, press the RESET button of the **Edimax*** for at least 5 seconds.

4. Connect the mobile to the **Edilife55*** WIFI, generated by the **Edimax*** plug and go to the **EdiLife*** APP.

5. Before integrating **p_smartplug.py** into **p_global.py,** it is highly recommended to start it in a test program, for example, **p_edimax.py** that is located in the /home/pi/home_auto/ folder.

6. Check that the IP that the Router assigns to **Edimax*** (for example in the **iMac*** with **Edimax*** **UpgradeTool** APP or with **Fing***) with MAC: **80:1f:02:xx:xx:xx.** This MAC should be set in the fixed IP assignment table of Router 192.168.1. [IP] or Main Router (already commented).

7. To test the operation, on the command line (terminal of the **Raspberry***_**home automation**), use:

python p_smartplug.py –H 192.168.1.[IP] –l[user]
–p[pass] –[a]
   Where:

[IP] is the correct IP of the **Edimax***.
[user] is the user registered in **EdiLife***
                        (by default **admin**).
[pass] is the password registered in **EdiLife***.
[a] can be:

   g   knows **Edimax*** status (ON/OFF)
   s ON   turns on
   s OFF   turns off

8. In **Python***, use the following lines of code:

```
from smartplug import SmartPlug
edimax=SmartPlug('192.168.1.[IP]',('[user]','[pass]'))
edimax.state            knows status
                                (returns'ON'/'OFF')
edimax.state='ON'       turns on
edimax.state='OFF'      turns off
```

TP-LINK WIFI Bulb LB100*

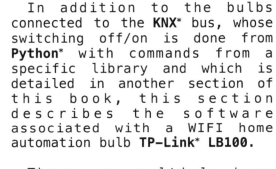

In addition to the bulbs connected to the **KNX*** bus, whose switching off/on is done from **Python*** with commands from a specific library and which is detailed in another section of this book, this section describes the software associated with a WIFI home automation bulb **TP-Link* LB100.**

There are multiple home automation bulbs on the market, this is an example, but anyone could use it. It is recommended to use those bulbs that have a simple software, accessible from a **Python*** library and are included in the **IFTTT*** integrator.

In this case, the software that controls it is the **Kasa*** APP of **TP-Link*.**

Here is a world of options and each WIFI bulb has its problem, both hardware and software, there is no standard established among manufacturers to access, via software, these elements.

The above argument is the reason why an integrator like **IFTTT*** (also explained below) becomes practically indispensable, allowing access to these bulbs easily and without writing any additional **Python*** code.

On the other hand, using **IFTTT*** adds the problem of third-party dependency (crashes of **IFTTT*** servers, modification of already written routines, updates, incompatible, etc.), but above all the biggest drawback is the introduction of delays in the execution of the **IFTTT*** commands, which are sometimes not acceptable in actions that must be online.

In this project the **TELEGRAM*** communication software is used, through a **BOT*** (also described below), as a communication chat with the home automation elements.

This chat is integrated into the **Python*** **p_telegram.py** program and it needs to know the status of the **TP-Link*** **LB_100** bulb.

To do this, do the following:

1. See https://github.com/konsumer/tplink-lightbub

2. **sudo apt-get update**
            (update the **Raspberry***_home automation**)

3. **sudo apt-get upgrade**

4. **sudo apt-get install nodejs npm**   (install **NPM***)

5. **sudo npm i -g tplink-lightbulb**
                (install **Tp-Link*** packages)

6. **tplight <command>** use the <command> as:

<scan>	see **Tp-Link*** bulbs connected
<on/off> [IP]	on/off WIFI bulb with the [IP]
<details> [IP]	details of the status of the bulb with the [IP]

In these details see:

line 19, position 14   0: off, 1: on

An example of **Python*** code, could be:

```
fbombilla='/home/pi/home_auto/p_bulb.txt'
#capture the state of light bulb

os.system ('tplight details [IP]>'+f_bulb)
#attention see if the IP is correct

file=open(f_bulb, 'r')
text=file.readlines()[19][14]        #line 19, pos 14
text=='0'                            #WIFI bulb OFF
text=='1'                            #WIFI bulb ON
```

As the tplight scan command does not have timeout, include your [IP] in the main Router table and turn it off/on to be assigned the [IP].

TP-LINK WIFI Extender

Additionally and to guarantee the existence of good WIFI coverage in the **Edimax*** plug (this plug is very close to the heater and therefore very hidden by the nearby walls), it was necessary to have a WIFI extender, in this case the **WA850RE*** of **TP-Link***, (it could be any other model of any other brand), which extends the WIFI range (**only 2.4GHz** but there are other models that support 5GHz), of the WIFI of the ground floor Bridge.

Red extendida

1. Install the **TP-Link*** **Tether*** APP to configure and manage the extender. **Important**: this APP can only be used in local mode by connecting to the main WIFI to be extended.

2. Add device and select the already mentioned **TL-WA850RE***

3. Create "extended" WIFI (or other name), using the "main" WIFI (or other name) as the host.

4. Review the type of password encryption and use **WAP*** encryption or the one required by the extender used.

135

5. Also connect to "extended" other devices that are close but not overcome, due to saturation problems of this WIFI, the 4 devices, or those indicated by the manufacturer of the extender.

6. In our case only the **Edimax***, one mobile (ever used to control the home automation system) and the **Sonoff*** switch that controls one of the kitchen light have been connected.

7. Attention: in some cases the MAC addresses of the devices connected to a WIFI extender are modified.

RM—MINI 3
Broadlink Converter

An interesting interface that relates the WIFI world to the infrared world is the one described below.

This interface allows it to manages from the home automation system, the switching off and on of TV, decoders, audio amplifiers, **Apple*** TV, old lamps managed by infrared remote control, etc., in summary, multiple existing equipment in the rooms of many homes.

Here we describe how to configure the **Broadlink*** **Mini Rm 3** (hereinafter **RM***) and it has been used for

its ease of use, both directly with its **IHC for EU*** APP (specific APP for infrared controls used in Europe, use **IHC*** APP for other places), as for the availability of **Python*** modules to be able to manage it and the versatility when it comes to having an interface with the vast majority of infrared remote controls.

For it:

1. Locate the **RM*** near the devices to be controlled: TV, decoder, colour lamp (in this case a **TAO—GLOW*** model), **Apple*** TV, audio amplifier, etc.

2. Install the **IHC for EU*** Android APP, (it also works with the **Broadlink*** **e-CONTROL*** APP, but the first one is better).

3. Customise the names of user (usually an e-mail) and password in the application.

4. Currently he **RM*** only supports **IFTTT*** for the on/off functions of the TV, decoder and WIFI lamps.

5. The rest of the operation with the **RM*** is implemented with the **Raspberry***_**home automation**, so we can change the channel or source on the TV and the decoder, adjust the volume on the audio amplifier, mute, select a screen concrete on the **Apple*** TV, turn on, off and change colour infrared lamps, etc.

For all of this we carry out the following operations:

✓ See https://forum.pimatic.org/topic/3074/
python-how-to-integrate-cheap-broadlink
-rm3-mini-ir-blaster-with-pimatic

✓ And in **Terminal*** execute:

```
sudo apt-get install python-dev
mkdir /home/pi/home_auto/infrared          (or other)
cd /home/pi/home_auto/infrared
sudo python -m pip install configparser
sudo python -m pip install netaddr
sudo python -m pip install pycrypto
sudo git clone
        https://github.com/mjg59/python-broadlink.git
cd python-broadlink
sudo python setup.py install
cd..
sudo git clone
        https://github.com/davorf/BlackBeanControl.git
cd BlackBeanControl
sudo nano BlackBeanControl.ini
```

And configure the following 4 parameters:

```
[General]
IPAddress=192.168.1.[IP]
Port=80
MACAddress=78:0f:77:xx:xx:xx
Timeout=10
[Commands]
```

✓ Where: [IP] is the IP address assigned to the **RM*** and MACAddress is its MAC address (can be viewed from **Fing*** or another similar APP).

✓ Add to the main router the fixed [IP] of **RM***, type 192.168.1.[IP]

✓ For the creation of the commands use Timeout=10 minimum and for execution it is enough with 2.

6. In the directory:

/home/pi/home_auto/infrared/ BlackBeanControl.py

ensure that the 4 parameters described are loaded, to do this edit line 167 as follows:

```
RM3Device=broadlink.rm((RealIPAddress,RealPort),
                        RealMACAddress,RealTimeout)
```

The operation mode is as follows:

1. The commands will be created, when they are not defined within the **BlackBeanControl.ini** file, using:

   sudo python BlackBeanControl.py −c [command]

2. And the commands will be executed, when they are already defined in **BlackBeanControl.ini**, using:

   sudo python BlackBeanControl.py −c [command]

3. If it wants to edit an existing command, it is better to delete it in the BlackBeanControl.ini

139

file and redefine it as indicated in point 1.

4. The commands are saved in the [Commands] section of BlackBeanControl.ini.

5. If a command is not yet invoked from **Python*** created the message "command not received" appears.

6. To link the commands created with actions to be chained, for example, by voice starting in **Google Home*** and through **IFTTT***, each command must be associated with a **[*].php** located in the **Raspberry*_home automation** in the folder /var/www/html/[*].php. These [*].php will be called from a **Webhook*** created in **IFTTT*** (we will see how later).

Next, by way of example, a table is defined with commands that are born by voice from **Google Assistant*** (**Google Home***), go through an **IFTTT*** **Webhook,** point to a [*].php and it executes a **Python*** module type [*].py.

When creating these commands, keep in mind that there are words reserved by the **Google Assistant*** Artificial Intelligence system and that they cannot be used, for example 'put', 'see', etc.

Google Assistant*	*.php	Description	Device
Program	p_1	Watch program	Decoder
TNT*	p_2	Watch **TNT***	Decoder
Energy*	p_e	Watch **Energy***	Decoder
Back	p_d_back	Go to previous situation	Decoder
Next channel	p_d_next	Next channel	Decoder
Previous channel	p_d_prev	Previous channel	Decoder

Google Assistant*	*.php	Description	Device
Colour $(*)	p_c_{{FieldText}}	Colour $	Bulb
More brightness	p_c_more_b	Change bulb to more brightness	Bulb
Less brightness	p_c_less_b	Change bulb to less brightness	Bulb
Increase volume	p_audio_more	Increase amplifier volume +5dB	Amplifier
Lower volume	p_audio_less	Lower amplifier volume −5dB	Amplifier
Remove silence	p_audio_sound	Remove mute	Amplifier
Remove sound	p_audio_mute	Remove sound	Amplifier
Right source	p_tv_s_right	Source and select right	TV
Left source	p_tv_s_left	Source and select left	TV
Turn on **Apple***	p_apple_on	Turn on Apple* TV	**Apple***
Turn off **Apple***	p_apple_off	Turn off Apple* TV	**Apple***

(*) **$** represents a variable word that is automatically loaded in the **{{FieldText}}** field of the **Webhook*** (detailed below).

The following **Webhooks*** with origin in **Raspberry***_**home automation** are also defined:

Name	*.php/Google*	Description	Device
apple_on/off	p_apple_on/off	On/off **Apple*** TV	**Apple***
tv_on/off	**Google Home***	On/off TV living room	**Samsung***
deco_on/off	**Google Home***	On/off decoder	**Arris***
colours_on/off	**Google Home***	On/off bulb	**TaoGlow***

1. To test a [*].php, it is best to run it by doing the following in **LXTerminal***: **php [*].php**

2. To create **Webhooks*** with variables, use the following sequence:

   ○ In **Google Assistant***, in the text field, add **$** as variable text.
   ○ In the **Webhook*** use {{TextField}} in the variable position.
   ○ Review spaces in URL (be careful when inserting {{TextField}})

Examples of URL to use in the **IFTTT*** **Webhook***, with variable text and pointing to a [*].php, located in /var/www/html/[*].php, which induces the execution of the corresponding **Python*** module:

/home/pi/home_auto/[*].py:

http://[user]:[pass]@[URL]/p_bulb_{{TextField}}.php

Where:

Parameter	Description
[user]	**Apache*** server (*) user in **Raspberry***_home automation** (we will see it)
[pass]	Idem for the password
[URL]	Address of he public page, hosted in **NO-IP*** (we will see)
{{TextField}}	File name [*].php captured by the **$** symbol

To use the UHD decoder (**Arris*** **VIP 5242**), load the following in the **IHC for EU*** APP:

1. <infrared> <add device> <set top box> <[operator]>

2. [operator] is the company that provides the telecommunications service.

3. Define the necessary buttons not included in the

previous file, using the learning option in the **IHC for EU*** APP and ensuring that the learned commands appear in the [commands] section of the BlackBeanControl.ini file.

4. **IMPORTANT:** For this system to function properly, the **RM*** must be at a concrete distance to the decoder (special case, does not happen with other devices).

   It is advisable to plug the **RM*** mini into a powerbank with +5v USB output and test positions until the best location is detected.

   A location that works well is positioning the **RM*** in the centre, under the TV, the decoder to the right of the TV being horizontal and somewhat lower than the **RM***.

5. Check that the public IP of the main router, in general 192.168.1.[IP], is properly assigned in **NO-IP*** (we will see later how) so that the **IFTTT*** commands are directed to the address, port, [*].php and [*].py suitable.

(*)   **Apache*** is a web server that allows us to access and run, via web, the necessary scripts located on the **Raspberry***_home automation.

Itead Sonoff Basic and eWelink

For switching off/on various devices: **Raspberry*_screen,** generic devices, ceiling lamp not accessible, **Tadoº*** Bridge, etc. **ITEAD*** switches of the **Sonoff Basic*** type have been chosen and managed by the **eWelink*** APP.

This choice basically responds to the ease of configuration of the APP, the availability of the material and the low price.

The great disadvantage of this product is its great complexity (possible need to implement a virtual server simulator, hacking of the control chips, etc.) that make it very difficult to integrate them into a simple **Python*** module. This English edition of the book describes a **Python*** solution to this complexity and it works perfectly.

However, this device it is easily managed by the **IFTTT*** integrator, which, in turn, has the great disadvantage of its slow execution. If the latter is a problem, it is recommended to use the **Edimax*** plug described above or implement the **Python*** script discussed.

To use **eWelink***, the first thing we must do is the pairing of the switches with the WIFI that will support them, this issue is critical because these switches need to be in the field of a 2.4GHz WIFI and with great coverage signal.

To do this, perform one of the following methods:

1) **Direct method:**
   ◦ Unplug and plug the power switch.
   ◦ Press the **Sonoff*** button, 6 seconds (it will start to flash slowly).
   ◦ Start the **eWelink*** APP on your mobile or tablet and select the WIFI (only 2.4Ghz, it does not work with 5Ghz) that covers the switch.
   ◦ Detected the switch, follow the rest of the steps. If this does not work go to method 2 described below.

2) **AP method:**
   ◦ Unplug and plug the switch into the mains.
   ◦ Press its button for 6 seconds and release it (the LED flashes slowly).
   ◦ Press the button again for another 6 seconds (the LED should flash quickly).
   ◦ Connect the mobile to the WIFI generated by switch, of the type **ITEAD***-**1000xxx** and initial password **12345678**
   ◦ Enter the APP **eWelink*** and wait for connection.
   ◦ Detected the switch, follow the rest of the steps and finish its configuration.
   ◦ If there are problems, deactivate the 5GHz WIFI of the Router or Bridge, to avoid interference and try pairing again.

The following describes how to operate with the **eWelink*** switches, **Sonoff*** Basic model, from **Itead***, without having to hack the firmware and integrate its management in a **Python*** module in a simple way and making the action on the **Sonoff*** switches much faster than using **IFTTT***.

See web: https://pypi.org/project/sonoff-python/ and perform the following steps:

```
sudo pip install sonoff-python
sudo pip install websocket-client
```

```
sudo cp /home/pi/.local/lib/python2.7/site-packages
                        /sonoff  /home/pi/home_auto
```

Switches, for example, can have the following configuration:

Device	Device id	Number
Screen	1000aaaaaa	[0]
Kitchen	1000bbbbbb	[1]
Ambient	1000cccccc	[2]
Bridge	1000dddddd	[3]

And in **Python*** use the following settings:

```
sss=sonoff.Sonoff('[user]','[pass]','[rr]')
```

Where:

[user] and **[pass]** are the user and password of the **eWelink*** APP and **[rr]** the region where the switches are located (us, eu, etc.)

```
devices=sss.get_devices()
dispo=devices[x]['deviceid']
sss.switch(action,dispo,None)
```

Where:

x is the [Number] and action is 'on' or 'off'

☉☉☉

14.–LINUX RASPBIAN*

The **Raspberry*** integrates a complete operating system of the **Linux*** family, called **Raspbian*** and which we have already mentioned previously.

On multiple occasions we will need to execute **Linux*** commands directly in the **Raspbian*** terminal application called **LXTerminal*** to act directly with the operating system.

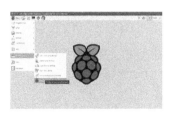

The following describes some common functions of this software, without pretending to be a comprehensive description of either **Linux*** or **Raspbian***, however there is ample information on both of them on the web.

For example see:

www.raspbian.org

*Basic Instructions

Remember the user and password that we have customised in the **Raspberry*** configuration and which by default are **user: pi** and **password: raspberry**

Linux command	Description
sudo shutdown -h now	Shut down system
sudo reboot -f	Reboot system
sudo rpi-config	Configuration mode
cat /proc/version	See **Raspbian*** version
cat /proc/partitions	See active partitions
cat /proc/cpuinfo	View hardware
sudo ssh-keygen -r[ip]	Generates host [IP] keys
sudo ssh -vvv pi@[ip]	Resets **Raspberry*** keys
lsusb	Connected usb list
sudo chmod 777 [file]	Gives full permission to [file]
sudo chown pi [file]	Assigns owner pi to [file]
htop	System processes information
rmdir	Delete directory
rm	Delete file
ls	List files
cd	Change to directory
mkdir	Create directory
cp	Copy file
mv	Move file
clear	Delete screen

*Script File Creation

When we need to execute several **Linux*** commands in **Raspbian***, it is very useful to create a file that includes them and that can be executed, for example, to create backup copies of certain important files in the **Raspberry*** configuration used here.

Example: we are going to create a script, called **save_home.sh** that backs up **Raspberry*_home automation** important configuration files.

/home/pi/home_auto/system_home_auto/save_home.sh

We will create it with **sudo nano save_home.sh** and add the following lines:

```
#!/bin/bash
echo "Copying files..."
sudo cp ~/.config/lxsession/LXDE-pi/autostart
        /home/pi/home_auto/system_home_auto/autostart
sudo cp /boot/config.txt
        /home/pi/home_auto/system_home_auto/config.txt
sudo cp /etc/fstab
            /home/pi/home_auto/system_home_auto/fstab
sudo cp /home/pi/.config/openbox/lxde-pi-rc.xml
   /home/pi/home_auto/system_home_auto/lxde-pi-rc.xml
sudo cp /etc/rc.local
        /home/pi/home_auto/system_home_auto/rc.local
sudo cp /etc/samba/smb.conf
        /home/pi/home_auto/system_home_auto/smb.conf
sudo cp /home/pi/home_auto/save_home.sh
   /home/pi/home_autos/system_home_auto/save_home.sh
echo "...copy made"
```

We could do the same in the **Raspberry*_ screen** with:

/home/pi/home_auto/system_rasp_screen/save_screen.sh

We will create it with **sudo nano save_screen.sh** and add the following lines:

```
#!/bin/bash
echo "Copying files..."
sudo cp ~/.config/lxsession/LXDE-pi/autostart
        /home/pi/home_auto/system_rasp_screen/autostart
sudo cp /boot/config.txt
        /home/pi/home_auto/system_rasp_screen/config.txt
sudo cp /etc/fstab
            /home/pi/home_auto/system_rasp_screen/fstab
sudo cp /home/pi/.config/openbox/lxde-pi-rc.xml
  /home/pi/home_auto/system_rasp_screen/lxde-pi-rc.xml
sudo cp /etc/rc.local
        /home/pi/home_auto/system_rasp_screen/rc.local
sudo cp /etc/samba/smb.conf
        /home/pi/home_auto/system_rasp_screen/smb.conf
sudo cp /home/pi/home_auto/save_screen.sh
    /home/pi/home_auto/system_home_auto/save_screen.sh
echo "...copy made"
```

Now we need the scripts save_[*].sh to be executable, for this we do:

sudo chmod +x save_[*].sh

And to test and execute them:

bash save_[*].sh

*Use of External Disks

Sometimes we will need to connect an external disk, be it a physical disk or a USB memory that is accessible as a hard disk, with a logical drive, which can be used, for example, to make backup copies of important system files of the project or very heavy multimedia files (photos, videos, etc.) that we need to use.

For this we do the following:

Command	Description
sudo fdisk —l	List of existing disks
sudo mkfs.ext3	Formats partition in **ext3** filesystem
sudo mkdir /media/[disk]	Creates access to [disk] in directory /media/
sudo nano /etc/fstab	Edit configuration initial mount of disks and add:
/dev/[partition]/media/[disk]	ext3 defaults 0
sudo chown pi /media/[disk]	Assign owner user pi to disk [disk]
sudo mount —a	Mount all disks (defined in fstab)
sudo umount /dev/[partition]	Unmount the disk in [partition]

⊖⊖⊖

15.-VNC*

For more convenience in accessing the **Raspbian*** operating system of both **Raspberry***, all its content and the home automation system and not to block other resources such as a TV (via **HDMI-CEC***), the need for a keyboard, a mouse, having to locate the **Raspberry*** very close to the TV, etc., it is recommended to use a remote connection via the **VNC*** software (local application or **Chrome*** plugin), which allows access to the **Raspberry*** from the mobile, a tablet, a computer, etc. and not only from the internal network of the home, it also allows access from outside the home.

To guarantee the connection from outside, even if the public IP is reassigned when the main Router is turned off/on, the **NO-IP*** environment and certain configuration are used on this Router and **Raspberry***, all with the following configuration:

1. Install the **VNC*** **Server** app on the **Raspberry***. In the latest versions of **Raspbian*** (**Stretch***) this software is already included.

2. Install the **Chrome*** plugin for **VNC*** on the **iMac*** (or PC) and also the **VNC*** **Viewer** APP (client) on mobile phones and tablets from which remote access will be performed. With the installation of **VNC*** **Viewer** on the mobile we can have several

access icons to the different devices: **iMac***, **Raspberry***_**home automation** and **Raspberry***_**screen** and with different types of access: LAN, WIFI or **NO-IP***

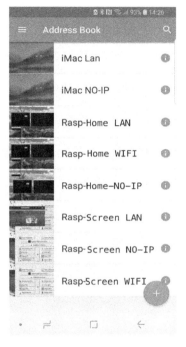

3. Open the ports on the main router: **5800, 5500** and **5900** in the **TCP** service.

4. To perform the operation of opening ports on the main router, follow the instructions of the router manufacturer or the telecommunications operator that provides the service.

5. To access from the internal network would be, for example: **192.168.1. [IP]:5900**. Where [IP] is the IP of the **Raspberry*** that it wants to access, it is therefore very convenient that this IP is fixed (it has already been seen how to assign it).

6. To access from the external network of the house, for example: **http://[URL]:5900** where [URL] is the public IP of the main Router or a URL assigned by some **DDNS*** dynamic assignment service, type **NO-IP***, which we will describe later.

7. Take note of the fixed IP of each **Raspberry***.

153

*General

As I mentioned earlier, by default **VNC*** is already installed on the **Raspbian*** **Stretch*** operating system, but with other version of this operating system can be installed with the following instructions:

```
sudo apt-get update install tightvncserver
tightvncserver
sudo reboot
sudo nano svnc.sh              and add:

#!/bin/sh
vncserver:0 -geometry 1920x1080 -depth 24 -dpi 96

chmod +x svnc.sh
./svnc.sh              to run
vncpasswd              to change or edit password or
                       from <vnc server>
                       <change password>
```

To ensure the proper configuration of **VNC***, in **Raspberry*** see:

```
vncserver:1 -geometry 2560x1600 -depth 16
                              -pixelformat rgb565
```

VNC pointer

On some occasion, for example when **VNC*** accesses an application that is only for viewing, that is: nothing is going to be executed remotely in it, or it is a query-only application, or it is a very sensitive application in which no input should be available, etc., we will need to disable the pointer so that it cannot make any unwanted keystrokes on the remote screen.

Important: this option is not advisable, unless it is not going to be used remotely, the mouse.

For this we enter **VNC*** of the **Raspberry*** and change:

```
<options> <expert> <AcceptPointerEvents> False
```

*Virtual Desks

If we want to work via **VNC*** with a **Raspberry*** remote desktop, different from the local desktop that is displaying or broadcasting the **Raspberry***, for example by HDMI output, the following can be done, although this option consumes many memory resources and CPU of the **Raspberry*** and its use is not advised:

1. Start:

   <preferences> <main editor menu> and add in these preferences: <Openbox Configuration Manager> <desktops> and define the necessary desktops.

2. In the top bar add/remove desktops and add <virtual desktops>

3. Configure the resolution in **VNC*** for desktop 1 with:

4. See:

   www.librebit.github.io

5. Search for "Enable **VNC*** Server on **Raspberry*** Pi" or:

   sudo nano /etc/init.d/vncboot

6. Change geometry and depth (1280x720) and run:

```
sudo chmot 755 /etc/init.d/vncboot
sudo update-rc.d lilghtm remove
sudo update-rc.d vncboot defaults
sudo reboot
```

7. Start **VNC*** with **192.168.1.[IP]:1** to access the new virtual desktop, with number 1.

8. Start **VNC*** with 192.168.1.[IP] to access the real **Raspberry*** desktop. In both cases [IP] is the fixed IP of the **Raspberry***.

9. In the virtual desktops we can use different display resolutions and for this we can configure resolutions such as:

```
DMT-85: 1280x700  60Hz 16:9
DMT-82: 1920x1080 60Hz 16:9
```

VNC on Another Tablet-Screen

As I mentioned earlier, an old **ZTE*** tablet has been reused to access the event viewer of the home automation application **p_global.py.**

The best way to make this access is precisely by installing **VNC*** on such a tablet.

This option is not essential for this project but it serves as an example of using **VNC*** and taking advantage of a disused tablet.

We do the following:

1. Copy the **Android*** application **Vnc-Viewer-Lite*** on the uSD card of the **ZTE*** to:

   /sdcard/Android/data

2. Install the **APK*** **Vnc-Viewer-Lite***.

3. On both **Raspberry***: **Raspberry***_**home automation** and **Raspberry***_**screen,** activate:

> <VNC> <options> <encryption>
> <prefer encryption>
> and <VNC password> <[password]>

4. On the **ZTE***, start the **Vnc-Viewer-Lite*** APK and configure:

Item	Raspberry*_home automation	Raspberry*_screen
IP	192.168.1.[IP_1]	192.168.1.[IP_2]
vnc_pass	Password_1	Password_2
vnc_port	5900	5900
SSH	Disable	Disable

5. Connect the **ZTE*** to the WIFI nearest.

6. Adjust the brightness and volume according to taste.

7. Adjust the **Python*** **Raspberry*_home automation** program that acts as an event viewer /home/pi/home_auto/**p_logfile.py** to be displayed in full screen of the **ZTE***.

⊖⊝⊖

16.-LXTERMINAL*

 We have already spoken that the **Raspbian*** operating system, which supports both **Raspberry***, contains a terminal emulator: **LXTerminal***.

This emulator allows the execution of fundamental **Linux*** commands to access multiple configurations and interactions with the basic functions of the operating system.

Like any direct access to an operating system, the use of **LXTerminal*** must be carried out with the necessary knowledge to avoid incurring critical operations that affect the operation of **Raspbian***.

In this sense it is recommended to make a backup copy of the uSD containing **Raspbian***, using, for example, the **ApplePI–Baker*** APP.

LXTerminal* can be configured with the following sections.

*General

It can adjust the sizes of open windows for **LXTerminal*** by doing the following:

sudo nano /usr/share /applications/lxterminal.desktop

And change:

Exec=lxterminal —geometry=60x25 (or oder size)

Or also:

sudo nano /home/pi/.config/lxterminal/lxterminal.conf

And add:

geometry_columns =60
geometry_rows   =25

Or also (I think it is the best solution):

1. Create program [*].sh for each program it wants to start.

2. Make them executable with: **sudo chmod +x [*.sh]**

3. Test them with: **bash [*.sh]**

4. Open with: **sudo nano ~/.config/lxsession/ LXDE-pi/autostart** and add:

   @/home/pi/home_auto/[*.sh]

5. Add the necessary @ ... for each [*.sh], for example, for **Raspberry*_home automation**, create the following programs in /home/pi/home_auto/*.sh:

Script	Description
p_start_global.sh	Starts p_global.py
p_start_telegram.sh	Starts p_telegram.py
p_start_logfile.sh	Starts p_logfile.py

6. The *.sh are like the following example:

```
#!/bin/bash
echo 'Booting p_logfile.py ...'
cd /home/pi/home_auto
lxterminal --command='sudo python p_logfile.py'
                    --geometry=105x25 -title='Logfile'
```

Other Options in LXTerminal

It can changes other details of the windows opened by **LXTerminal***, for example, run:

sudo nano ~/.config/lxterminal/lxterminal.conf

And change:

hide: scrollbar, menubar, closebutton, pointer to True, depending on how it wants each parameter.

.cache/lxsession/LXDE-pi/run.log, allows to see the boot log of **LXTerminal***.

Or to eliminate the decoration of the window (title, maximise, minimise and close buttons), it can be achieved with:

sudo nano /home/pi/.config/openbox/lxde-pi-rc.xml

And add:

```
<applications>
        <application name="*">
        <decor>no</decor>
        </application>
</applications>
```

☺☺☺

163

17.-NO-IP*

We have already commented that every time we turn off and on the main Router (unless we have a fixed public IP contracted with the telecommunications operator and usually has a monthly fee), the public IP of our main Router will change. This is a problem when we want to access our Router remotely because we do not know, if we are outside the home, what is that IP.

There are multiple solutions in the market to help us with this problem, one of them is to use a third-party service (there are free and paid), which basically keeps an allocation table updated between a domain they provide us and the public IP of our main router.

To perform this update it is necessary to install on the **Raspberry*** a software that is responsible for this update or also configure the main Router so that, when its public IP changes, it automatically communicates with the company that gives us the public domain and update the pair: domain vs public IP.

Here we will see one of these solutions, **NO-IP***, which until the time of writing of this book (January 2020), has a free version that only has as an inconvenience the need to update periodically, via e-mail, the decision to continue using the free version, unsubscribe or change modes.

Finally we will also see how the main router is configured so that it is who updates the pair: public domain vs public IP, although as we will see, this configuration will depend a lot on the brand of the main router used but all the necessary information is available on the manufacturer's website.

*General

Register on the **NO-IP*** website, www.noip.com and the **FreeDyn*** (NOIP) APP, configure it as follows:

```
<my accounts>
        service:    no-ip.com
        name:       [our URL]
        username:   [our e-mail]
        password:   [our password]

<my hostnames>
        service:    [our URL]
        hostname:   [our URL]
        <auto update> <refresh>
```

Where [our URL] will be the domain assigned to us by the **NO-IP*** server, in the general format

http://[URL].hopto.org

This [our URL] is the domain that allows us to access our main Router and therefore our project (home automation files, destination of **IFTTT***, destination o f **Webhook***, destination of [*].php, etc). [our e-mail] and [our password] are the parameters used to register in **NO-IP*** and it is highly recommended that they be customised.

In the **iMac*** (or another computer) it can also use the **No-IP DUC*** application and update the public IP in <Update Now>.

Some data as a summary, to enter the **Raspberry***:

[public IP of the Router]:5900

Or also:

http://[URL].hopto.org   URL assigned by **NO-IP***

    Or also:

http://[user]:[pass]@[URL].hopto.org   If username
                                       and password are used.

5800, 5500, 5900 Ports open to the TCP service such
as:

192.168.1.[IP]/5800/TCP   with local **Raspberry*** IP
192.168.1.[IP]/5500/TCP
192.168.1.[IP]/5900/TCP

*Installation

In general, install **NO–IP*** on the **Raspberry*** only if the public IP is to be updated from the **Raspberry***, otherwise update from the mobile (with **FreeDyn***) or from the **iMac*** (with **No–IP DUC***).

As it was said, if we want to use the free version of **NO–IP***, at www.noip.com it must update the host name, at least weekly, to maintain the domain assigned to us. Otherwise we will permanently unsubscribe this domain and we will have to rewrite the code again. Luckily, the **NO–IP*** service will remind us in our email that we must perform this operation.

To install **NO–IP*** on the **Raspberry***, we will do the following:

```
mkdir noip
cd no ip
wget http://www.no-ip.com/client/linux/
                          noip-duc-linux.tar.gz
tar vzxf noip-duc-linux.tar.gz
sudo apt-get install build-essential
make
sudo make install
sudo nano /etc/rc.local            and add:

     /usr/local/bin/noip2

ps aux | grep noip2                to check.
```

In addition and very important, so that when accessing the main Router with the URL assigned by **NO–IP***, the access to the **Raspberry*** is directed, the NAT table of the main Router must be configured as follows:

```
<network configuration> <NAT>
<Port Forwarding>
```

And add the following rules: two lines for each destination (**PLEX***, **Raspberry***_**home automation**, **Raspberry***_**screen**, **iMac***, etc.), a line with the **TCP** service and another line with the **UDP**

For example:

Service	External	Internal	IP server	Name
plex_TCP	[p1]–[p1]	[p1]–[p1]	192.168.1.[IP]	Raspberry*_ screen
plex_UDP	[p1]–[p1]	[p1]–[p1]	192.168.1.[IP]	Raspberry*_ screen
rasp_h_TCP	[p2]–[p2]	5900–5900	192.168.1.[IP]	Raspberry*_ home automation
rasp_h_UDP	[p2]–[p2]	5900–5900	192.168.1.[IP]	Raspberry*_ home automation
rasp_s_TCP	[p3]–[p3]	5900–5900	192.168.1.[IP]	Raspberry*_ screen
rasp_s_UDP	[p3]–[p3]	5900–5900	192.168.1.[IP]	Raspberry*_ screen
imac_TCP	[p4]–[p4]	5900–5900	192.168.1.[IP]	iMac* LAN
imac_UDP	[p4]–[p4]	5900–5900	192.168.1.[IP]	iMac* LAN
NOIP1	80–80	80–80	192.168.1.[IP]	Raspberry*_ home automation
NOIP2	443–443	443–443	192.168.1.[IP]	Raspberry*_ home automation

Where [IP] is the IP address of the destination device and px is the internal or external port of the main Router that it wants to use for the service described.

With this **NAT*** table, the shortcuts for **VNC*** with **NO-IP*** would be, for example, the following:

169

Device or Service	Full URL
PLEX*	http://[URL].hopto.org:p1
Raspberry*_home automation	http://[URL].hopto.org:p2
Raspberry*_screen	http://[URL].hopto.org:p3
iMac*	http://[URL].hopto.org:p4

Where px is the port assigned to the service it wants to access.

*Important

Port **80 (http://)** and **443 (https://)** must be open for action requests to enter the **Raspberry*_home automation** (origin in **IFTTT*** and destination **Apache*** server, which we will see later).

On the **iMac***, the **OSX*** firewall may be enabled, but it must disable the firewall created by the antivirus (for example **Avira***, **McAfee***, etc.) or write exception rules. For example, for **McAfee*** antivirus:

```
<settings> <firewall> <unlock with password> <add
rule> <name allow VNC> <TCP> <local ports> <5900>
<block>
```

In addition, **iMac*** must be configured to share like:

```
<system preferences> <share> <enable screen sharing>
<computer settings> <enable both options: everyone
can ... and viewers ...>
```

Check that the public IP of the main router is collected in **NO-IP***, for this look at:

www.no-ip.com as:

```
<log in> <[e-mail]> <[password]> <Dynamic DNS>
<Modify> <[Public router IP]> <update hostname>
```

Finally, it can activates the **NO-IP*** update, from the main Router itself as indicated below, however this configuration depends on the brand of the Router.

This is the best solution because it is the main router itself that is responsible, automatically, for updating any change in its public IP (for example, when the power supply is lost or when a reset occurs) and therefore it is a convenient solution and safe.

```
<network configuration> <Dynamic DNS> <Dynamic DNS:
enable> <Service Provider:

                www.no-ip.com>

<Host Name: [URL] <Username: [e-mail]> <Password:
[password] > <Apply>
```

And verify that the public IP is accepted and confirmed.

☉☉☉

18.-COLORAMA*

Next we talk about **Colorama***, an additional **Python*** software module and that allows to improve the presentation of the screens of the home automation program, **p_global.py**, making it more attractive, readable, clear and friendly.

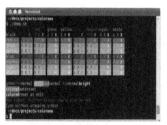

Specifically, this module, which is only valid in the environment of the **Raspbian*** terminal emulator, this is in **LXTerminal***, allows it to position text in a specific and fixed place in a window, assigning it a series of attributes: colour of the text, colour of the background, font, brightness, flickering, etc.

In this way, the [*].py program that runs with this software will have a semi-graphic environment in rows and columns mode.

It is very simple to use. See the following:

*Installation and Commands

Install the **Python*** module **Colorama***, with the following instructions:

See: http://nullege.com/

```
from colorama import <function>
from colorama import init()
python setup.py install
```

Let's see some basic instructions of **Colorama***:

Instruction	Action
Fore.GREEN+'Text'	Displays 'Text' with green letter
Back.RED+'Text'	Displays 'Text' with red background
Style.NORMAL+'Text'	Displays 'Text' with normal brightness
Style.BRIGHT+'Text'	Displays 'Text' with high brightness
Style.RESET_ALL	Restores all settings
Style.BLINK	Blinks text
Style.UNDERLINED	Underlines text
init(autoreset=True)	Restores style after writing
Cursor.BACK(x)	Goes back x characters
Cursor.FORWARD(x)	Goes forward x characters
Cursor.UP(x)	Goes up x characters
Cursor.DOWN(x)	Goes down x characters
Cursor.POS(c,r)	Positions the cursor on c=column & r=row

*Examples

```
print (Cursor.POS(48,23)+Fore.YELLOW+'Hello')
print (Cursor.POS(1,2)+Style.BRIGHT+Fore.RED+'Start:')
print (Cursor.POS(2,5)+Fore.WHITE+Back.GREEN+write(x))
print (Cursor.POS(10, 5)+''*27)
print (Cursor.POS(10.5)+Fore.BLUE+Back.WHITE+
                               time.strftime('%X'))

trace (Cursor.BACK(20.30)+'P'+str(write(5)))
```

Where write() & trace() are user defined functions.

☻☻☻

19.-TKINTER*

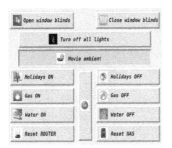

Another very interesting **Python*** module and that in this project is used in t h e **p_screen.py** program (which we will see later), is **Tkinter***, which basically allows to create and locate buttons on the screen, with different formats, colours, sizes, fonts, associated gifs, motion effects, etc. and that pressing them can execute additional **Python*** scripts.

In our case, **Tkinter*** module runs on the **Raspberry*_screen** to present the different management options of the home automation program in the form of buttons, which when pressed from the touch screen or from **VNC***, execute a specific home automation action.

Let's see it below:

*General Information

To install it follow the next guide:

See www.guia-tkinter.readthedocs.io

```
from tkinter import <Label>    imports module <Label>
widget=Label(None,text=<text>)
widget.pack()
widget.mainloop()
```

These three widgets (definition of buttons, grouping of them and execution of actions), should always be used and in this order for the creation of any button or group of buttons.

Next we will see how they are created, grouped, configured, added content, gifs and even sound and some concrete examples.

*Buttons Creation

The buttons, whose activation from the touch screen execute a specific **Python*** module, are necessary to define them previously: position, text source, associated icon, action to be executed etc., for this we can do the following:

Install the necessary functions with:

```
from Tkinter import *
import tkFont
```

And add in the **Python*** module **p_screen.py,** the following instructions:

To create in this example a button, called open_button, with the text **'Open window blinds',** adjusted to the **left** of the button, with the **Helvetic*** font, size 20, on a 800x600 pixel resolution screen, shifted 100 pixels to the right, which cannot be resized, minimised, or maximised, that no pointer is displayed, with **cyan background** colour, with button with 5 pixel size border, with raised relief, which at press it simulate its sinking, which executes the **Python*** module **[opens],** which with the click changes the colour of the background to **green,** which is positioned in the coordinates [left]-[height], with a width [width_short], with a height [height_short] and an image obtained from the file **blinds.gif,** etc.

We would do:

```
window=Tk()
source=tkFont.Font(family='Helvetic',size=20,)
                #the height and width are in lines

window.geometry('800x600+100+0')
     #width and height adjustment and right-hand shift

window.resizable(width=False,height=False)
                        #to avoid changing screen size

window.config(cursor="none")
          #to avoid displaying the cursor in the screen

window.config(background='cyan')
                          # background screen colour

button_open=Button(window,text='Open window blinds',
               anchor='w',compound=LEFT,font=source,
                relief='raised',overrelief='sunken',
                       borderwidth=5,command=open,
               activebackground=green,cursor=type_cur)

button_open.pack()
button_open.place(x=left,y=height+offset,
               width=width_short,height=height_short)

image1=PhotoImage(file='/home/pi/home automation/
                              photos/blinds.gif')
button_open.config(image=image1)
mainloop()
```

Where type_cur, left, height, offset, width_short & height_short are variables previously defined by the user.

*Use of Images
on Buttons

To make the presentation of a **Tkinter*** button more attractive, it can add an icon on each button, which represents in some way the action that is going to perform this button, here the creativity is infinite.

See the following:

1. The format to be used is *.**gif** at 60x60 pixels maximum (to fit the size of our buttons).

2. Use <preview> <tools> <adjust size> to 40x40 pixels.

3. Position button with **COMMAND**

4. See www.online-convert.com if the conversion of *.jpg to *.gif is necessary and resize to be usable with **Tkinter***.

*Hide Cursor
on Screen

Here are described actions to hide the cursor in **LXTerminal***, so that we only see the buttons created b y **Tkinter***, leaving the window much cleaner, intuitive and above all safe, so as not to press inappropriate buttons because the cursor is positioned there by mistake.

Do the next:

1. **os.system**('setterm –cursor off')
                        #hides the cursor of **LXTerminal***

2. **os.system**("xte 'mousemove 0 0'")
                        #positions the cursor point
                        outside the active screen.

3. Use the DECORATE function in **LXTerminal*** with:

sudo nano /home/pi/.config/openbox/lxde–pi–rc.xml

And add:

```
<applications>
      <application name="*">
      <decor>no</decor>
      </application>
</applications>
```

*Include Sound when Pressing Buttons

Finally, if it wants to press a button to sound a 'beep' or other sound and thus acoustically feedback that we have pressed such a button, we can do the following, for this we must have the necessary hardware to activate the sound.

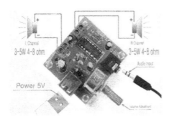

There are several options to activate the sound: connect a small speaker to the audio output by jack (very low volume), add a small amplifier, **Bluetooth*** connection etc.

There are amplifiers for **Raspberry***, such as **Winwill PM2038*** (USB power and 2x5w audio power), or pair the audio via **Bluetooth*** with any speaker or device that has this type of connection, etc.

In the **Python*** module, in our case **p_screen.py,** add the following:

```
from pygame import mixer        #to reproduce sounds.
sound='/home/pi/home_auto/conga.wav'
                               #wav file with the sound.
mixer.init()
beep=mixer.Sound (sound)
beep.play()
```

In **Raspbian*** activate the sound with:

<audio> <devices settings>

182

And select:

–bcm2835 ALSA (mixer)
–PCM

And in **Raspberry*_screen** configuration review:

sudo raspi-config
<advance options> <audio> <AUTO>

If it wants to do it by BT **(Bluetooth***), it is only necessary to activate the BT speaker and put it in pairing mode, enter the top bar of **Raspbian*** and select the BT icon:

```
<manage bluetooth devices> <turn on bluetooth>
<add device> <select device> <pair>
and increase the volume as desired.
```

☺☺☺

20.—SAMBA*

We had already commented previously, that to manage home automation commands from the **Raspberry*** touch screen, it is necessary to have information exchange files between both **Raspberry***.

This information exchange files are located on one device, but must be accessible, both for reading and writing, from other devices.

Also if we want to make a backup of the two **Raspberry*** (home automation & screen) home automation software and important files, for example from the **iMac***, we will need to share information bidirectionally as if they were disk drives.

All this tasks are implemented by the **SAMBA*** module, as we will see.

*General

To implement this sharing of information, software, configurations, etc., this project uses the configuration of a **virtual disk** defined in **/etc/fstab** and resident in the **Raspberry*_home automation**.

The content of /etc/fstab in the **Raspberry*_home automation** was previously discussed. For the /etc/fstab of the **Raspberry*_screen**, something similar should be added to this:

```
#Network disks
//192.168.1.[IP[/public        /home/pi/disks/public
                    cifs username=1,password=1 0 0
//192.168.1.[IP[/pi_home_auto/home_auto     /home/pi/
          disks/home_auto cifs file_mode=0777,
        dir_mode=0777,username=1,password=1 0 0
//192.168.1.[IP]/sirio      /home/pi/disks/sirio
                cifs username=1,password=1,vers=1.0 0 0
```

Where **public** and **sirio** are physical disks in network and **pi_home_auto** is a virtual disk, located in the **Raspberry*_home automation**, from which the /home/pi/disks folder on which the physical disks are to be mounted.

To be able to share information without problems, run **Python*** as **ROOT** as follows:

sudo su
python /home/pi/home_auto/p_screen.py

And add this information at startup as follows:

sudo nano ~/.config/lxsession/LXDE-pi/autostart

And add:

```
@lxpanel --profile LXDE-pi
@pcmanfm --desktop --profile LXDE-pi
@xscreensaver -no-splash
@point-rpi
@chromium-browser            http://192.168.1.[IP]:
                                [port]/web/index.html
@sudo su
@sudo python /home/pi/home_auto/p_screen.py
@sudo mount -a
```

The shared disk **/home/pi/disks/[shared disk]** contains all the necessary files, of the style **[*].txt,** and among them **p_actuators.txt** (or another name), with the following actions and with values YES or NO:

Action	Description
Turn off lights	Turns off all lights
Lights living room sofa	Lights the living room lamp in the sofa area
Watch movie	Actives movie mode
Close window blinds	Closes a group of window blinds
Open window blinds	Opens a group of window blinds
Open living room window blinds	Opens living room window blinds
Open all window blinds	Opens all window blinds
Holidays ON	Activates Holidays mode
Holidays OFF	Deactivates Holidays mode
Water ON	Opens the electro valve of the water
Water OFF	Closes the electro valve of the water

Action	Description
Gas ON	Opens the gas electro valve
Gas OFF	Closes the gas electro valve
Heating ON	Sets thermostat in PRESENCE
Heating OFF	Sets thermostat in ABSENCE
Clear screen	Resets the p_global.py screen
Reset NAS	Resets de home NAS
Reset **ONT***	Resets **ONT*** communication
Reset ROUTER	Resets the main ROUTER
Reset **RASPBERRY***	Resets **Raspberry***_home automation

On the other hand and to share information between both **Raspberry*** and between them and the **iMac*** (or another computer at home), a network disk management program must be installed.

In our case, the **SAMBA*** module has been installed in each **Raspberry***, as described below.

*Samba Installation

To install the **SAMBA*** module on each **Raspberry***, we perform the following:

```
sudo apt-get install samba samba-common-bin
sudo nano /etc/samba/smb.conf
```

And add in the [global] section:

```
workgroup           =WORKGROUP
wins support        =yes
```

and at the end, in section [pi], add:

✓ **For Raspberry*_home automation:**

```
[pi_home_auto]
comment             =user directory
path                =/home/pi
browseable          =Yes
writeable           =Yes
read only           =no
only guest          =no
create mask         =0777
directory mask      =0777
public              =Yes
```

✓ **For the Raspberry*_screen:**

```
[pi_screen]
comment             =user directory
path                =/home
browseable          =Yes
writeable           =Yes
read only           =no
only guest          =no
```

```
create mask        =0777
directory mask     =0777
public             =Yes
```

And finally use:

```
sudo smbpasswd -a pi            add customise password
sudo systemctl restart smbd         to restart SAMBA*
sudo systemctl stop smbd            stop SAMBA*
sudo systemctl stop start           start SAMBA*
```

With this configuration we have **SAMBA*** installed on all devices and we can already share information between them, via **Python*** even via **Raspbian*** file manager on any **Raspberry*** or **OSX*** of the **iMac*** or **Windows*** of the **PC***.

☺☺☺

21.-TELEGRAM*

In order to interact with the home automation of the house, in addition to using **VNC*** or acting with the buttons of the **Raspberry***_ screen, a Telegram **BOT*** has been added, which with the execution of a simple **Python*** module in the **Raspberry***_home automation allows to execute a series of commands to perform the most important and fundamental home automation actions. To do so, both from home and from outside it, we only need an Internet access.

Telegram* has been used because it allows the easy creation of the **BOT***, without problems of "banning" by the managers of **Telegram***, (**WhatsApp*** is not valid for automatic **BOT***).

There are multiple examples available on the web and its stability is proven.

Let's see how to do it below:

*General

There is a lot of literature and web sources that explain how to implement a **Telegram*** **BOT** in a **Raspberry*** to control various issues.

I recommend, for example, to see the following examples links, they describe step by step the installation and configuration of **Python*** modules and examples of operation are attached.

https://geekytheory.com/tutorial-raspberry
                    -pi-use-of-telegram-with-python

https://www.fwhibbit.es/controla-tu-raspberry
                    -pi-via-telegram

In this **BOT*** 4 fundamental options have been included: **Raspberry***, System, Home Automation and Info.

1. I n **Raspberry***: Temperatures, HD, RAM and CPU options.
2. I n **System:** IP, Clear, Reset NAS/ONT /Router/**Raspberry***.
3. I n **Home Automation:** State, Action, Lights/Others, Window blinds, Heater, Devices, Holidays and Movie scene.
4. In **Info:** available commands and help.

Each option indicates the situation and status of the affected elements and in the case of the Status section, it is also indicated by voice via **Google Home*** (something similar could be done with **Alexa***). We will see later how it is configured.

*Install
System Features

We need to install specific modules following the instructions on the previous websites and with the commands described below:

Install Telebot*	BOT of **Telegram***.
Install sysstat	To see% CPU usage.
Install psutil	To view system variables.

```
sudo apt-get install build-essential python-dev
                                        python-pip
sudo pip install psutil
sudo apt-get install sysstat
```

The Botfather

Then we enter in **Telegram***, we register following the instructions and activate the **BotFather*** that will guide us, step by step, in the configuration of the **BOT***.

token in @BotFather
rasp in @Rasp [user]Bot

Finally:

To install **Telegram*** on the **Raspberry*_home automation**:

sudo pip install pyTelegramBotAPI

In our example, we will have the following commands:

/start	Starts communication with the **BOT***.
/help	List of available commands.
/exec	Executes **LXTerminal*** commands.
/others	Rejects invalid commands, etc.

In the **Python*** module, which runs the **BOT*** in the **Raspberry***_**home automation** (in parallel with **p_global.py**) and in our case we have named **p_telegram.py,** we will use the following instructions:

import telebot   #Import necessary modules.
from telebot import types

```
TOKEN ='[token_id]'    #View the Token on Telegram*
idi   ='[user_id]'     #View the user code
text  =m.text          #Load on text button pressed BOT*
cid   =m.chat.idi      #Load on cid BOT* user code
Bot.send(cid,'Text')   #Send Text to the BOT*
```

Now we will see some interesting alternatives and functions, which we can use to format the visualisation and generate the **BOT*** orders.

*Change Type
of Text in the BOT*

By default, all the texts displayed on the **BOT***
in **Telegram*** have the same typeface, the same format
and the same size, that makes the **BOT*** boring to see
and not very clear.

So that the **BOT*** present in **Telegram***, the text
with several formats (there are not many
alternatives), we can do the following, in this case
'[text]' will be displayed in **bold** or *italic*:

bold	bot.send_message(cid,'*text*', parse_mode='Markdown')
italic	bot.send_message(cid,'_text_', parse_mode='Markdown')

We may use **bold** or *italic*, for example, to
highlight the name of the device, its status, its IP
address, the main menus, the purposes of executing
listings, etc. Here creativity is infinite.

*Device List

One of the functions implemented in the **BOT*** is to visualise the home automation devices, with WIFI or LAN connectivity, connected to the system.

There are multiple ways of doing this function, the safest is to order the **Raspberry***_**home automation** by **BOT*** to perform a **PING** to all possible local IP addresses, but it would take a long time.

In our example a mixed solution has been proposed, on the one hand the content of **ARP*** is listed (file containing the local IP detected by the **Raspberry***) and on the other a PING to the devices considered critical. Let's look at a specific example in each case:

✓**According to the MAC accessible by ARP***

First we are going to visualise all the possible devices connected using the **ARP*** table of **Raspbian***:

1. Only the IP segments that are the usual scope of our devices, are going to be analysed, in our example: 192.168.1.1/101

2. Install the **nmap** application with:
   sudo apt-get install nmap

3. Update **ARP*** table with:
   nmap -sn 192.168.1.*

4. And use the following instructions in **Python***:

```
pid    =Popen(["arp","-n",host],stdout=PIPE)
s      =pid.communicate()[0]
```

```
mac   =re.search(r"(([a-f\d]{1,2}\:){5}[a-f\d]
                              {1,2})",s).groups()[0]
```

✓**By pre-scanning the [IP]** and using ARP-SCAN, as follows:

```
sudo apt-get install arp-scan
arp-scan -r 1 -I eth0 --localnet -t 300>[file]
```

Where:

[IP] first characters to the '\t'
[MAC] tab next 18 characters

The last option, the most reliable, but the slowest, is to directly scan all IP where we suspect a device may be connected, but as it is necessary to enable a timeout, minimum of 2 seconds, to give each device time to answer the PING command, if we scan a large IP range, the process can take several minutes and becomes unmanageable.

To make PING scanning practical, in our case it has been limited exclusively to critical devices:

TV that can stay on.

Router and Bridges that support the connectivity of the entire system.

Equipment with fixed IP, which usually support devices that we need to be enabled before a power failure: **Edimax***, **Tadoº***, **RM***, Decoders, WIFI Bulb, **Google Home***, etc.

We use the following commands:

```
x=os.system('ping -c 1'+host+'> /dev/null 2>&1')
```

Where:

if x=0 the device is connected.
if x#0 the device does not respond.

And in our case we only do PING about:

Living room TV
Bedroom TV
PS4* WIFI
Main Router
Each Bridge
Edimax*
Tadoº*
WIFI bulbs
RM* mini
Google Home*
Alexa*
Both **Raspberry***
iMac*

IMPORTANT: it is very useful to have updated the IP assignment table in our network and which we have described in previous chapters.

*Public and Local IP Detection

We have added a function that allows us to visualise the **public IP** (we may need it at any time to update **NO-IP*** if we are not at home) and confirm the **private IP** of our **Raspberry*_home automation** which is what we use as an entry point to our installation.

For the detection of our **public IP** we ask the **Raspberry***, via **Telegram*** **BOT***, to extract this IP, for example, from one of the following websites (it can be any other):

http://miip.es
https: //www.cual-es-mi-ip.net/
http://www.cualesmiip.com/

And in **p_telegram.py** we extract the IP using the following functions:

```
import urllib2
ip=urllib2.urlopen(url_ip).read()[a:b]
```

Where **a** and **b** are the location of [IP]
To obtain the **private IP** of the **Raspberry*_home automation** we use:

```
x=[l for l in ([ip for ip in socket.gethostbyname
                _ex(socket.gethostname())[2]if not ip
    .startswith("127.")][:1],[[(s.conect(('8.8.8.8',53))
            ,s.getsockname([0],s.close())for s in [socket
                            .socket(socket.AF_INET,socket
                            .SOCK_DGRAM)]][0][1]])if l][0][0]
```

And we validate the content of x so that it has the format of an IP type 192.168.1.[IP]

☺☺☺

22.-IFTTT*

With the emergence of multiple home automation hardware manufacturers, with diverse parameters and protocols, various action integrators have also appeared.

These integrators allow to easily create applets that relate specific situations in sensors, variables, orders, etc., with specific actions, actuators, files, software, APPS, etc.

Here the **IFTTT*** integrator (**if this, then that**) is described because its ease of use, gratuity and endless possibilities of operation with multiple hardware and home automation software manufacturers in a simple way to create and maintain.

This integrator is available in both web version and in APP version.

*General

To configure access to **IFTTT*** from the **Raspberry***_home automation,** do the following:

Enter at:

https://ifttt.com/maker_webhooks

And create the **Webhooks***, such as:

if MakerEvent [x] **then** turn [on] [device]

See the required key at:

https://ifttt.com/maker_webhooks

[documentation] and use:

curl −X POST https://maker.ifttt.com
                    /trigger/[webhook]/with/key/[key]

Or from **Python***:

os.system ('previous instruction')

To add it in **Python***:

```
import requests
requests.post('https://maker.ifttt.com/
          trigger/'+[webhook]+'/with/key/'+/[key])
```

To include parameters add to the end of the previous order:

−H "Content − Type:application/json"
                    −d'{"value[1]":"[parameter]"}
                    ...−d'{"value[n]":"[parameter]"}

To update the [key] from **IFTTT**[*]:

<Webhooks Settings> <Edit connection>

To avoid text-to-screen output from the **IFTTT**[*] order, add at the end of the instruction:

> /home/pi/home_auto/ifttt.log 2>&1

Webhooks Created

Here the creativity is infinite, some examples
are described below:

Webhook*	Description
ambient_on/off	On/off switch **Sonoff*** ambient
bridge_on/off	On/off switch **Sonoff*** **Tadoº***
bulb_on/off	On/off lamp **TP-Link*** WIFI
kitchen_on/off	On/off switch **Sonoff*+RF** kitchen
colours_on/off	On/off colours lamp
deco_on/off	On/off living room decoder
tv_on/off	On/off living room TV
screen_on/off	On/off switch **Sonoff*** screen
tado_auto	**Tadoº*** goes to automatic mode
tado_on_18	**Tadoº*** goes to 18°C (64,4°F) setpoint
tado_on_22	**Tadoº*** goes to 22°C (71,6°F) setpoint
tado_off	**Tadoº*** turns off heating
log_dropbox	Adds /home/pi/home_auto/ p_logfile.txt to **DropBox***
send_sms	Send an SMS
rasp_calendar	Adds specific event to calendar

☺☺☺

23.-GOOGLE ASSISTANT*

Google Assistant

In this section we will see how, using **Artificial Intelligence** integrated in a speaker with a personal assistant, we can provide the entire system with much more added value.

The integration of **Google Assistant*** discussed here, use this device to dictate the home automation orders we need at any time: open the window blinds, turn off lights, turn on the TV, put on such a channel, turn up the volume, set up such environment, put 20°C/°F on the thermostat, turn off the heating, etc., dictate routines: good morning, good night, I'm leaving, I'm here, etc., (we'll see them in detail) and also receive and issue system status messages, automatic actions, alarm situations, etc., and all of this with voice and in a friendly and fun environment.

T h e **Amazon*** assistant could have been used but it is more difficult to integrate with **Python*** a n d i t i s m o r e complicated to obtain using a two-way voice system. For a basic home automation system **Alexa*** is equally useful.

The device used here is **Google*** **Home Mini** for its excellent interpretation of voice commands, the excellent relationship with the **IFTTT*** integrator, the availability of forums, information, tutorials, etc. about its operation, its affordable price, the reception and transmission of voice messages as if it were a **Chromecast***, etc.

Important: place this device in a little noisy place and close to the user.

To improve the integration of the **Google*** **Home Mini** with other devices, especially with the TV, **Google*** **Chromecast** is used connected to an HDMI port of the TV in the living room. This allows to manage with voice commands: turn on/off the TV, play songs from **Spotify*** or **YouTube*** **Music**, watch a series of **Netflix***, watch photos from **Google*** **Photos,** watch a **YouTube*** video, watch a movie from **HBO***, watch a **TED Talk*** chat, listen to a radio station on **TuneIn Radio***, etc.

In order for this device to turn off and on the TV, it must have its own power, therefore DO NOT power it from a USB port on the TV.

*General

On the web there is a lot of literature on how to interconnect **Google Assistant*** with a **Raspberry***, here it proposes to see the following:

www.sistemasorp.es

Next we will review an example of detailed configuration of this system, based on the integration with the **APACHE*** server, to which we will also protect its access with username and password (we will see it in detail later) and the execution of modules of the type **[*].php,** located in the **Raspberry***_home **automation** and launching home automation orders.

Personally I think this is the part that brings more value and perhaps the most playful (send verbal orders and receive, also verbally, information on the status of devices, sensors, actuators, variables, alarms, performances, guard dog barking simulation, etc.), I hope you enjoy the same as me.

*Important

Ports **80 (http://)** and **443 (https://)** must be open on the main Router, so that requests for action, originating in **IFTTT*** and destination **Apache*** server, are directed to the **Raspberry***_home automation** and can run there without any problem.

In the tutorial on the previous website it talks about installing **NGROK*** to direct the **IFTTT*** request to the **APACHE*** server. In this case, install **NGROK*** and create a public host with https://[code].ngrok.io, but this option forces to obtain an **NGROK*** code and write the IP address of the main router in the script every time it changes.

In our case it has been preferred to use the domain provided by **NO-IP*** (already described) for greater stability and for not needing to rewrite any code or modify the **Python*** script every time it changes to the IP address of the main Router.

*Script Creation

It must creates a series of **scripts, in [*].php** format, which are targeted by the **IFTTT** * applets started by the **Google Assistant** *. These [*].php will contain instructions to start the **Python** * [*].py modules, which are the ones that finally execute the home automation actions indicated by voice in the **Google** * **Home Mini.**

In our example several [*].php have been created, but here the creativity is infinite (I repeat myself a lot). Let's look at some examples:

*.PHP	Description
p_open.php	Opens all window blinds
p_open_living.php	Opens living room window blinds
p_ambient_on/off.php	Adds/removes ambient to p_devices.txt
p_turn_off.php	Turns off all the lights
p_turn_on/off_sofa.php	Turns on/off sofa lamp
p_apple_on/off.php	Turns on/off **Apple** * TV
p_audio_more/less.php	Increases/decreases +5dB audio amplifier volume
p_audio_mute.php	Puts mute in the amplifier
p_audio_on/off.php	Turns on/off amplifier
p_close.php	Closes all window blinds
p_colours_auto.php	Puts colour lamp in auto
p_colours_[colour].php	Puts colour lamp in a concrete colour

*.PHP	Description
p_colours_more/less_br.php	Puts colours lamp with maximum/minimum brightness
p_colours_on/off.php	Turns on/off colours lamp
p_deco_back.php	Goes back decoder screen
p_deco_more/less.php	Advances/goes back program
p_deco_mute.php	Decoder mute
p_turn_on_sofa.php	Turns on the sofa lamp
p_bridge_on/off.php	Adds/removes bridge **Tadoº*** to p_devices.txt
p_put_[number].php	Puts desco on channel number [number]
p_put_[name].php	Puts desco con channel name [name]
p_screen_on/off.php	Adds/removes screen to p_devices.txt
p_tado_away/home.php	Adds/removes **Tadoº*** away/home to p_devices.txt
p_tado_more/less22.php	Adds **Tadoº*** >22°C, <22°C to p_devices.txt (71,6°F)
p_tado_more/less50.php	Adds **Tadoº*** >50%, <50% HR to p_devices.txt
p_tv_more/less.php	Advances/goes back living room TV channel
p_tv_source.php	Activates input sources from the living room TV
p_tv_source_right.php	Advances right in the source selection
p_tv_source_left.php	Advances left in the source selection
p_watch_movie.php	Activates movie ambient

*Topics to Review

1. By configuration of **Raspbian*** and the **Apache*** server, the [*].php must necessarily be located in the **/var/www/html/[*].php** folder of the operating system.

   Give total permits with:

   sudo chmod 777 /var/www/html

   And review them with:

   sudo ls –l

2. **IMPORTANT:** Also give full permissions to all the exchange files used: (**p_devices.txt, p_actuators.txt,** etc.), with:

   sudo chmod 777 /home/pi/home_auto/p_[*].txt

3. To check the correct functioning of the [*].php, we can do:

php p_[*].php	with the [*].php
sudo python p_[*].py	with the [*].py

4. We must make the **Apache*** server and the **UART*** serial port of the **Raspberry***_home **automation** compatible with:

   sudo usermod –a G video,dialout www_data

5. Change the extension or name of this file:

   /var/www/html/index.html

So that it doesn't start with the [*].php.

6. To start/stop the **Apache*** service use:

```
sudo /etc/init.d/apache2 restart
sudo /etc/init.d/apache2 stop
```

Protect Apache
with User & Password

With the creation of the **NO-IP*** domain http://[URL].hopto.org the **NAT*** portforwarding table of the main Router and the installation of **Apache***, the files located in /var/www/html/ become public access (try typing the previous URL)

As in this directory there are critical home automation actions that only we should be able to use, next we will see how to protect access to **Apache*** with a personalised **[user]** and **[password]**, avoiding unwanted access and maintaining our information totally sure.

To do this:

```
sudo apt-get update
sudo apt-get install apache2 apach2-utils
sudo htpasswd -c /etc/apache2/.htpasswd
                              [user] [password]
sudo nano /etc/apache2/.htpasswd
                          to see if it is created.
sudo nano /etc/apache2/sites-enabled/
                              000 -default.conf
```

And add before the end of the file, just before </virtualHost>, the following information:

```
<Directory "/var/www/html">
      AuthType        Basic
      AuthName        "For administrators only"
      AuthUserFile    /etc/apache2/.htpasswd
      Requires    valid-user
</Directory>
```

211

In addition user:password must be added in **IFTTT*** applet URL such as:

http://[user]:[password]@[URL].hopto.org:80/[x]

Where [x] can be:

```
p_turn_off.php
p_close.php
p_open.php
p_open_living.php
p_turn_on/off_sofa.php
p_[*].php
any *.php defined in the previous tables
```

In **IFTTT***, the method must be kept in GET and the rest of the applet options blank.

Applets Created in IFTTT

In www.ifttt.com, to correctly configure voice commands, it is recommended to include in each of the applets, three words without articles in an option of the three provided by the applet.

With this issue we must have a lot of patience because **Goggle Assistant*** or **Alexa*** reserve many specific words for their internal system and that we cannot use in **IFTTT***

Examples of **IFTTT*** applets are shown below:

Name	Origin	Destination	Action
ambient on/off	**Raspberry***	**eWelink***	On/off ambient light switch
kitchen_on/off	**Raspberry***	**eWelink***	On/off kitchen light switch
bridge_on/off	**Raspberry***	**eWelink***	On/off **Tadoº*** bridge switch
screen_on/off	**Raspberry***	**eWelink***	On/off screen switch
bulb_on/off	**Raspberry***	**Tp-Link***	On/off WIFI bulb
logfile_dropbox	**Raspberry***	**DropBox***	Upload logfile to **DropBox*** at 12:00 am

The following group of Applets is defined in the APP **Home*** itself that manages the **Google Home*** device and it is not essential to use **IFTTT***:

Name	Origin	Destination	Action
Turn on/off ambient	Google*	eWelink*	On/off ambient light switch
Turn on/off kitchen	Google*	eWelink*	On/off kitchen light switch
Turn on/off bridge	Google*	eWelink*	On/off Tadoº* bridge switch
Turn on/off screen	Google*	eWelink*	On/off screen switch
Turn on/off bulb	Google*	TP-link*	On/off WIFI bulb
Bulb to 10%	Google*	TP-link*	Turns on WIFI bulb to 10% of brightness
Open living room window blinds	Google*	KNX*	Opens blinds of living room
Movie ambient	Google*	KNX*	Activates movie mode
Open window blinds	Google*	KNX*	Opens all blinds
Close window blinds	Google*	KNX*	Closes all blinds
Turn on/off sofa	Google*	KNX*	Turn on/off sofa lamp
Turn off lights	Google*	KNX*	Turns off all lights
Turn on heating	Google*	Tadoº*	Sets Tadoº* to 22°C (71,6°F)
Turn off heating	Google*	Tadoº*	Turns off Tadoº* thermostat
Customer response	Google*	Google*	Says a phrase through the speaker
ambient_on/off	eWelink*	Raspberry*	Acts with ambient in p_lights.txt
kitchen_on/off	eWelink*	Raspberry*	Acts with kitchen in p_lights.txt
bridge_on/off	eWelink*	Raspberry*	Acts with bridge in p_lights.txt
screen_on/off	eWelink*	Raspberry*	Acts with screen in p_lights.txt
ambient_on/off	Raspberry*	Raspberry*	On/off ambient in p_lights.txt
kitchen_on/off	Raspberry*	Raspberry*	On/off kitchen in p_lights.txt

Name	Origin	Destination	Action
bridge_on/off	Raspberry*	Raspberry*	On/off bridge in p_lights.txt
screen_on/off	Raspberry*	Raspberry*	On/off screen in p_lights.txt
bulb_on/off	TP-Link*	Raspberry*	Acts with WIFI bulb in p_lights.txt
Temperature>/<22°C	Tadoº*	Raspberry*	Adds >/<22°C to p_devices.txt (71,6°F)
Humidity >/<50%	Tadoº*	Raspberry*	Adds >/<50% HR to p_devices.txt
Away/home mode	Tadoº*	Raspberry*	Adds away/home mode to p_devices.txt
tado_away	Tadoº*	eWelink*	Turns off ambient, screen & WIFI lamp
tado_off	Raspberry*	Tadoº*	Turns off heating
tado_on_22/18	Raspberry*	Tadoº*	Turns on heating on 22/18°C (71,6/64,4°F)
tado_auto	Raspberry*	Tadoº*	Set Tadoº* thermostat on auto mode
Close	Button widget	KNX*	Closes all blinds
Sofa on/off	Button widget	KNX*	Turns on/off living room sofa lamp
Movie	Button widget	KNX*	Activates and acts with movie ambient
[channel]	Button widget	RM*	Sets [channel] on decoder
[colour]	Button widget	RM*	Sets colours lamp in [colour]

It is also convenient to create some Applet to perform various tests and test various devices and systems, for example: **DropBox***, **RM***, **KNX*** **Tadoº*** & **Google*** **Assistant:**

Name	Origin	Destination	Action
Save test	**Google***	**DropBox***	Saves p_logfile.txt to DropBox
Colours test	**Google***	**RM* mini**	Turns on colours lamp

Name	Origin	Destination	Action
Open test	**Google***	**KNX***	Opens window blinds via **Raspberry*** & **KNX***
Talk test	**Google***	**Google***	Activates **Google*** **Mini** answers

IMPORTANT: do not create **IFTTT*** with **eWelink*** with more than one user (type e-mail and password), since there can be no **eWelink*** devices associated with two different **Gmail*** accounts and that manage an **IFTTT*** account with only one e-mail.

Examples of texts to be included in an **IFTTT*** widget/trigger:

Option A	Option B	Option C
Turn off the lights	Off lights	Off all lights
Close window blinds	Close blinds	Close all blinds
Open window blinds	Open blinds	Open all blinds
Turn on/off sofa lamp	On/off sofa	On/off lamp of the sofa
Set on lights for movie	On movie lights	Watch movie
Open living room window blinds	Open living room blinds	Open only living room blinds
On/off screen	–	–
On/off ambient	–	–
On/off WIFI bulb	–	–

Sometimes it will have to use the error proof technique until it gets the right word combination because, as we said, **Google Home*** or **Alexa***, certain words are reserved for their own internal functioning.

216

Routines in Google Home

In the APP that configures the **Google* Mini, Chromecast***, etc., called **Home***, it is very interesting to group several sequential actions initiated from **Google Assistant*** and that are triggering various home automation actions called **Routines.** These routines help the user to chain actions without having to repeat several instructions verbally to **Google Home***.

Here are some routines and how to access them:

<appHome> <account> <settings> <assistant> <routines>

Let's see some examples:

Routine	Description
[turn on/off the TV]	Turns on/off the amplifier via **RM*** (infrared) and turns on the TV via **Chromecast***
[watch movie]	Activates movie ambient and runs **[turn on the TV]** routine
[good morning]	Announces weather forecast, agenda, the reminders for today and opens all blinds.
[good evening]	Runs **[turn off the TV]** routine, announces the weather forecast & agenda for tomorrow, closes all the blinds and turns off all the lights

Routine	Description
[good bye]	Turns off **Raspberry*_ screen** & all the lights and runs **[turn off the TV]** routine
[i'm home]	Turns on **Raspberry*_ screen,** reads the reminders and runs **[turn on the TV]** routine

Where **[text]** is the only thing the user has to say to **Google Home*** to trigger the execution of the actions described in each option.

Personally, I prefer **Google Home*** t o **Alexa***, because on **Alexa*** the orders must start with the word "trigger" and it's tedious and not natural, but this is only a personal matter.

Google Home APP

Previously there was talk of the **Google Home*** APP, which manages the configuration of the **Google*** **Home Mini** device and **Google*** **Chromecast,** but in this same APP many other interesting actions are carried out such as the following and that add value to the project:

1. Configure the voice interpreter.

2. Configure the house, rooms, etc.

3. Add compatible devices with **Home***

4. Create and maintain routines.

5. Associate third-party applications: **Netflix***, **Spotify***, **Youtube***, **TED***, **HBO***, etc.

6. Associate home automation managers : **eWelink***, **TP-Link***, **Broadlink***, etc.

Below are some actions to perform with this APP.

1. Download and register in the APP.

2. Create the house, for example, <my_house>

3. Create the rooms, for example: <living room>, <kitchen>, <garage>, etc.

4. Configure the rest of the parameters.

5. Add the devices to each room as follows:

Room	Devices
Kitchen	eWelink*
Room	Ewelink*, Tadoº* bridge
Living Room	Tp-Link* bulb, Chrome*, Google* Mini, eWelink* ambient, Raspberry*_screen, Tadoº* thermostat, TV, decoder etc.

Act with:

1. Add devices in:

```
<add> <configure device> <works with Google>
<add new>
```

2. **TP-Link Kasa*** for WIFI Bulb.

3. Smart **eWeLink*** for ambient light, Bridge, Kitchen and **Raspberry*_screen.**

220

Google Broadcasting

A very interesting functionality, which at the time of writing the first edition of this book was pending implementation, but that in this one is already implemented and 100% operational, is to be able to send a text (or a [*].mp3 file) to **Google Home*** from the **Raspberry*_home automation** let it announce it by voice.

Thus, when an automatic action is performed, for example, if the room temperature is higher than 26°C (78,8°F) and the **Raspberry*_home automation** decides to close its window blinds, or start or end the day and proceed to open or close these window blinds or there is an error with any device or an alarm situation occurs, etc. **Google Home*** announces it, for example, "close the window blinds for temperatures above 26°C (78,8°F)", etc. This announcement is made at the volume level that is selected in **Google Home*** at any time.

Likewise, when an action is requested (via **Google Home*** itself, **Telegram*** or by the touch screen), a notice is issued by **Google Home*** when the action is completed.

Similarly, the **Raspberry*_home automation** can send an [*].mp3 to **Google Home*** to play a sound and simulate, for example, the barking of a guard dog, etc.

Finally and very interesting, with this system it can check the status of a situation: **Google Home*** is asked, for example, the status of the water valve, it runs a script [*].php that links to another script [*].py that collects the information and send it to **Google Home*** to announce it.

Various options were tested but the simplest and most effective is using **gTTS***, **Pychromecast***, **mySQL*** and **Apache***, with some small limitations (translate text to mp3, broadcast from a URL, only work in **Python*** **3.5,** somewhat slow, etc.).

Below are the basic instructions to be able to send these messages whose origin is texts defined in the **Python*** program **p_global.py,** translated to [*].mp3 by **gTTS***, select by **mySQL***, indexed by **Apache*** and reproduced by **Pychromecast*** as voice messages or [*].mp3 sounds, played on **Google Home***.

1. Update **Python*** 3.5, Pip3* and install **Pychromecast*** with:

```
sudo apt-get install python3
sudo apt-get install python3-pip
sudo pip3 install pychromecast
```

2. Review permissions on **/var/www** with:

```
sudo chown -R www-data:www-data html
sudo find html -type d -print -exec chmod 775 {}\;
sudo find html -type f -print -exec chmod 664 {}\;
                                        www-data pi
sudo usermod -a -G www-data pi
```

3. Install **PHP7*** with:

```
sudo apt install -t stretch -y php7.0 libapache2-
                        mod-php7.0 php7.0-mysql
```

4. Restart **Apache*** with:

```
sudo /etc/init.d/apache2 restart
     And to know the status of the web server:
sudo /etc/init.d/apache2 status
```

5. Install the **mySQL*** database manager with:

222

```
sudo apt-get install mysql-server mysql-client
sudo apt-get install -y phpmyadmin
```

6. Change the name of /var/www/html/index.php so that the **Apache*** info does not start when pointing to that website.

7. Create the [*].mp3, with the voice of **Google Home*** and in English, installing **gTTS*** with:

```
git clone https://github.com/pndurette/gTTS.git
cd gTTS
sudo python setup.py install
gtts-cli'[text]' -l en -o [text].mp3          where:
```

The [text].mp3 file is created with [text] moved to the **Google Home*** voice, in the -l language, in this case in English (-l en).

8. Configure the following in **/gTTS/p_ghome_say.py**:

The files [*].mp3 will be located in the folder '/var/www/cache/' and should be called through a URL (they cannot be invoked as files in local and this is the reason to use **Apache***), in addition they cannot be in a location protected by user and password, for this reason we will code them in **MD5*** without extension to hide them to the maximum. We control the excess files with the **Glob*** library.

To invoke them we will do:
mc.play_media ('http://**[URL]**.hopto.org/cache/'
                              +**[file]**,"audio/mp3")

Where **[URL]** is the address provided by **NO-IP*** (it cannot take special characters) and **[file]** is the file that will locate the audio, in mp3 format and that generates the **p_ghome_say.py** script with the **gTTS*** software and that we have installed.

9. Make **p_ghome_say.py** executable with:

```
sudo chmod + x p_ghome_say.py
And copy it to /usr/bin/
```

10. To execute the script we will do from **p_global.py** the following:

```
os.system (./p_ghome_say.py [IP] [text])
```

Where **[IP]** is the **Google*** **Home Mini** IP and must be set in the main router table and **[text]** is the *.mp3 file that is generated by **gTTS*** and will be issued verbally.

11. It is proposed to locate the [*].mp3 in /var/www/cache/[*].mp3, encoded by **MD5*** and without extension to be less exposed.

    The [*].php of **IFTTT*** will continue to be located at /var/www/html/[*].php and will be protected by [user] and [password].

12. It must change the security settings of [user] [password] of /var/www/html with:

```
sudo nano /etc/apache2/sites-enabled/000-default.conf
```

```
<VirtualHost *:80>
    ServerAdmin webmaster@localhost
    DocumentRoot /var/www

    <Location /html>
       AuthType basic
       AuthName "Authorisation is required"
       AuthUserFile /etc/apache2/.htpasswd
       Require valid-user
    </Location>
    ErrorLog ${APACHE_LOG_DIR}/error.log
    CustomLog ${APACHE_LOG_DIR}/access.log
                                        combined
</VirtualHost>
```

13. **IMPORTANT:** since now the **Apache*** server points to /var/www, (instead of pointing to /var/www/html), we will have to change in all

IFTTT* **webhooks*** the following:

***Previous situation:**

http://**[user]**:**[password]**@**[URL]**.hopto.org/**[*]**.**php**

***New situation:**

http://**[user]**:**[password]**@**[URL]**.hopto.org/html/**[*]**.**php**

Where **[user]** and **[password]** are the users and password which protect the **Apache*** server, which we have already seen and are created with:

sudo htpasswd −c /etc/apache2/.htpasswd [user] [pass]

Where: **[URL]** is the address provided by **NO−IP*** and [*].php is the destination php script that will execute the **Python*** script, which will perform the appropriate home automation action.

Note: adjust the names of the [*].php to those generated by **Google Home***, especially when using the **$** wildcard (use, for example, a mobile phone and see what text the **Google Assistant*** generates).

With all this installed correctly it can generate, for example, the following ads directly controlled by **p_global.py:**

Starting home automation control program.
Performing setup.
Performing initial test.
Program started successfully.
It is day/night, the blinds are opening/closing.
Closing/Opening blinds due to excess/lack of temperature.
It is 12pm, the daily report is being sent.
Attention: NAS/CPU temperature/humidity excessive/correct.
Attention: error/correct in **EDIMAX***/**GPIO***/**SMTP***/ LOGFILE/SENSORS/ACTUATORS/LIGHTS/BLINDS/DEVICES/ TRIGGER/**POPEN***/TEMPFILE/**DHT22***/KEYS/SYSTEM/I−O/ **KNX***/REQUESTS/etc.

Alarm: power/smoke/gas/flood/$C0_2$/bell.
Recovered from Internet shutdown.
KNX* thermostat absence/presence.
Lights off.
Living room lamp off/on.
Window blinds/gate opened/closed.
Water/gas valve opened/closed.
Movie/holiday atmosphere on/off.
System screen cleared.
NAS/ONT/**Raspberry*** reset.
Reset/Delete/Send key pressed.
Long/Short reset pressed.
Barks de guard dog (or other *.mp3 sound)

Finally, we can create an **IFTTT*** applet, with origin in **Google Home*** and destined a **Webhook*** that points to an [*].php and this one to an [*].py, that executes the capture of system information and announces it by voice in the **Google Home*** system, for example, an **IFTTT*** **Status $,** where $ can be:

$	Status information
Water	Open/Closed water valve
Gas	Open/Closed gas valve
Holidays	Holidays on/off
Ambient	Ambient scene on/off
Garage	Garage gate open/closed
NAS	**DHT22*** temperature and humidity
Raspberry*	CPU and GPU temperatures
Summary	Summarise all the above

☺☺☺

24.-PYTHON 2.7*

For programming control modules, management, monitoring, reports, etc. of this home automation system, in the two **Raspberry***, the most famous every day, **Python 2.7*** programming language has been used, running on the **Raspbian*** operating system, especially for being a modern, powerful language, for its greater ease of implementation, for the existence of multiple libraries, manuals, tutorials, forums, integration with home systems, easy integration with **Raspberry*** hardware, etc.

There are other versions of **Python*** higher than 2.7, but also, for most scripts, it is more than enough for this project.

In some scripts (conditioned by existing libraries)it is indicated if it is necessary to use **Python 3.5***.

Next we will see some details:

*General

1. **Python 2.7*** (and in few cases **Python 3.5***) in this project is running on **Raspbian*** **Stretch** (**Linux 9***), although it also works on previous versions of this operating system.

2. If you don't have basic knowledge of **Python***, you can make easy online learning about the training environment, for example, **www.codecademy.com** or others, by registering and obtaining the corresponding username and password. This web environment is very simple to handle, has theory and very practical examples, both parts very well guided and tutored by the web.

3. Used editors: **IDLE*** and **PyCharm*** to edit the programs [*].py used.

4. Programs created in **/home/pi/home_auto/*.py**:

Python* module	Description	Location
p_global.py	Home automation management	**Raspberry*_home automation**
p_telegram.py	Communication	**Raspberry*_home automation**
p_logfile.py	Event viewer	**Raspberry*_home automation**
p_screen.py	Action buttons	**Raspberry*_screen**

*Added Libraries

To complete the designed **Python*** modules, already configured **Python*** libraries are necessary. The most commonly used in this project are indicated below:

1. **rpi.gpio***: **Raspberry***_**home automation** pin management.
2. **pigpio***: **GPIO*** timing management for sensors.
3. **colorama***: semi graphic interface with addressing by rows and columns.
4. **tkinter***: graphical interface for button management vs actions.
5. **tkfont***: font control for Tkinter*.
6. **time*** and **locale***: management of temporary variables, time, year, week, etc.
7. **pygame***: sound handling.
8. **ramdom***: random number generation.
9. **os*** and **sys***: access to operating system management.
10. **serial***: interface with the **UART*** for connection with **KNX***.
11. **termios*** and **fcntl***: keystroke control on touch screen and keyboards.
12. **mimetext*** and **smtp***: e-mail management.
13. **mimebase***: e-mail attachment management.
14. **encoders***: encryption of attachments.
15. **dht22***: temperature & humidity sensor controller.
16. **telebot***: **Telegram*** **BOT** manager.
17. **urllib2***: file display manager via URL.
18. **psutil***: interface with RAM usage data.
19. **socket***: to identify the local IP.
20. **smartplug***: **Edimax*** WIFI plug manager.
21. **subprocess***: system manager for access to IP vs MAC table.
22. **logging***: **Python*** error handling.

23. **requests***: use direct access to URL.
24. **knxcomobject***: home automation operation with **KNX*** bus.
25. **knxdevice***: device manager associated to **KNX***.
26. **knxdpt***: **KNX*** parameter manager.
27. **knxtelegram***: **KNX*** bus telegram manager.
28. **sonoff***: communication manager with **Itead*** **Sonoff*** switches.
29. **traceback***: display **Python*** lines in execution.
30. **pychromecast***: sender of verbal messages to **Google Home***.
31. **gtts**: text converter to *.mp3 format with **Google Home*** voice.
32. **haslib**: created from files in **MD5*** format.
33. **glob**: controls the number of files.
34. **func_timeout**: **Python2.7*** process timeout control.
35. **threading**: **Python3.5*** process timeout control.

Summary Python Commands

The following are the most common **Python** 2.7 and **Python** 3.5 commands used in this project.

At all this list wants to be a **Python** course or a reference guide or something exhaustive on the subject, it is only a list of commands with a very brief description and that can serve as a reminder when a very simple program is being written.

For more detailed information, it is recommended to go to the official guide:

https://www.python.org/

It can also uses any of the online learning websites, many of them free, tutorials, forums, explanatory videos, etc.

Command	Description
#	Comments 1 line
'''…'''	Comments several lines
print text	Displays text on screen
print '%s'%var	Var formats print in %s
var=raw(input)	Enters text & load variable var
=	Assigns int, real, boolean variables
+,-,*,/	Basic operations
**	Exponent
%	Module, residue

Command	Description
//	Entire division
\	Escape character, example '\n' line break
var[x]	Retrieves position x in variable var, counts from 0
len(x)	Length string x
string.isalpha()	Sees if variable is string
x.lower()	Passes string x to lowercase
x.upper()	Passes string x to uppercase
str(x)	Converts x to a string
x+y	Concatenates the strings x & y
==	Compares in if statements. Do not confuse with =
!=	Not equal in if statements
-=,+=,*=	Operates & assigns in the same function
and, or, not	Basic logical operations
a>>b	Shifts 1 bit to the right
a<<b	Shifts 1 bit to the left
a&b	AND operation between bytes
a|b	OR operation between bytes
a^b	XOR operation between bytes
~a	NOT operation
0bx	Transforms x to binary
bin(x)	Transforms string x to binary
oct(x)	Transforms string x to octal
hex(x)	Transforms string x to hexadecimal
int(x)	Transforms string x to integer
int(x,s)	Transforms string x to integer into base s

Command	Description
if[exp]:	If expression [exp] is true, the following instruction is executed
elif[exp]:	Else if following instruction is executed
else:	Other instructions are executed
s[i:j]	Extracts from the string s from i to j-1. Counts form 0
s[i:]	String s from i to the end
s[:j]	String s from the beginning to j-1
def fn(a,b):	Defines de fn function with arguments a & b
return(x)	Returns the local variable x of the function fn
fn(a,b,c)	Calls the function fn with parameters a, b & c
import x	Imports library x
from m import f	Imports f function from library m
dir(m)	Sees libraries included in m
math.sqrt(x)	Invokes the square root of x
type(x)	Returns data type of x
list=[x,...,z]	Defines list as a data list from x to z
list.append(e)	Adds the element e to list
list.remove(e)	Deletes item e from list
len(list)	Number of list items
list[a:b]	Truncates the list from position a to position b-1. Counts from 0
list.index(x)	Position of x in list
list.insert(x,s)	Inserts the string s in the x position
list.sort()	Sorts the list items and creates an ordered list

Command	Description
sum(list)	Adds elements of the list
zip(l_1,l_2)	Creates a list with pair of lists l_1 & l_2
for x in list:	Cycle through the list
while condition:	Executes while condition is true
break	Exits loop for or while
dic={x:a,...,z:b}	Creates dic dictionary with keys x...z and values a...b
dic[x]	Returns value of the key x in the dictionary dic
del dic[a]	Deletes the key a & its value in dictionary dic
dic={}	Empty dictionary
dic[x]=a	Adds key x and value a to dic
dic.items()	Returns value_key from dic, unordered
dic.keys()	Returns keys from dic
dic.values()	Returns values from dic
print dic[x]	Prints key value x in dic
range(x)	Element x of the list
range(x,y)	Range from x to y with increment 1 by default
range(x,y,z)	Range from x to y and increase z
import random	Imports random number management library
random.randint(x,y)	Generates random between integers x & y
round(x,y)	Rounds x to y decimals
s.split()	Transforms string s into list
pass	Does nothing
open([file],'w')	Opens file [file] for writing

Command	Description
open([file],'r')	Opens file [file] for reading
open([file],'a')	Opens file [file] for append
open([file],'r+')	Opens file [file] for reading and writing
[file].readline()	Reads a line in file [file] ('\' included)
[file].close()	Closes de file [file]
with open([file],'r') as var	Automatically opens/closes [file] in var object

*Error Handling
with try...except

In addition to the instructions that handle inputs vs outputs according to the algorithm described in each **Python*** program and as the complexity of the program grows, the use of an error manager is essential, so that when an error occurs, it is not paralyse the program, on the contrary, the flow of the program is redirected to a specific module where it is treated and if it is possible to redirect the flow to the point where the execution of the main program should continue.

For this, we can include in our **Python*** program a structure similar to:

```
import logging
logging.basicConfig(filename='/home/pi/home_auto
                    /p_global.py',level=logging.INFO)
```

And a **try vs except** block like the following:

```
try:
        [...]
except Exception as e:
        logging.exception(str(e))
        print sys.exec_info()
```

In this way the instructions contained in the **try body** are executed, and if an error occurs (an exception), the flow is directed to the **body except:** and here it is treated accordingly.

There are multiple options to deal with exceptions, for example, depending on the type of error:

236

Keyboard interrupt,
System error
I/O error
Import error
Value error
EOF error
OS error
General exception,
Etc.,

The flow can be redirected to a specific body except and there treated as desired.

If it wants to direct the output of the program to a file, it can do the following:

```
sudo python /home/pi/home_auto/p_global.py
                                    &>p_error_log.txt
```

☺☺☺

25.-KNX*

The **KNX*** interface may not be used in many home automation developments, because it is more oriented to the office environment than to the home environment due to its high price, the complexity of installation and maintenance, the need for a dependency on professional experts integrators and officials, because of the difficulty in obtaining devices, because it is a very closed and proprietary system, with little or no security, nothing friendly, very difficult to integrate with other solutions, expensive, etc.

On the other hand, we can find some single-family homes that have a home automation installation based on this standard, especially for the management of lights and window blinds.

Thus, having a **KNX*** system in the home will allow automating multiple actions:

- Turn off/on lights.

- Dimmer lamps.

- Open/close window blinds.

- Open/close electric valves.

- Presence control switches.

- Interact with analog alarms: flood, fire, smoke, gas, etc.

- Manage the setpoint temperature and actual temperature of a **KNX*** thermostat.

- Twilight sensors.

- LCD display as control centre.

- **NFC*** proximity card detectors.

- Interface with the **Raspberry*_home automation**

- Interface with the **ETS*** software.

Therefore, it is interesting to know how to integrate this bus into our home automation project.

Some topics are summarised below.

✴Configuration

We need, on the one hand, a small **Raspberry**✴ to **KNX**✴ interface, using an **ADUM_1201**✴ level isolator and converter, which adapts the electrical signals between the **KNX**✴ bus and the **Raspberry**✴ **UART**✴ and a **KNX**✴ interface, for example the **5wg-1117-2ab11**✴ of **Siemens**✴ or equivalent to access the bus.

On the other hand we need **Python**✴ modules that manage the bus. See on the websites:

1. For the hardware:

http://michlstechblog.info/blog/raspberry-pi -eibknx -ip-gateway-or-router-with-the-pi/

2. For the software:

https://github.com/ThingType/KNX_Python_library/blob /master/example_script.py

In the software check the following:

1. See group address and add to KnxDevice. G_ADDR (x,y,z)

2. See data type in the 'Group Addresses' object, see Data Type and analyse KnxDPT.py in KnxDPT_ID.

3. See FLAGS by clicking on 'Group Adresses' by adding the values of the next table:

Key	Description	Value
C	Communication	0x20
R	Reading	0x10
W	Writing	0x08
T	Transmission	0x04
U	Update	0x02
I	Init read	0x01

4. Examples:

```
CWTU=20+8+4+2    =0x2E       (button)
CWT =20+8+4      =0x2C       (bulb)
```

Parameters in the Raspberry

To connect the **UART*** of the **Raspberry***_home **automation** to the interface with the **KNX*** **BTI*** bus and for the sending and receiving of the **KNX*** Telegrams to work correctly, we have to do the following:

1. Disable the **Bluetooth***, BT interface in **Raspberry***_home **automation.**

2. Use, in the **SERIAL*** configuration and we will see in the next point:

/dev/ttyAMA0 instead of /dev/serial0 and also instead of /dev/ttyS0.

3. **sudo nano /boot/config.txt** and add:

   dtoverlay=pi3-disable-bt

4. **sudo systemctl disable hciuart**

KNX connection to Raspberry* UART

The **Raspberry** * to **KNX** * connection, as we have already mentioned, must be totally and electrically isolated without any ground common GND, and the logic levels must be adapted between the **KNX** * **BTI** * bus, which operates at +5v and the **UART** * of the **Raspberry*_home automation**, which operates at +3.3v.

The +5v can be obtained directly from the **KNX** * bus, in the **PEI-10** * adapter, while the +3.3v are taken from the dual power supply described in previous sections.

For all this, it is proposed to use the **ADUM1201** * module, which ensures that the **KNX** * bus has symmetrical coupling to the bus, there is no fixed reference point to GND, that the transmission is symmetrical free of GND and thus the device does not detect voltage regarding GND, it detects the tension within the twisted pairs and everything works perfectly.

In addition, the **ADUM1201** * module is very cheap and easy to get, for example, on **Aliexpress** * web.

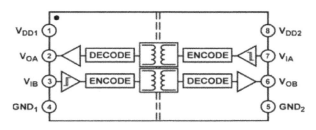

243

Serial Installation

The management of the **UART*** integrated in the **Raspberry***_home **automation** rests with the **SERIAL*** module, to configure it we have to perform the following:

1. **sudo rpi-config**

   <advanced options> <series> <shell session> <NO>

2. **sudo nano /boot/config.txt**   and add:

   enable_uart=1

3. **dmesg | grep tty**   must be active:

   /dev/tty AMA0 and /dev/serial0

4. **sudo apt-get install python-serial**

5. Download software from:

https://github.com/ThingType/KNX_Python_library.git

https://github.com/atdt/monotonic.git

Communication with the UART

The **UART*** of the **Raspberry*** must be configured with a series of parameters to specify speed, transmission format, communication protocol etc.:

```
ser=serial.Serial(port='/dev/ttyAMA0',
                        #for Raspberry* PI 3 without BT
port='/dev/serial0',    #for Raspberry* PI 3 with BT

baudrate=9600,                  #speed (1.200 to 19.200)

parity=serial.PARITY_EVEN,      #even parity
                                #(_none,_even,_odd)

stopbits=serial.STOPBITS_ONE, #bits stop(_one,_two)

bytesize=serial.EIGHTBITS,      #bits total
                                #(.eightbits,.sevenbits)

xonxoff=False,                  #xonxoff disable

rtscts=False,                   #rtscts disable

dsrdtr=False)                   #dsrdtr disable

#ser.timeout=0                  #block read
ser.timeout=1                   #non-block read
#ser.timeout=2                  #timeout block read
```

*Various

Some additional details to review:

1. In 1 **KNX*** line there can only be 64 devices maximum.

2. Only 15 lines can operate in each area.

3. In each installation there can only be 15 areas.

4. Pair **KNX*** sensor-actuator from the same manufacturer.

5. The **KNX*** bus=**EIB*** bus with +29 volts of power supply.

6. Always use the 10-pin **PEI10*** external interface.

The following describes in detail how the **KNX*** protocol is, it is only for informational or pedagogical purposes.

If it has the **Python*** libraries that handle it, this information is not necessary, but if it wants to design libraries that manage the telegrams of this bus, it is highly recommended to know these structures.

See www.knx.org

Structure of the KNX Telegrams

The **KNX** bus is used by **KNX** devices, both sensors (light bulb and shutter switches, thermostat temperature sensor, twilight sensor, binary inputs, LCD display control centre, presence sensors, control buttons, etc.) and actuators (LED status, light bulb relays, window blinds motors, electro gas and water valves, heater switch, etc.), to send information in telegram mode.

These telegrams must have a specific structure and are discussed below:

Part of the telegram	Length
Control	8bit 1byte
Source address	16bit 2byte
Target address	16bit+1 2byte+1bit
Routing counter	3bit
Length	4bit
Usage data	Up to 8x16bit
Check	8bit 1byte

Examples:

hex: BC–11–10–18–20–E1–00–81–1A: closes left large living room blind
dec: 188–17–16–24–32–225–0–126–26
hex: BC–11–10–18–20–E1–00–80–1B: open left large living room blind

control: =BC
source: 1.1.10   =11–10

247

```
destination:                    1.8.20              =18-20
routing counter:                1110
length:                         0001
routing counter+length:         1110-1110           =E1
TPCI                            000000              =0
APCI                            0010
data use                        000001
APCI+usage data:                0010000001          =81
check                           00011010            =1A
```

*Detail in the Telegram Fields

If we continue to deepening each section of the telegram, we can see:

Part of the telegram	Description
control:	1byte with position (d7...d0)
7-6	10 always
5	1 doesn't repeat & 0 repeats
4	1 always
3-2	Priority:
00 Maximum	System functions
01	Alarm functions
10	High priority orders (normal)
11 Minimum	Low priority orders (auto)
Example:	
1011-1100	=xBC=188
1-0	00 always
Example:	
B0,B4,B8,BC	Without repetition
90,94,98,9c	With repetition
origin:	2byte
16bit	Example: 1/1/10 (area/line/device)
destination:	2byte+1bit (0 physical address, 1 group)
16bit+1(in **NPCI*** field)	Example: 1.8.20

Part of the telegram		Description
control:		8bit+6bit+4bit=18bit where:
	8bit	**NPCI***: Network Protocol Control Information
	6bit	**TPCI***: Transport Protocol Control Information
	4Bit	**APCI***: Aplication Protocol Control Information
NPCI*		8bit, where:
	7	0 individual, 1 group
	6-4	110, which is decremented by coupler
	3-0	**EIS*** with data length after control
TPCI*		6bit, where:
	5-0	000000 always
ACPI*		4bit, where:
	0000	Read value
	0001	Answer value
	0010	Write value
	1010	Write memory
data:		1 to 32bit, according **EIS*** protocol

Examples:

Part of the telegram	Description
EIS*=1 switching	1bit window blind
EIS*=2 dimming	4bit light
EIS*=5 float value	16bit thermostat
hexBC-11-10-18-20-E1-00-81-1A dec188-17-16-24-32-225-0-129-26	Closes left large living room window blind
hexBC-11-10-18-20-E1-00-80-1B	Opens left large blind

Part of the telegram	Description
control:	xBC, where:
1011-11001	W=1 no retry
10W1-PP00	PP=11 minimum priority
origin:	0001-0001-0001-0000 1.1.10
destination:	0001-1000-0010-0000 1.8.20
NPCI	RC+1110+LONG =0001
NPCI	1110-0001 =xE1
TPCI	000000 =x00
APCI	0010 =x80
data:	000001 =x01
validation:	00011010 =x1A with:
xBC	1011-1100
x11	0001-0001
x10	0001-0000
x18	0001-1000
x20	0010-0000
xE1	1110-0001
x00	0000-0000
x81	1000-0001
xE5	1110-0101
x1A	0001-1010

Another example: downstairs garage light

BC-11-1F-28-02-E1-00-81-07

Part of the telegram		Description
xBC	1011-1100	Control
x11	0001-0001	Origin
x1F	0001-1111	Origin

Part of the telegram		Description
x28	0010-1000	Destination
x02	0000-0010	Destination
xE1	1110-0001	RC+LONG
x00	0000-0000	Data
x81	1000-0001	Data
x07	0000-0111	Data
xF8	1111-1000	CRC

*Communication Sequence

The sending of the telegrams must comply with a specific protocol, specifically the **CSMA/CA*** protocol, which basically has the following sequence:

1. Wait t1=50bit for NO BUSY bus =xC0=192=1100-0000

2. Send the telegram.

3. Wait t2=13bit for ACK=x0C=12=0000-1100 1bit start+8bit data+1bit even parity+1bit stop.

4. Retry up to 3 times if NACK=xCC=204=1100-1100

5. If the bus is busy, the device with the highest priority and same priority is prioritised the device with the lowest group address is prioritised too.

6. t1=50bits=5.20ms   (with 9.600 bauds)

7. t2=13bits=1.35ms

8. d0+...+d7+parity=0

Now we will see how the **KNX*** address assignment of the devices connected to the bus is structured. The names and addresses used here are just an illustrative example.

The locations have been named with: **f_r_o**, where **"f"** represents the floor, **"r"** the room and **"o"** the order of the device in room **"r"** of the floor **"f"**. The following describes the sensors (push buttons, twilight sensor, etc.) and the actuators (window blinds, lights, valves, etc.)

253

KNX* buttons: 17/x or 1.7.x

Where x=

x	Description	x	Description
1	2_room_b1	2	2_stair landing
3	2_room_a1	4	2_bathroom
5	1_room_a1	6	1_room_b1
7	1_stair landing	8	Free
9	Free	10	1_bathroom
11	0_entry	12	Free
13	0_living room terrace	14	-1_garage
15	-1_laundry	16	0_living room lamp & blind
17	0_bathroom	18	-1_cellar
19	2_room_b2	20	2_room_a2
21	Free	22	1_room_a2
23	1_room_b2	24	Free
27	0_kitchen	28	0_thermostat
31	0_garage stairs up	32	Free
55	-1_**Raspberry*_home**	56	Free
75	0_all	76	0_all
77	0_twilight sensor	78	2_LCD display
124	0_living room wall lights	125	0_living room little blinds

KNX* blockers: 17/x or 56/x

Where x=

x	Description	x	Description
7	2_stair landing	8	2_room_b1

x	Description	x	Description
9	Free	10	2_bathroom ceiling
11	2_room_a1	12	Free
13	Free	14	1_bathroom ceiling
15	Free	16	1_stair landing
17	1_room_b1	18	1_room_a1
19	Free	20	0_kitchen
23	-1_garage	24	0_garage stairs up
25	Free	26	-1_garage stairs down
27	Free	28	0_entry
31	Free	32	0_bathroom ceiling

KNX* lights: 8/x or 1.0.x

Where x=

x	Description	x	Description
1	2_room_b1	2	2_stairs landing
3	2_room_a1	4	Free
5	Free	6	2_bathroom ceiling
7	2_bathroom mirror	8	1_room_a1
9	1_room_b1	10	1_stairs landing
11	0_living room sofa wall	12	0_living room table wall
13	1_bathroom ceiling	14	1_bathroom mirror
15	0_kitchen	16	0_entry
17	0_garage stairs up	18	0_bathroom ceiling
19	0_terrace	20	-1_cellar
21	-1_garage	22	-1_garage stairs down
23	-1_laundry	24	0_all

x	Description	x	Description
25	-1_gym	26	0_hall
29	Free	30	0_bath mirror

KNX* lights: 16/x or 2.0.x

Where x=

x	Description	x	Description
1	0_living room table lamp	2	0_living room table lamp dimmer
3	0_living room room sofa lamp	4	0_living room sofa lamp dimmer
5	0_living all lamps	6	0_living room all lamps dimmer

KNX* lights: 48/x or 6.0.x

Where x=

x	Description	x	Description
1	2_room_b1	2	2_stairs landing
3	2_room_a1	4	2_bathroom ceiling
5	1_room_a1	6	1_room_b1
7	1_stairs landing	8	Free
9	Free	10	1_bathroom ceiling
11	0_entry	12	Free
13	Free	14	-1_garage
15	0_garage stairs up	16	0_kitchen
17	0_bathroom ceiling	18	0_living room lamps

KNX* blinds: 24/x or 3.0.x

Where x=

x	Description	x	Description
15	1_room_a1	17	1_room_b1
19	0_living room small left	21	0_living room small right
25	0_kitchen	27	0_living room large right
29	0_all blinds	31	0_living room large left

Making x+1 generates an up or down pulse.

KNX* living room lamps 16/x or 2.0.x

Where x=

x	Description	x	Description
1	0_right lamp	2	0_right dimmer lamp
3	0_left lamp	4	0_left dimmer lamp
5	0_both lamps	6	0_both dimmer lamps

To perform DIM (dimmer) decrease by (2.0.2/4) with 5 successive ones from 100% to 0%.

KNX* thermostat: 32/x or 4.0.x

Where x=

x	Description	x	Description
1	0_heater	2	0_presence/absence

x	Description	x	Description
3	0_real temperature	4	0_setpoint temperature

KNX* valves: 40/x or 5.0.x

Where x=

x	Description	x	Description
9	–1_gas	10	–1_water

KNX* Relay Physical Addresses

To have **KNX*** relays well identified, which are the ones that finally provide the electric power to the actuator devices for their operation and since it is necessary to physically access their learning button when they are associated with the group address and the actuator that active, it is important to number each relay and identify its position.

For example:

- **In closet 0_1:** [floor 0, place 1]

28	thermostat	
57	A: terrace	B: kitchen
58	A: cellar	B: laundry
59	A: garage stairs	B: garage
60	A: entry	B: heater
61	A: hall	B: gym

- **In closet 0_2:**

62	A: sofa wall light	B: table wall light
67	living room small right window blind	
68	living room small left window blind	
87	living room large left window blind	
64	living room large right window blind	

- **In closet 1_1:**

71 A: room_a1 light   B: room_b1 light
72 A: room_a1 blind   B: room_b1 blind

- **In closet 2_1:**

73 A: room_b1 light   B: room_b2 light
74 A: ceiling bathr. light   B: mirror bathroom light

- **In closet 2_2:**

75 A: 2_stairs landing   B: 1_stairs landing
76 A: 2_room_b2

Home Automation with Raspberry, Google & Python: KNX* Elements

Control display

Thermostat

KNX*-RS232 interface

Twilight sensor

Light/blinds/dimmer/valves relay

Binary inputs

Lights switch

Lights/blinds switch

Blinds/Light/Dimmer

*Configuration in p_global.py

In the **Python*** module that manages **KNX***, the KnxDevice.G_ADDR, is necessary the configuration described in the previous tables.

It is important to know that:

- lights: 1,0,x   1:on   0:off
- lamps: 2,0,x   1:on   0:off
- dim: 2,0,x   5 successive on
- window blinds: 3,0,x   1:close   0:open
- blinds advance: 3,0,x   1/0 to x+1
- thermostat (∗)   4,0,2   presence/absence
- valves: 5,0,x   1:close   0:open

(∗) KnxComObject(KnxDevice.G_ADDR(4,0,2),1,0x2E/ 0x2C)

To act from **Python***, we can group devices, for example as follows:

Group	Devices
Window_blinds_without alarm	Living room, kitchen, room_1/2
Window_blinds_living	Living room small/larger
Window_blinds_auto	Living room small, room_1/2
Window_blinds_movie ambient	Living room small & larger_50%
Window_blinds_holiday even days	Living room small, room_1

261

Group	Devices
Window_blinds_holiday odd days	Living room small & room_2
lights_holiday even days	Living room right, kitchen, room_1
lights_holiday odd days	Living room left, kitchen, room_2

☉☉☉

26.-ETS3/4*

To configure **KNX*** devices, the official **ETS*** software, version 3, 4 or 5 could be used.

This software is only available for **Windows***, hence the need to use a **Windows*** virtual machine with **VirtualBox*** to use this software from an **iMac*** or similar.

Depending on the knowledge, the needs and the size of the **KNX*** installation, we will choose the appropriate version of the **ETS*** software.

For small installations it is sufficient with the first versions 3 or 4, less heavy and easier to use.

Here are some basic aspects of this application.

It is recommended to access:

www.knx.org

KNX Work
Sequence with ETS*

There is multiple information on the web about official, general and specific courses of **KNX*** and **ETS*** and in this book it is not intended to create a manual more of these two tools, it is only a very very brief guide that focuses only on the essentials for help the reader to use them.

The basic sequence in the use of **ETS*** is as follows:

1. After paying the corresponding license, download and install the application.

2. Download the sensor & actuator catalog from the official websites of the manufacturers of each device (it is recommended that all devices be from the same manufacturer).

3. Create the project with friendly name.

4. Create housing structure: house, floors, rooms, closets, etc.

5. Add the devices (power supply, interfaces, binary inputs, switches, relays, window blinds motors control, twilight, thermostat, LCD display and so on)

6. Select correct parameters to each device. This task is essential because it defines what can be configured and therefore the behaviour of each device.

7. Create the connections (group addresses) between devices and actions, that is, specify

what tasks each device should perform.

8. Program each device, selecting its programming mode and sending, via **ETS*** to **KNX*** bus, its configuration (address & parameters).

9. If possible, it is highly recommended to perform tests of the **KNX*** bus operation on a test bus electrically separate from the home bus and periodically make backup copies of the **ETS*** database to avoid errors.

10. It is highly recommended, on the one hand, to build a table with the description of each device (device, location, type, **KNX*** code, description, and its associated actions or group addresses) and on the other hand to build another table with the description of each action (name, explanation, etc.)

Device vs Group Addresses

Device	Floor	Type	KNX	Group Addresses			
1.1.6	1st	Button	230–22	3/0/18	3/0/17	1/0/9	6/0/6
1.1.51	2nd	Relay	562–11	1/0/1 1/0/2	1/0/1	7/0/7	7/0/8
1.1.63	Main	Motor	520–11	3/0/25 3/0/29	3/0/26 3/0/30	–	–

Explanation of the tasks of the group addressses

Group Addresses	Explanation
1/0/1_2	Blocks billiard/stairs landing lights
1/0/9	Blocks room_1a lights
3/0/17_18	Closes/opens room_1a window blind
3/0/25_26	Closes/opens kitchen window blind
3/0/29_30	Closes/opens all window blinds
7/0/7_8	Billiard/stairs landing lights status

*Various

Here are some interesting points to consider in the installation and configuration of the **ETS*** software.

The example has an old **KNX***–**RS232*** interface and this is the reason for using previous versions of both **ETS*** and the operating system.

If a more modern **KNX*** interface (USB or Ethernet) is available, more recent software versions could be used.

1. It is possible install this software version on **Windows XP–Professional*** or on **Windows–7***.

2. If using SERIAL–USB converter, use **ETS4*** or higher.

3. Activate **SERIALPEI16–COM1***
4. Mask $0012 in physical address a.b.c reserved.

5. Standard **RS232*** connection in COM1.

6. Use <diagnostic><group monitoring>

USB-Serial Converter

In this example, a **VirtualBox*** virtual machine was used to run **ETS4*** on **Windows*** (nowadays there is no **ETS*** for **MAC-OSX***) and an RS232-USB converter connected to an **iMac***. Consider the following:

1. To view the RS232-USB adapter on the iMac*:

<applications> <PL2303_MacOSX_1_6_1_2017018> <about this Mac> <USB> <Hub> <USB-SerialController>

2. In terminal:
   cd /dev
   ls tty.usbserial*

3. <Preferences><NET> <USB-SerialController>

4. To check the communications, it can use software **CoolTerm*** with the following parameters:

   (9600|E|1|8|xo=F|rts=F|dsr=F)

5. The RS232-USB converter is the **UGREEN*** **20210,** but any other could be used if the corresponding drivers are available.

6. Download the driver for the **iMac*** at: www.ugreen.com

7. Install the **PL2303_MAC*** or **Windows*** software.

267

8. To use this converter, **ETS4*** or higher must be used.
9. For **Windows*** do the following:

–See which **MAC*** driver is installed in:

<system report> <USB> <USB 2.0 bus> <Hub> <USB–Serial Controller>

–Check in **iMac*** Terminal:

<cd /dev> <ls tty.usbserial*> <system preferences> <red> <USB–Serial...>

–Configure ports for **Windows*** (**VirtualBox***) as:

<virtualbox> <ports> <serial ports> <port 4> <enable port> <COM4> <host device> <path> </dev/cu.usbserial>

–Check that:

```
        /dev/cu.serial              exists
        /dev/tty.usbserial          exists
        in lsof|grep usbserial      no session started
                                       (exit or restart)
        with null–modem            bypass the DB9
                        in CoolTerm (in MAC*) see TxD–RxD
```

☺☺☺

27.-ADDITIONAL SOFTWARE

To optimise the process of creating software, design and testing of electronic circuits, it is proposed to use the software detailed below and which helps in:

- The installation of the **Raspbian*** operating system in the **Raspberry***.

- Basic operations with **Linux***.

- The process of editing, proofreading, testing and execution of **Python*** programs.

- Prior simulation of electronic circuits before real implementation.

- The graphic register of schemes, diagrams, circuits, etc.

- The routing of the circuits for the possible creation of the optimised printed circuit boards.

- The update and access to **NO-IP***.

- Use of other operating systems.

- Network access utilities.

Applepi-Baker and Etcher*

To make the recording of the uSD cards with the basic boot software and operating systems for the **Raspberry***, it is necessary to have some tool that allows, both to record the card with this software, and to backup the card content on the computer.

This second option is fundamental especially in the development phase and when the **Raspberry*** are updated to new versions and it is necessary to make a "backwards".

Both software examples allow recording of [*].**ISO** and [*].**ZIP**, as well as backing up the contents of the uSD card to the computer.

In the case of **ApplePi-Baker***, it also allows it to format the uSD to load the **NOOBS*** multi-boot system, which allows to have a boot menu with several operating systems. We have not used it in our project to make it faster to boot because unnecessary packages are not loaded.

LXTerminal and Terminal*

These two semi-graphic environments create a window in text mode (rows and columns), which allows the introduction, execution and monitoring of **Linux*** or **OSX*** system commands, for the basic configuration of the operating system.

The **LXTerminal*** application is used for the **Raspbian*** system and **Terminal*** for the **OSX*** system.

In previous sections we have already seen a list of the most used commands for the construction of this project, however on the web there are extensive manuals of the commands for both operating systems.

IMPORTANT: the commands used in these two environments act directly on the operating system, so it must have adequate knowledge to perform certain critical operations and avoid errors that impair the operation of these operating systems.

Pycharm

This is a program text editor and advanced software debugger written in **Python***.

It is quite evolved and with an advanced graphic environment, with a clear visualisation of the ideation (something that should be displayed very clearly) and the different blocks: functions, loops, conditions, etc. and all of this in different colours and formats (definitions, import body, comments, instructions, functions, constants, variables, etc.) to offer the greatest clarity.

Easily detect programming, writing, etc. errors and has excellent programmer support. It also includes interesting additional functions: autocomplete, syntax control, analysis tool, web integration, integration with other software, support over virtual environments, export and import tools, text formatting, etc.

It allows many more functions than the basic **Python*** editor, in the **Raspbian*** environment, called **IDLE*** (Integrated Development Environment), so it is more advisable to use it when using very long program texts with a lot of ideation, or when it wants to use it as a source to transfer documents such as this book.

Icircuit

This software allows the simulation of electrical and electronic operation in simulated, theorists or test circuits, both digital and analog.

It has a large database with all kinds of devices: switches, relays, transformers, power supplies, signal generators, speakers, microphones, buzzers, resistors, capacitors, coils, diodes, transistors (**TTL***, **Mosfet***, etc.), logic gates, counters, "flip-flops", encoders, A/D converters, integrated circuits, etc.

Electrical parameters can be displayed in voltmeters, ammeters, frequency meters, or in a virtual oscilloscope (voltage, intensity, frequency, etc.), in real time and make the necessary changes to simulates any kind of situations.

This software is really interesting for projects like this, where it has to define small designs and test them before building a prototype, so it saves a lot of time in the implementation phase because it already knows that the circuit can work as expected, avoiding, in this way, errors of design and operation.

Eagle

This application allows the design and graphic registration of electronic circuits and the generation of files to manufacture **PCB*** boards of printed circuits and **PDF*** for both tasks, performing the functions (always very tedious & with a lot of mistakes) of auto router tracks fully automatically, both on single-sided or double-sided **PCB*** with all type of devices.

The free version is limited to a certain small volume of circuits and printed card area, but for the prototypes described here it is very useful and sufficient.

It also has a large community of users who provide help forums, tutorials or circuit projects already designed, which allows a quick learning curve.

It includes a large database of all types of components, both active and passive.

It is very simple to use, both in virtual wiring and in the assignment of labels to devices and tracks.

NO-IP Duc

No-IP DUC

DUC* (Dynamic Update Client) is a software that includes a very simple **NO-IP*** web interface, running on the **iMac*** over **OSX***, to manage the maintenance of access to external IP Main router of the home automation installation, for remote access from **VNC***, managing the IP changes caused by reboots of this Router or for power failures.

In order for the Router external IP changes to be reflected online in the URL assigned by **NO-IP***, the **DUC*** program must be running, for example in the background, on the computer at the time that such change occurs.

If this is the case, activate the automatic start of **DUC*** when the computer starts up. For this reason it is more advisable, as long as the Router allows it, to enable the management of the update of the external IP by the Router itself with the **NO-IP*** web via http (described in previous chapters).

275

VirtualBox

This software manages the virtual machines necessary for simulating access to the system, both from **Windows*** environments, and from **Ubuntu***, **Debian***, etc. environments.

It is interesting to use it for when we have an operating system, for example **MAC OSX***, but we need to try some management software of a device in a different operating system, for example the **KNX*** **ETS*** device management software that is not available for **MAC OSX***, **USB–RS232*** interface drivers, etc.

This software is free and very easy to handle whenever we have an ISO with the operating system that we want to install as a virtual machine, we can even have several operating systems running simultaneously (for this reason it is necessary to have a sufficiently powerful computer with enough RAM).

On the web we can find all the necessary information about this application and how to find the [*].iso or [*].zip operating system files.

Ipscanner Home

This software allows scanning of a certain range of active IP throughout the system and identification of devices connected to the network via WIFI or LAN, specifying both IP, MAC, open ports, services, etc.

It is very useful to quickly detect and visualise which devices are active in any of our interior networks of our home.

Although the free version only scans a section of the network, we can define several sections, so that in two or three scans we will have the global vision of our entire internal network.

We can assign friendly names to each device associated with an IP or a MAC and assign an easy-to-view icon, so that all connected devices will be perfectly identified.

It also allows us to perform direct PING, port scanning, wake on lan, etc. procedures.

☺☺☺

28.-EXCHANGE FILES

As it has said in previous chapters, for the correct communication of parameters between t h e **Raspberry*_home automation** and the **Raspberry*_screen,** a series of information exchange files are used, which allow writing and reading the commands that are generated on the **Raspberry*_screen, Telegram*** or **Google Home*** and run on the Raspberry*_home automation.

It is important that all these exchange files are located in the right place and that the necessary read and write permissions are available on all affected devices.

These exchange files are:

* p_sensors.txt
* p_actuators.txt
* p_blinds.txt
* p_lights.txt
* p_devices.txt
* p_logfile.txt

A possible structure, for example, of these files is described below.

*P_Sensors.txt

Located at:

Raspberry*_home automation:

> /home/pi/home_auto/p_sensors.txt

Enable permissions with:

sudo chmod 777 p_sensors.txt

In this file the **Raspberry*_home automation** records online the status of the sensors, alarms and variables.

Parameter	Description
NAS temperature: xx °C/°F	External NAS temperature
NAS humidity xx %RH	External NAS humidity
Power: yes/no	There is or not 220v power supply in the house
Internet: yes/no	There is or not Internet access
Garage gate: open/close	Garage gate status
Doorbell: on/off	Doorbell rings or not
Smoke: yes/no	Smoke alarm status of floors with sensor
Water: yes/no	Flood alarm status of wet areas
Gas: yes/no	Leak alarm status of the kitchen
CO_2: normal/danger	Alarm status by toxic gases of the garage

Parameter	Description
Heater: on/off	Heater status by schedule or thermostat
Holidays: on/off	Holidays mode status
Movie: on/off	Movie ambient mode status
Thermostat: presence/absence	**KNX*** thermostat status
Water_valve: open/close	Valve of the water status
Gas_valve: open/close	Valve of the gas status
Origin: xx	Origin of the alarm or action: **Telegram***, **Google***, etc.
Setpoint temperature: xx °C/°F	Setpoint temperature in the living room **KNX*** thermostat
Real temperature: xx °C/°F	Real temperature in the living room **KNX*** thermostat

*P_Actuators.txt

Located at:

Raspberry*_home automation:

/home/pi/home_auto/p_actuators.txt

Enable permissions with:

sudo chmod 777 p_actuators.txt

In this file the **Raspberry*_home automation** reads the action to be performed with origin in **Telegram*, Google Home* or Raspberry*_screen.**

Parameter: Value	Description
Turn of lights: yes/no	Turns off all lights
Turn on living room sofa: yes/no	Turns on the living room lamp, sofa area
Turn off kitchen yes/no	Turns off kitchen light
Watch movie: yes/no	Activates MOVIE=ON/OFF
Close blinds: yes/no	Closes blinds without alarm
Close all blinds: yes/no	Closes all blinds
Open blinds: yes/no	Opens blinds without alarm
Open living room blinds: yes/no	Opens all living room blinds
Open all blinds: yes/no	Opens all blinds
Holidays on/off	Activates HOLIDAYS=ON/OFF
Water on/off	Opens/closes water valve
Gas on/off	Opens/closes gas valve
Heater on/off	Sets presence/absence status

Clear screen	yes/no	Clears p_global.py screen

Parameter: Value		Description
NAS reset	yes/no	Resets NAS
ONT reset	yes/no	Resets ONT communication
Router reset	yes/no	Resets the main Router
Raspberry* reset		R e s e t s **Raspberry*_home automation**

*P_blinds.txt

Located at:

Raspberry*_home automation:

/home/pi/home_auto/p_blinds.txt

Enable permissions with:

sudo chmod 777 p_blinds.txt

In this file the **Raspberry*_home automation** adds the **OPEN** window blinds and eliminates the **CLOSED** window blinds. Can contain:

Open window blind	Description
Kitchen	Kitchen, main floor
Room 1_a	Bedroom_a 1st floor
Room 1_b	Bedroom_b 1st floor
Living_room_l_r	Living room large right, main floor
Living_room_l_l	Living room large left, main floor
Living_room_s_r	Living room small right, main floor
Living_room_s_l	Living room small left, main floor

*P_lights.txt

Located at:

Raspberry*_home automation:

/home/pi/home_auto/p_lights.txt

Enable permissions with:

sudo chmod 777 p_lights.txt

In this file the **Raspberry*_home automation** adds the lights ON and eliminates the lights OFF. This can be:

Light ON	Description
Terrace	Led focus on terrace, main floor
Living room table lamp	Lamp near table of living room, main floor
Living room sofa lamp	Lamp near sofa of living room, main floor
Living room wall table	Wall light table of living room, main floor
Living room wall sofa	Wall light sofa of living room, main floor
Entry	LED ceiling entry house, main floor
Hall	Lamp outside, main door
Entrance bathroom ceiling	Bathroom ceiling, main floor

Light ON	Description
Entrance bathroom mirror	Bathroom mirror, main floor
Garage stairs up	Garage stairs, main floor
Gym	Garage, gym area
Laundry	Garage, laundry area
Garage	Garage, cars area
Cellar	Garage, cellar area
Stairs landing 1st	Stairs landing 1st floor
Bathroom 1st ceiling	Bathroom ceiling 1st floor
Bathroom 1st mirror	Bathroom mirror 1st floor
Room_1a	Bedroom_a 1st floor
Room_1b	Bedroom_b 1st floor
Stairs landing 2nd	Stairs landing 2nd floor
Room_2a	Bedroom_a 2nd floor
Room_2b	Bedroom_b 2nd floor
Bathroom 2nd ceiling	Bathroom ceiling 2nd floor
Bathroom 2nd mirror	Bathroom mirror 2nd floor

*P_devices.txt

Located at:

Raspberry*_home automation:

/home/pi/home_auto/p_devices.txt

Enable permissions with:

sudo chmod 777 p_devices.txt

In this file the **Raspberry*_home automation** records the ON devices and removes the OFF ones. These might be:

Activated device	Manufacturer	Description
Bridge	**eWelink***	Turns on/off **Tadoº*** bridge switch
WIFI bulb	**Tp-Link***	Turns on/off bulb
Kitchen	**eWelink***	Turns on/off kitchen switch
Raspberry*_screen	**eWelink***	Turns on/off screen switch
Tadoº* home/away	**Tadoº***	**Tadoº*** thermostat status
Tadoº* ><22 °C (71,6°F)	**Tadoº***	**Tadoº*** temperature
Tadoº* ><50 %RH	**Tadoº***	**Tadoº*** humidity

*P_logfile.txt

Located at:

Raspberry*_home automation:

/home/pi/home_auto/p_logfile.txt

Enable permissions with:

sudo chmod 777 p_logfile.txt

In this file the **Raspberry*_home automation** records the actions that happen in **p_global.py** and that is sent daily as a summary of the system activity and on the other hand, they are displayed online in the system event viewer. Example:

Day	Time	Event	Origin()
mm—dd—yy	hh:mm:ss	garage gate opens	status_door
mm—dd—yy	hh:mm:ss	garage gate closes	status_door
mm—dd—yy	hh:mm:ss	Switches off all lights	**Telegram***
mm—dd—yy	hh:mm:ss	Opens all window blinds	**Google Home***
mm—dd—yy	hh:mm:ss	Real temperature 22°C (71,6°F)	Thermostat
mm—dd—yy	hh:mm:ss	Turns on screen	Automatic
mm—dd—yy	hh:mm:ss	"It's day"	Say
mm—dd—yy	hh:mm:ss	Sounds doorbell	status_bell
mm—dd—yy	hh:mm:ss	Barks de guard dog	Say
mm—dd—yy	hh:mm:ss	Acts with ambient	**IFTTT***
mm—dd—yy	hh:mm:ss	"It's a new day"	**Gmail***

☉☉☉

29.-PYTHON*
MODULES

This chapter describes the **Python* modules** that make up the entire system: home automation, control, messaging and event viewer.

Each module details the functions created with: description, inputs, outputs, observations and definitions of the most important components.

I have decided not to include all the **Python*** code as it is, because it is specific to the installation of the example housing, because it is very extensive and with a personal wording, however I am convinced that, with the attached information and basic knowledge of **Python***, readers can complete and/or expand the necessary functions. The modules are as follows:

Python module	Description	Location
p_global.py	Home automation management	R_home
p_telegram.py	Communication program	R_home
p_logfile.py	Event viewer	R_home
p_screen.py	Action buttons management	R_screen

Next we will go into detail of each of these modules.

*P_global.py

This is the main program that manages all system inputs: sensors, alarms, variables, keyboard commands, voice originating in **Google Home***, message originating in **Telegram***, etc. and that generates the outputs: actuators, blinds, lights, thermostat, variables, WIFI equipment, voice broadcast on **Google Home***, messages to **Telegram***, **Gmail***, acoustics, etc. This module integrates the "intelligence" of the system, containing the automatic actuation algorithms, which, depending on the day, time, variables, sensors, alarms, etc., make the decisions to be made, freeing the user from repetitive and tedious tasks, ensuring optimisation in the operation of the home. The following screen shows the use of **Colorama***

MAIN MODULE RUNNING IN RASPBERRY*_HOME AUTOMATION

*P_telegram.py

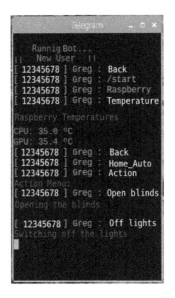

In this module resides the **Telegram*** **BOT,** which acts between the user and the system in a friendly way, allowing to know the state of the set: lights on, window blinds open, devices activated, state of the **Raspberry*_home automation**, temperatures, humidity, alarms, etc., and act on the systems: window blinds, lights, WIFI devices, valves, etc.

The display shows the communication between the BOT and the **Raspberry*_home automation**, one instruction per line without formatting with **Colorama***

The BOT that runs on **Raspberry*_home automation**, interacts with **Telegram*** that runs as an APP on a mobile or tablet.

Here, in **Telegram*** we have a special chat, created by **Botfather*** assistant, where we communicate with the BOT and we can visualise the home automation action buttons: open, close window blinds, turn off and on lights, see connected devices, etc., and all this both from home and from anywhere else.

*P_logfile.py

This module controls the **System Event Viewer**, that is, a **Python*** script that displays in the **Raspberry***_home automation, by screen, what happens: day, time, line number, event, origin, etc.

This information is extracted from the last lines of the **Raspberry***_home automation /home/pi/home_auto/**p_logfile.txt** file and is designed to be displayed, both on the **ZTE*** tracking tablet and on **VNC***

It is highly recommended to use this system to know what happens in the main program **p_global.py**, especially in the debugging phase: execution of orders, situation of variables, errors, etc.

EVENTS VIEW RUNNING ON THE RASPBERRY*_HOME AUTOMATION

*P_screen.py

This is the module that manages the software that runs on the **Raspberry*_screen** and that allows us to manage basic actions of the home automation system: turn off all the lights, open all the blinds, close and open the electro valves, reset devices, etc. This module is completed with the **PLEX*** server and the **XscreenSaver*** photo frame simulator, which also controls the transitions between these applications. Here you can see the buttons created with **Tkinter***

SCREEN MODULE RUNNING ON THE RASPBERRY*_SCREEN

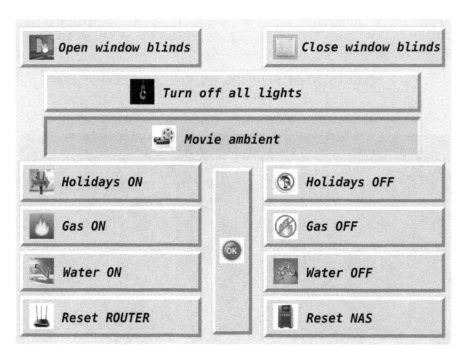

⊝⊙⊝

30.–DETAIL OF PYTHON* MODULES

B elow is a summary of the most important functions that make up the **Python*** modules described above and that allow this project to work properly.

There is not 100% of the code (almost 5,000 lines o f **Python*** code), since it is concrete for the installation of the project housing, with personal information and adapted to real and existing devices in that house, but it contains more than enough information to, with basic knowledge of **Python*** programming, complete them and adapt them to the desired home automation project implement.

*P_global.py

```
#=====================================================================
# P_BLOBAL v.09 January 2019 with home automation actions
# in KNX* WIFI devices, Tadoº* & RM*
# verbal announcements & status questions by Google Home*
# Home Automation-Raspberry Integration Modules
# @ Gregorio Chenlo
#=====================================================================

# GENERAL CONFIGURATION
#!/usr/bin/env python -u
# -*- coding: utf-8 -*-
version='v.09'

# IMPORT BODY
import sonoff                    #Sonoff devices management
import RPi.GPIO as GPIO
from colorama import init, Style, Fore, Back, Cursor
init(autoreset=True)            #reset colorama style after writing
from datetime import datetime #to know the month
import time,random
time.strftime("%H:%M:%S") #24 hours format
import locale                   #for local names
locale.setlocale(locale.LC_ALL,'en_EN.UTF-8')
import os, sys, serial    #system & UART control
os.system('setterm -cursor off') #hidden cursor in terminal screen
import termios, fcntl         #key press capture
import requests                #direct use of curl -X POST in IFTTT()
import KnxComObject            #KNX actuation modules
import KnxDevice               #for bulbs and window blinds
import KnxDPT
import KnxTelegram
import traceback               #ejection line visualisation
import logging                 #mistakes management
from func_timeout import func_timeout, FunctionTimedOut   #timeout
                                              function controller
try:                           #on error in p_global.log da error,
                                              creates it again
    logging.basicConfig(filename='/home/pi/home_auto/
    p_global.log',level=logging.ERROR)
except:
    os.system('sudo rm /home/pi/home_auto/p_global.log')
    logging.basicConfig(filename='/home/pi/home_auto/p_global.log',
                                          level=logging.ERROR)
```

```python
#------------------------------------------------------------------
# Delete these instructions and keys() to run program
# in interpreter mode
#------------------------------------------------------------------

fd = sys.stdin.fileno()      #variables to read keyboard
oldterm = termios.tcgetattr(fd)
newattr = termios.tcgetattr(fd)
newattr[3] = newattr[3] & ~termios.ICANON & ~termios.ECHO
termios.tcsetattr(fd, termios.TCSANOW, newattr)
oldflags = fcntl.fcntl(fd, fcntl.F_GETFL)
fcntl.fcntl(fd, fcntl.F_SETFL, oldflags | os.O_NONBLOCK)


#------------------------------------------------------------------
from email.mime.text import MIMEText    #to send email
from email.mime.multipart import MIMEMultipart
from smtplib import SMTP
import smtplib, socket, getpass
from email.MIMEBase import MIMEBase     #to send files by email
from email import encoders              #to encrypt files
import pigpio # to DHT22 temperature sensor, daemon must be started
import DHT22  # DHT22 module should be in same folder as program

#RASPBERRY PIN ASSIGNMENT
# pin 8 & 10 for UART-RS232, do not occupy or activate serial en
                                                      raspi-config
pines_relays  =[29,33,35]
pin_nas       = 29                      #NAS with 74ls14 inverter
pin_ont       = 33                      #ONT with 74ls14 inverter
...
pin_sensor    = 2        #IMPORTANT: serial data by GPIO0
pin_buzz      = 7        #active buzz, see polarity deactivate
                             #1-Wire in raspi-config/interfaces
boton_reset   = 16       #boton reset, configuration: pull_up_down=
                                     #gpio.pud_up y falling
                         #short_reset: clear screen, long_reset
                                 #(more than 3 seconds): total reset
# GLOBAL VARIABLES
ledR =        32         #red LED
ledA =        5          #yellow LED
...
close_blind=14           #seconds close living room left blind in
                                                      ambient mode
key_ifttt='-------------------------'  #Webhook IFTTT key
order_colour='sudo python /home/pi/home_pi/infrared/
                 BlackBeanControl/BlackBeanControl.py -c colours_'
jump='\n'*3
title='DAY:       HOUR:     ALARM:'+' '*54+'ORIGIN:\n'  #head of file
                                                #p_logfile.txt
ip_tv      ='192.168.1.xx'       #fixed ip tv living room lan
...
#AUTOMATIC CONTROL OF BLINDS/LIGHTS & HOLIDAYS MODE
day1 ='11:00:00' #start hour day automatic, blinds & holiday mode
...
dayi_4='20:15:00' #end  afternoon lights odd day
```

```
act_a=True        #act or not in automatic mode
act_v=True        #act or not in holidays mode

#SCHEDULE ON/OFF WIFI EDIMAX HEATER SWITCH
schedule={0:'08:30:00-12:00:00/16:30:00-23:55:00', #Sunday
...
          6:'08:30:00-12:00:00/16:30:00-23:55:00'} #Saturday

#PUSH BUTTONS KNX 17-x type where  x can be:
push_button={
1:  'billiard              ',2:   'stair landing 2nd floor       ',
...
124:'living wall lights    ',125: 'living small blinds          '}

#PUSH BUTTON KNX BLOCKERS 17-x -> 56/a, type where a can be:
blocker={
7: 'stair landing 2nd floor ',8:   'billiard                 ',
...
28:'entry                  ',32:  'bathroom main floor ceiling '}

#LIGHTS KNX 8/x type, simple & double push button, where x can be:
bulb_A={
1: 'billiard               ',2:   'stair landing 2nd floor      ',
...
30:'bathroom main floor mirror '}

#LIGHTS KNX 48/x type double push buttons, where x can be:
bulb_B={
1: 'billiard              ',2:  'stairs landing 2nd floor       ',
...
17:'bath. main f. ceiling ',18: 'living room lamps            '}

#LIGHTS 16/x type, push button dimmer, where x can be:
bulb_C={
1: 'living room table lamp',2:  'living room table DIM lamp   ',
3: 'living room sofa lamp ',4:  'living room sofa DIM lamp    ',
5: 'living room lamps     ',5:  'living room lamps DIM        '}

#WINDOW BLINDS 24/x type, simple push buttons, where x can be:
blind= {
15: 'room_b 2nd floor      ',16:  'room_b 2nd floor-stop       ',
...
31: 'living large left    ',32:  'living large left-stop      '}
#
OTHER ACTUATORS 32/x type, where x can be:
others=    {1:  'Heater'}

#-------------------------------------------------------------
# Configuration off KnxDevice.G_ADDR for home automation actuation
# see https://thingtype.com/blog/hacking-a-knx-network-with-
# a-raspberry-pi/
#-------------------------------------------------------------
# LIGHTS 1,0,X (1:on, 0:off)
#-------------------------------------------------------------
# LIVING LAMPS 2,0,X (1:on, 0:off)
```

```
# DIM: do 5 successive on
#------------------------------------------------------------
# BLINDS 3,0,X (1:close, 0:open) (X+1=one pulse)
#------------------------------------------------------------

blinds_without_alarm    =[15,17,19,21,25]
...
lights_holidays_odd     =[15,9,11]


#------------------------------------------------------------
# THERMOSTAT KNX 4,0,2 type absence/presence with:
# KnxComObject(KnxDevice.G_ADDR(4,0,2),1,0x2E/0x2C)
#------------------------------------------------------------
# VALVES 5,0,X type (1:close, 0:open)
#------------------------------------------------------------

# CONFIGURATION UART FOR KNX
ser=serial.Serial(
    port='/dev/ttyAMA0',               #for Raspberry 2
                                       #& Raspberry 3 without BT
#port='/dev/serial0',                  #for Raspberry 3 with BT
    baudrate=19200,                    #speed (1200-19200)
    parity=serial.PARITY_EVEN,         #parity (_none,_even,_odd)
    stopbits=serial.STOPBITS_ONE,      #bits stop (_one,_two)
    bytesize=serial.EIGHTBITS,         #total bits
                                       #(.eightbits,.sevenbits)
        xonxoff=False,                 #xonxoff disable
        rtscts= False,                 #rtscts  disable
        dsrdtr= False)                 #dsrdtr  disable
ser.timeout=1                          #non-block read

#Data exchange files with Telegram BOT p_telegram.py
f_sensors  ='/home/pi/home_auto/p_sensors.txt'     #sensors status
f_actuators='/home/pi/home_auto/p_actuators.txt'   #actions
f_lights   ='/home/pi/home_auto/p_lights.txt'      #lights on
f_blinds   ='/home/pi/home_auto/p_blinds.txt'      #blinds open
f_devices  ='/home/pi/home_auto/p_devices.txt'     #devices online

#Controls for garage gate
garage_gate_open=garage_gate_close=time.time()
still_open=False
f_open=True

#GMAIL parameters
origin      = "xx@gmail.com"
address1    = "reci1@gmail.com"            #addresses
address2    = "reci2@gmail.com"
smtp_server = 'smtp.gmail.com'
smtp_user   = 'xx@gmail.com'
smtp_pass   = 'pass'
server = smtplib.SMTP(smtp_server)
diary='/home/pi/home_auto/p_logfile.txt'    #log file storage

try:
  outfile=open(diary,'a')
```

297

```
except:
  os.system('sudo cp /home/pi/home_auto/p_logfile.ok
                      /home/pi/home_auto/p_logfile.txt')
  outfile=open(diary,'a')
outfile.write('DAY:      HOUR:    ALARM:'+' '*54+'ORIGIN:\n')  #add
                                                    #file header
outfile.write(separator)
outfile.close()

#-----------------------------------------------------------------
# COLOUR CLASS: Acts with colours lamp
# INPUTS:  on, off, brightness & colour
# OUTPUTS: turn on/off, set colour
# add > /dev/null 2>&1 to avoid error messages on the screen
#-----------------------------------------------------------------
class colour:
  global orig
  try:              #don't change the green text
    on=             order_colour+'on > /dev/null 2>&1'
...
    less_bright=  order_colour+'less_bright > /dev/null 2>&1 '
  except:
    orig='Class colour'
    line(traceback.extract_stack()) #set num_line with current line
    write_outfile('Colours isn't available, review NO_IP')

#-----------------------------------------------------------------
# MODULE ON_OFF_SONOFF() turns on/off un sonoff switch
# INPUTS:  on/off, switch
# OUTPUTS: on/off Sonoff switch
#-----------------------------------------------------------------
def on_off_sonoff(accion,device):
  global y_on
  try:
    if accion=='on' and device=='screen':
      y_on=True
    if accion=='off' and device=='screen':
      y_on=False
    dispo=devices[switch[device]]['deviceid']
    sss.switch(accion,dispo,None)
    orig='on_off_sonoff()'
    line(traceback.extract_stack())
    write_outfile('Set '+device+' in '+accion)
  except:
    orig='on_off_sonoff()'
    line(traceback.extract_stack())
    write_outfile('Sonoff isn't available, review eWelink')

#-----------------------------------------------------------------
# MODULE SEE_MONTH(): look if is summer or winter
# INPUTS:  datetime.now()
# OUTPUTS: variable dia2 to "21:00:00" or "22:00" for automatic()
#          April-August closes at 22:30, September at 21:30 & 21:00
#          the rest of the months
#-----------------------------------------------------------------
```

```python
def see_month():
  global day2
  month=datetime.now().month
  if month>=4 and month<=8:
    day2='22:30:00'
  elif month==9:
    day2='21:30:00'
  else:
    day2='21:00:00'


#-----------------------------------------------------------
# MODULE LINE(): take the current line of execution
# takes into account he level on nesting: main, function, function
# in function, etc...
# INPUTS:   stack situation
# OUTPUTS: num_line from function call is
#-----------------------------------------------------------
def line(x):
  global num_line                              #function output
  level=len(x)                                 #nesting level
  line=str(x)                                  #find line number
  for j in range(0,level):                     #repeat as level
    line=line[line.find('p_global.py')+13:]  #& set format
  num_line=line[line.find(' ')+1:line.find(',')]
  num_line=str(int(num_line)+1)
  num_line='#'+('000'+num_line)[len(num_line)-1:]+' '
  return (num_line)


#-----------------------------------------------------------
# MODULE SEE_COLOUR(): turns on colours with the select colour
# INPUTS:   select colour
# OUTPUTS: if is possible, colours turns on
#-----------------------------------------------------------
def see_colour(x):
  global orig
  orig='see_colour()'
  try:
    if '&&' in x:                              #look for several actions
      j1=x[x.find('colours_')+8:x.find('/dev')-3]
                                               #1st action in j1
      j2=x[x.find('&&'):]
      j2=j2[j2.find('colours_')+8:j2.find('/dev')-3]
                                               #2nd action in j2
      jf=j1+' & in: '+j2
    else:
      jf=x[x.find('colours_')+8:x.find('/dev')-3]    #only one
    write_outfile('Set Colours in: '+jf)
    os.system(x)  #acts with Colours and action x
  except:
    line(traceback.extract_stack())
    write_outfile('Colours isn't review NO_IP')


#-----------------------------------------------------------
# MODULE START_EDIMAX(): act with Edimax SP1101W plug
# Based on smartplug.py script (available SP1101W FW 2.02)
```

299

```python
# set the correct Edimax ip & Ediplug password
# edimax.state        know status ('ON'/'OFF')
# edimax.state='ON'   turn on
# edimax.state='OFF'  turn off
#----------------------------------------------------------------
def start_edimax():
  global orig,edimax,error_edimax
  line(traceback.extract_stack())
  see_colour(colour.orange) #turn colours on orange
  orig='start_edimax()'
  ip_edimax='192.168.1.xx'
  line(traceback.extract_stack())
  write_outfile('Activates Edimax connection in: '+ip_edimax)
  from smartplug import SmartPlug  #Edimax status
  try:
    edimax=SmartPlug(ip_edimax,('[user]','[password]'))
    line(traceback.extract_stack())
    write_outfile('Edimax connection correct activate')
    error_edimax=False
  except:
    error_edimax=True
    line(traceback.extract_stack())
    say('Attention: Edimax error')
    line(traceback.extract_stack())
    see_colour(colour.red)

#----------------------------------------------------------------
# MODULE START_SONOFF(): acts with Sonoff switches
# INPUTS:   Sonoff parameters
# OUTPUTS: Sonoff detected switches are init
#----------------------------------------------------------------
def start_sonoff():
  global sss,switch,devices,orig
  try:
    sss=sonoff.Sonoff('[user]','[password]','us')
    switch={'screen':0,'ambient':1,'kitchen':2,'bridge':3}
    devices=sss.get_devices()
    orig='start_sonoff()'
    line(traceback.extract_stack())
    write_outfile('Sonoff started successfully')
  except:
    orig='start_sonoff()'
    line(traceback.extract_stack())
    write_outfile('Sonoff isn't available, review eWelink')
    see_colour(colour.red)

#----------------------------------------------------------------
# MODULE SETUP_GRAL(): starts el GPIO
# INPUTS:   any
# OUTPUTS: GPIO configuration & warnings
#----------------------------------------------------------------
def setup_gral():
  global orig
  try:
    GPIO.setmode(GPIO.BOARD)     #GPIO numbers by physical location
```

```
      GPIO.setwarnings(False)        #Remove unnecessary warnings
   except:
     orig='setup_gral()'
     line(traceback.extract_stack())
     say('Attention: GPIO error')
     line(traceback.extract_stack())
     see_colour(colour.red)

#--------------------------------------------------------------------
# MODULE TRACE(): display GPIO status
# INPUTS:  GPIO pin situation
# OUTPUTS: GPIO pin formatted situation
#--------------------------------------------------------------------
def trace(x_trace):
   print (Cursor.POS(48,23)+Fore.YELLOW + str(x_trace))

#--------------------------------------------------------------------
# MODULE ENLARGE(): change str to str+blank of a certain length
# INPUTS:  x_enlarge, length_text
# OUTPUTS: x_enlarge formatted str
#--------------------------------------------------------------------
def enlarge(x_enlarge):
   x_enlarge=x_enlarge+' '*(length_text-len(x_enlarge))
   return(x_enlarge)

#--------------------------------------------------------------------
# MODULE CLEAR_ACTUATORS() Start p_actuators.txt
# INPUTS:  p_actuators.txt with actions
# OUTPUTS: p_actuators.txt with actions initiated to NO
#--------------------------------------------------------------------
def clear_actuators():
   global orig
   try:
     acts=open(factuators,'w')
     acts.write('Turns off lights: NO\n')
...
     acts.write('Turns off living room sofa: NO\n')
     acts.close()
   except:
     orig='clear_actuators()'
     line(traceback.extract_stack())
     say('Attention: ACTUATORS error')
     line(traceback.extract_stack())
     see_colour(colour.red)

#--------------------------------------------------------------------
# MODULE CLEAR_LIGHTS(): empty p_lights.txt
# INPUTS:  p_lights.txt
# OUTPUTS: p_lights.txt empty except hall if is on
#--------------------------------------------------------------------
def clear_lights():
   global switched_on,orig
   try:
     if 'hall                    ' in switched_on:
       lights=open(flights,'w')
       lights.write('hall                    ')
```

```
      switched_on=[]
      switched_on.append('hall                        ')
      lights.close()
    else:
      switched_on=[]                    #switched on lights
      lights=open(flights,'w')
      lights.close()
  except:
    orig='clear_lights()'
    line(traceback.extract_stack())
    say('Attention: LIGHTS error')
    line(traceback.extract_stack())
    see_colour(colour.red)

#---------------------------------------------------------------------
# MODUE CLEAR_BLINDS(): adds open blinds to p_blinds.txt
# INPUTS:  p_blinds.txt
# OUTPUTS: p_blinds.txt full with open blinds
#---------------------------------------------------------------------
def clear_blinds():
  global open,orig
  try:
    open=[]                          #open blinds, alphabetical order
    blinds=open(fblinds,'w')
    for x in [25,15,27,31,21,19,17]:    #starts with all open
      open.append(blind[x])
      blinds.write(blind[x]+'\n')
    blinds.close()
  except:
    orig='clear_blinds()'
    line(traceback.extract_stack())
    say('Attention: BLINDS error')
    line(traceback.extract_stack())
    see_colour(colour.red)

#---------------------------------------------------------------------
# MODULE RECORD_LIGHTS(): switched_on[] to p_lights.txt transfer
# INPUTS:  p_lights.txt & switched_on[]
# OUTPUTS: p_lights.txt
#---------------------------------------------------------------------
def record_lights(switched_on):
  global orig
  try:
    switched_on.sort()               #switched on lights sort
    lights=open(flights,'w')
    for x in switched_on:
      lights.write(x+'\n')
    lights.close()
  except:
    orig='record_lights()'
    line(traceback.extract_stack())
    say('Attention: LIGHTS error')
    line(traceback.extract_stack())
    see_colour(colour.red)
```

```
#------------------------------------------------------------
# MODULE RECORD_BLINDS(): open[] to p_blinds.txt transfer
# INPUTS:  p_blinds.txt & open[]
# OUTPUTS: p_blinds.txt
#------------------------------------------------------------
def record_blinds(open):
  global orig
  try:
    open.sort()
    blinds=open(fpersianas,'w')
    for x in open:
      if 'stop' not in x:          #delete stops
        blinds.write(x+'\n')
    blinds.close()
  except:
    orig='record_blinds()'
    line(traceback.extract_stack())
    say('Attention: BLINDS error')
    line(traceback.extract_stack())
    see_colour(colour.red)


#------------------------------------------------------------
# MODULE RECORD_SENSORS(): states[] to p_sensors.txt transfer
# INPUTS:  states[] y p_sensors.txt
# OUTPUTS: p_sensors.txt
#------------------------------------------------------------
def record_sensors(states):
  global orig
  try:
    sensors=open(fsensors,'r')
    k=[]                           #to save data
    while True:                    #record states[] except states[16]
      x=sensors.readline()
      if x!='':
        k.append(x)
      else:
        break
    sensors.close()
    if len(k)<18:
      os.system('sudo cp /home/pi/home_auto/p_sensors.ok
                          /home/pi/home_auto/p_sensors.txt')
      sensors=open(fsensors,'r')
      k=[]
      while True:
        x=sensors.readline()
        if x!='':
          k.append(x)
        else:
          break
      sensors.close()
    sensors=open(fsensors,'w')
    for x in range (0,16):
      sensors.write(states[x]+'\n')
    sensors.write(k[16])
    sensors.write(states[17]+'\n')
```

```
      sensors.write(states[18]+'\n')
      sensors.close()
    except:
      orig='record_sensors()'
      line(traceback.extract_stack())
      say('Attention: SENSORS error')
      line(traceback.extract_stack())
      see_colour(colour.red)


#-------------------------------------------------------------
# MODULE RECORD_open(): p_blinds.txt to open[] transfer
# INPUTS:   p_blinds.txt y open[]
# OUTPUTS: open[]
#-------------------------------------------------------------
def record_open():
  global open,orig
  try:
    open=[]
    blinds=open(fblinds,'r')
    while True:
      x=blinds.readline()
      if x!='':
        open.append(x[:len(x)-1]) #watch out with \n
      else:
        break
    blinds.close()
  except:
    orig='record_open()'
    line(traceback.extract_stack())
    say('Attention: BLINDS error')
    line(traceback.extract_stack())
    see_colour(colour.red)


#-------------------------------------------------------------
# MODULE RECORD_SWITCHED_ON(): p_lights.txt, switched_on[] transfer
# INPUTS:   p_lights.txt & switched_on[]
# OUTPUTS: switched_on[]
#-------------------------------------------------------------
def record_switched_on():
  global switched_on,orig
  try:
    switched_on=[]
    lights=open(flights,'r')
    while True:
      x=lights.readline()
      if x!='':
        switched_on.append(x[:len(x)-1]) #watch out with \n
      else:
        break
    lights.close()
  except:
    orig='record_switched_on()'
    line(traceback.extract_stack())
    say('Attention: LIGHTS error')
    line(traceback.extract_stack())
```

```
    see_colour(colour.red)

#-------------------------------------------------------------
# MODULE RECORD_ACTIVTED(): p_devices.txt to activated[] transfer
# INPUTS:  p_devices.txt
# OUTPUTS: activated[]
#-------------------------------------------------------------
def record_activated():
  global activated,orig
  try:
    activated=[]
    devices=open(fdevices,'r')
    while True:
      x=devices.readline()
      if x!='':
        activated.append(x[:len(x)-1]) #watch out with \n
      else:
        break
    devices.close()
  except:
    orig='record_activated()'
    line(traceback.extract_stack())
    say('Attention: DEVICES error')
    line(traceback.extract_stack())
    see_colour(colour.red)


#-------------------------------------------------------------
# MODULE RECORD_STATES(): updates current sensor status
# INPUTS:  each sensor status by GPIO & p_sensors.txt
# OUTPUTS: p_sensors.txt y states[]
#-------------------------------------------------------------
def record_states():
  global states,tempo,orig
  try:
    tempo=[]
    inter=open(fsensores,'r')
    while True:
      x=inter.readline()
      if x!='':
        tempo.append(x[:len(x)-1])
      else:
        break
    inter.close()
  except:
    orig='record_states()'
    line(traceback.extract_stack())
    say('Attention: SENSORS error')
    line(traceback.extract_stack())
    see_colour(colour.red)

  if len(tempo)<18:                    #p_sensors.txt corrupt?
    os.system('sudo cp /home/pi/home_auto/p_sensors.ok
                        /home/pi/home_auto/p_sensors.txt')
    tempo=[]
    inter=open(fsensores,'r')          #tmp[] with p_sensors.txt
```

```
    while True:
      x=inter.readline()
      if x!='':
        tempo.append(x[:len(x)-1])
      else:
        break
    inter.close()
    states=[]
    states.append  ('Temp NAS:    '+str(tem)+' °C')
    states.append  ('Hum  NAS:    '+str(hum)+' %HR')
    if GPIO.input(pin_power)=='0':      #POWER
      states.append('Power:       No')
    else:
...
    if GPIO.input(pin_co2)=='1':        #CO2
      states.append('Co2:         Excessive')

#-----------------------------------------------------------
# MODULE UPDATE_STATES(): updates states[] with real data
# INPUTS:  sensor, gpio, connected, garage_gate, heater
# OUTPUTS: states[]
#-----------------------------------------------------------
def update_states():
  global states
  states[0]='Temp NAS:    '+str(tem)+' °C'
  states[1]='Hum  NAS:    '+str(hum)+' %HR'
  if GPIO.input(pin_power)=='0':  #POWER
    states[2]='Power:       No'
  else:
    states[2]='Power:       Yes'
...
#-----------------------------------------------------------
# MODULE KNXEVENTS(): read knx bus
# INPUTS:  KNX bus telegrams
# OUTPUTS: information load into KnxDevice script
#-----------------------------------------------------------
#Function called from previous (KnxDevice) to allow the script
# to be notified of a telegram event.
def KnxEvents(index):
    pass


#-----------------------------------------------------------
# MODULE KNX_ONOFF(): acts with KNX bus with several parameters
# INPUTS:  (x,0,y),z,0x2E/0x2C (x,0,y) group addresses, z flag &
#          k='ON' or k='OFF'
# OUTPUTS: action with KNX bus
#-----------------------------------------------------------
def knx_onoff(x,y,z,k):
  global orig
  try:
    Knx=KnxDevice.KnxDevice()
    Knx._comObjectsList=[KnxComObject.KnxComObject(
        KnxDevice.G_ADDR(x,0,y),z,0x2E),KnxComObject.KnxComObject(
                            KnxDevice.G_ADDR(x,0,y),z,0x2C)]
    Knx._comObjectsNb=len(Knx._comObjectsList)
```

```python
    #1,0,55 is reserved for raspberry pi 3
    Knx.begin("/dev/ttyAMA0", KnxDevice.P_ADDR(1, 0, 55), Knx,
                                                          KnxEvents)
    if k=='ON':
      Knx.write(1,1)
    if k=='OFF':
      Knx.write(1,0)
    for j in range(1,100):
      Knx.task()

  except:
    orig='knx_onoff()'
    line(traceback.extract_stack())
    say('Attention: KNX error')

#---------------------------------------------------------------------
# MODULE SAY(): announces by Google Home text with 15s timeout
# INPUTS:   text/[*].mp3
# OUTPUTS: announces text by Google Home
# Call to p_ghome_say.py script that runs in Python 3.5 who needs
# PHP 7.0, Apache & Mysql to management *.mp3 URL
# generated with gTTS. The *.mp3 are in /var/www/cache on
# MD5 format & without protection with user/pass
#---------------------------------------------------------------------
def say(text):
  global orig
  orig='say()'

  try:
    line(traceback.extract_stack())
    value=func_timeout(15,talk,args=(text))    #15s
    #watch out: this function sends text as a list, it has convert
                                  #it as str with: ''.join(text)
    time.sleep(3)                     #wait to avoid problems

  except FunctionTimedOut:
    line(traceback.extract_stack())
    write_outfile('Function say() error, Google Home resets')
    location='/home/pi/home_auto/gTTS/'
    os.system(location+'./p_ghome_reset.py '+' > /dev/null 2>&1')

#---------------------------------------------------------------------
# MODULE TALK(): called by say() with timeout
# INPUTS:   text
# OUTPUTS: text to talk on Google Home
#---------------------------------------------------------------------
def talk(*text):
  global orig
  orig='talk()'
  ttt=''.join(text)                    #*text parameter to one variable
  ip_google='192.168.1.xx'
  location='/home/pi/home_auto/gTTS/'
  write_outfile('Announce: '+ttt)
  os.system(location+'./p_ghome_say.py '+ip_google+' "'+ttt+'"
                                          > /dev/null 2>&1')
```

```
#------------------------------------------------------------------
# MODULE IFTTT(): acts with IFTTT widgets
# INPUTS:   name=widget name. Available are:
# log_dropbox, WIFI_bulb_on/off, ambient_on/off, screen_on/off,
# bridge_on/off, colours_on/off, tv_on/off, desco_4k_on/off,
# tado_off, tado_auto, tado_on_22, tado_on_18
# Adds: +'> /dev/null 2>&1' to avoid screen messages
# OUTPUTS: turns on/off select widget
# In terminal use: curl -X POST https://maker.ifttt.com/trigger
#                                  /[webhook]/with/key/[clave]
# See key en www.ifttt.com->select: webhooks->webhooks->settings
#------------------------------------------------------------------
def ifttt(name):
  global orig
  orig='ifttt()'
  error_ifttt=False
  line(traceback.extract_stack())
  write_outfile('Acts on WIFI with '+name)
  if name=='tv_on':     #look if tv is off to switch it on
    res=os.system("ping -w 1 "+ip_tv+'> /dev/null 2>&1')
    if res!=0:          #tv is OFF
      try:
        requests.post('https://maker.ifttt.com/trigger/
                                '+name+'/with/key/'+key_ifttt)
      except:
        error_ifttt=True
  elif name=='tv_off':
    res=os.system("ping -w 1 "+ip_tv+'> /dev/null 2>&1')
    if res==0:          #tv is ON
      try:
        requests.post('https://maker.ifttt.com/trigger/
                                '+name+'/with/key/'+key_ifttt)
      except:
        error_ifttt=True
  ...
      try:
        requests.post('https://maker.ifttt.com/trigger/
                                '+name+'/with/key/'+key_ifttt)
      except:
        error_ifttt=True
  if error_ifttt:
    line(traceback.extract_stack())
    say('Attention: REQUESTS error')
    line(traceback.extract_stack())
    see_colour(colour.on+' && '+colour.red)

#------------------------------------------------------------------
# MODULE LOG_DROP(): upload on Dropbox p_logfile.txt
# INPUTS:  p_logfile.txt
# OUTPUTS: p_logfile.txt on Dropbox in /logfile
# It has record in www/cache/ and invoke in IFTTT only with:
# [URL].hopto.org/cache/p_logfile.txt (NO-IP URL)
#------------------------------------------------------------------
def log_drop():
```

```
global orig
orig='log_drop()'
try:
  os.system('sudo cp /home/pi/home_auto/p_logfile.txt
                          /var/www/cache/p_logfile.txt')
except:
  line(traceback.extract_stack())
  say('Attention: SYSTEM error')
ifttt('log_dropbox') #upload p_logfile.txt on DROPBOX/logfile/
line(traceback.extract_stack())
write_outfile('Upload p_logfile.txt on DROPBOX/logfile/')

#--------------------------------------------------------------
# MODULE AUTOMATIC(): acts, every day except HOLIDAYS=ON
# INPUTS:  holidays mode true/false, movie mode true/false
# OUTPUTS: acts with blinds like:
# At 11:00-21:00(22:30 summer) opens: room_a/b & living room small
# At 21:00 (22:30 summer)-11:00 closes room_a/b % living room small
#--------------------------------------------------------------
def automatic():
  x=states[12]
  global orig,open,close_high
  if (not holidays and x=='Movie:    OFF'):
    global acts_a
    if y_on==False and 'tado home           ' in activated:
      if devices[0].get('params').get(u'switch')=='off':
        on_off_sonoff('on','screen')
        orig='automatic()'
        line(traceback.extract_stack())
        write_outfile('Switch on screen')
        say('Tadoº is in Home mode, switch on screen')
    if y_on==True and  'tado away           ' in activated:
      if devices[0].get('params').get(u'switch')=='on':
        on_off_sonoff('off','screen')
        orig='automatic()'
        line(traceback.extract_stack())
        write_outfile('Switch off screen')
        say('Tadoº is in Away mode, switch off screen')
    t=time.strftime("%X")      #look the time
    if ((t>=day1 and t<=day2) and 'hall             ' not in
                                  switched_on):#is day

      if acts_a and closes_high:        #it has to open blinds
        see_colour(colour.on+' && '+colour.red)
        orig='automatic()'
        ifttt('ambient_off')     #switch off ambient
        ifttt('WIFI_bulb_off')   #switch off WIFI bulb
        ifttt('colours_off')     #switch off colours

        #if Tadoº home then switch on screen
        if tado_state=='home' and y_on==False:
          on_off_sonoff('on','screen')
          orig='automatic()'
          line(traceback.extract_stack())
          write_outfile('Switch on screen')
          say('Tadoº is in Home mode, switch on screen')
```

```
        if not movie:        #look if ambient mode is activated
          for j in blinds_auto:
            knx_onoff(3,j,0,'OFF')
            time.sleep(.5)     #update open[]
          if 'room_a                        ' not in open:
            open.append('room_a                        ')
...
          orig='automatic()'
          line(traceback.extract_stack())
          say('It's day, open the blinds')
          acts_a=False
          close_high=False
        else:
          for j in blinds_auto_pelicula:
            knx_onoff(3,j,0,'OFF')
            time.sleep(.5)     #update open[]
...
          acts_a=False
          close_high=False
    if ((t>=day2 or t<=day1) and 'hall              ' in switched_on):
                                  #it's night or hall is on
      if not acts_a:
        see_colour(colour.on+' && '+colour.red)
        for j in blinds_auto:
          knx_onoff(3,j,0,'ON')
          time.sleep(.5)       #update open[]
        if 'room_a                        ' in open:
          open.remove('room_a                        ')
...
        see_colour(colour.off)
        orig='automatic()'
        line(traceback.extract_stack())
        say('It's night, close the blinds')
        acts_a=True
        close_high=True
    record_blinds(open)

#----------------------------------------------------------------
# MODULE INITIAL_TEST(): initial test on start or after RESET
# INPUTS:   start o RESET
# OUTPUTS: LED R,A,V, blink, sounds, sensors values, send mail
#          adds event to p_logfile.txt
#----------------------------------------------------------------
def initial_test():
  global orig
  line(traceback.extract_stack())
  try:
    os.system('clear')       #clear main screen
    orig='initial_test()'
    write_outfile('Do the initial test')
    print (Cursor.POS(10, 2)+Style.BRIGHT+Fore.RED+'INITIAL TEST:')
    print (Cursor.POS(25,3)+Fore.GREEN  +'Temperature: ')
    print (Cursor.POS(25,4)+Fore.GREEN  +'Humidity: ')
    print (Cursor.POS(25,6)+Fore.RED    +'Red LED: ')
    print (Cursor.POS(25,7)+Fore.YELLOW +'Yellow LED: ')
```

```
      print (Cursor.POS(25,8)+Fore.GREEN  +'Green LED: ')
      for i in range(0,1):
        print(Cursor.POS(25+i, 2) + Style.BRIGHT + Fore.RED + '.')
        sensor()
        ae_LED('R','E',long)
...
        sound(short)
    except KeyboardInterrupt:
      line(traceback.extract_stack())
      see_colour(colour.red)
      destroy()


#---------------------------------------------------------------------
# MODULE SETUP_RELAYS(): nas, ont, router, hub
# Acts with 8 RELAY-kkmoon
# L=OFF (C+NC), H=ON (C+NA) with 74ls14 inverter
# power RELAY x8 module, whit external power
# INPUTS:  pin, time ON, time OFF
# OUTPUTS: on/off, display pin on/off & screen messages
#---------------------------------------------------------------------
def setup_relays():
  global orig
  orig='setup_relays()'
  try:
    for i in pins_relays:
      GPIO.setup(i, GPIO.OUT)                # Set i mode is output
    GPIO.output (pin_nas,     GPIO.LOW)
...
    write_outfile('Switch off all relays')
  except:
    line(traceback.extract_stack())
    say('Attention: GPIO error')
    line(traceback.extract_stack())
    see_colour(colour.on+' && '+colour.red)


#---------------------------------------------------------------------
# MODULE SETUP_LED(): start led, reset button & buzz
# INPUTS:   led (R:red, Y:yellow, G:green) E/A(on/off), reset button
# OUTPUTS: sounds buzz x seconds, LED status on the screen
#---------------------------------------------------------------------
def setup_led():
  global orig,num_line
  orig='setup_led()'
  try:
    nom_LED=[ledR,ledY,ledG]
    for i in nom_LED:
      GPIO.setup(i, GPIO.OUT)                # output mode for led
      GPIO.output(i,GPIO.LOW)                # switch off led
    GPIO.setup(pin_buzz,  GPIO.OUT)          # output mode
    GPIO.output(pin_buzz, GPIO.LOW)          # switch off buzz
    GPIO.setup(boton_reset, GPIO.IN, pull_up_down=GPIO.PUD_UP)
    line(traceback.extract_stack())
    write_outfile('Starts LED')
  except:
    line(traceback.extract_stack())
```

```python
      say('Attention: GPIO error')
      see_colour(colour.on+' && '+colour.red)

#-----------------------------------------------------------------
# MODULE SETUP_ALARMS(): house alarms detection
# INPUTS:  Garage(12), Smoke(13), Water(15), Gas(18), Power(37),
#          Doorbell(40), CO2(31)
# OUTPUTS: sound, screen messages & email
#-----------------------------------------------------------------
def setup_alarms():
  global orig
  try:
    orig='setup_alarms()'
    for i in pines_alarms:
      GPIO.setup(i, GPIO.IN, pull_up_down=GPIO.PUD_UP)
    GPIO.setup(pin_power, GPIO.IN, pull_up_down=GPIO.PUD_DOWN)
...
    GPIO.add_event_detect(pin_garage, GPIO.BOTH,
                    callback=ac_alarm_garage, bouncetime=bounce*4)
...
    write_outfile('Starts GPIO of alarms')
  except:
    line(traceback.extract_stack())
    say('Attention: GPIO error')
    line(traceback.extract_stack())
    see_colour(colour.on+' && '+colour.red)

#-----------------------------------------------------------------
# MODULE START_ALARMS(): start variables to False
# INPUTS:  variables to start
# OUTPUTS: variables started to  False
#-----------------------------------------------------------------
def start_alarms():
  global error,reset_pressed,reset_long,wait,
                          cut_internet,a_sensor_bad,t_wait
  v=[]
  i=0
  while i<8:
    v.append(False)
    i+=1 (error,reset_pressed,reset_long,wait,cut_internet,
                          a_sensor_bad,a_reset,t_wait)=v

#-----------------------------------------------------------------
# MODULE AE_LED(): on/off specified LED
# INPUTS:  LED (R:red, Y:yellow, G:green), E/A(on/off), time
# OUTPUTS: on/off LED
#-----------------------------------------------------------------
def ae_LED(LED, action, time):
  global error,cur,orig,jj
  if accion == 'E':
    accion = GPIO.HIGH              # LED on with  HIGH
    n_accion='Switched_on'
  elif accion == 'A':
    accion = GPIO.LOW               # LED off with LOW
    n_accion='Switched_off'
```

```python
  else:
    print (Cursor.POS(10, 20) + Fore.RED + enlarge('ERROR: action
                                    '+str(accion)+' wrong'))
    orig='ae_LED()'
    line(traceback.extract_stack())
    write_outfile('ERROR: action '+str(accion)+' wrong')
    error = True
    destroy()
  if LED == 'R':
    GPIO.output(ledR, accion)
    n_LED='Red'
    if accion==GPIO.HIGH:
      print (Cursor.POS(40, 6) + Fore.RED + 'Yes')
    else:
      print (Cursor.POS(40, 6) + Fore.RED + 'No')
    print (Cursor.POS(10, 19) + Fore.GREEN + enlarge('LED: '
                                    +n_LED+' is: '+n_accion))
...
  else:
    print (Cursor.POS(10, 20) + Fore.RED + enlarge('ERROR:
                                    LED'+str(LED)+' wrong'))
    orig='ae_LED()'
    line(traceback.extract_stack())
    write_outfile('ERROR: LED'+str(LED)+' wrong')
    error = True
    destroy()
  time.sleep(time)              #Don't delete, it's ck speed controller

#----------------------------------------------------------------
# MODULE ON_DEVICE(): set ON on GPIO & time
# INPUTS:   pin & time to on
# OUTPUTS: pin of GPIO activation
#----------------------------------------------------------------
def on_device(pin,time):
  global orig
  n_pin=pin
  if pin==  'NAS':
    pin=pin_nas
    fil=10
...
  else:
    print (Cursor.POS(10, 18) + Fore.RED + enlarge('ERROR: relay
                                    '+str(n_pin)+' wrong'))
    orig='on_device()'
    line(traceback.extract_stack())
    write_outfile('ERROR: relay '+str(n_pin)+' wrong')
    return()
  try:
    if (pin==pin_ont or pin==pin_nas or pin==pin_router):
      GPIO.output(pin, GPIO.LOW)
    else:
      GPIO.output(pin, GPIO.HIGH)
  except:
    orig='on_device()'
    line(traceback.extract_stack())
```

```
    say('Attention: GPIO error')
    see_colour(colour.red)
  time.sleep(time)
  print (Cursor.POS(10, 17)  + Fore.GREEN + enlarge('Switch on
                                              relay: '+str(n_pin)))
  orig=ori
  line(traceback.extract_stack())
  write_outfile('Switch on relay: '+str(n_pin))
  print (Cursor.POS(51, fil) + Fore.CYAN  + 'ON ')

#----------------------------------------------------------------
# MODULE OFF_DEVICE(): OFF on GPIO with time
# INPUTS:  pin & off time
# OUTPUTS: switched off specified GPIO pin
#----------------------------------------------------------------
def off_device(pin,time):
  global orig
  n_pin=pin
  if pin==  'NAS':
    pin=pin_nas
    fil=10
...
  else:
    print (Cursor.POS(10, 18) + Fore.RED + enlarge('ERROR: relay
                                        '+str(n_pin)+' wrong'))
    orig='off_device()'
    line(traceback.extract_stack())
    write_outfile('ERROR: relay '+str(n_pin)+' wrong')
    return()

  try:
    if (pin==pin_ont or pin==pin_nas or pin==pin_router):
      GPIO.output(pin, GPIO.HIGH)
    else:
      GPIO.output(pin, GPIO.LOW)

  except:
    orig='off_device()'
    line(traceback.extract_stack())
    say('Attention: GPIO error')
    see_colour(colour.red)
  time.sleep(time)
  print (Cursor.POS(10, 17)  + Fore.GREEN + enlarge('Switch off
                                          relay: ' + str(n_pin)))
  orig=ori
  line(traceback.extract_stack())
  write_outfile('Switch off relay: ' + str(n_pin))
  print (Cursor.POS(51, fil) + Fore.RED   + 'OFF')

#----------------------------------------------------------------
# MODULE MESSAGE(): send e-mail with gmail
# INPUTS:  topic, message_see (screen), message_rest (full) address
# OUTPUTS: message to address with topic and message_see/rest
#----------------------------------------------------------------
def message(topic, message_see, message_rest, address):
  global orig
```

```python
orig='Gmail'
try:
  line(traceback.extract_stack())
  see_colour(colour.on+' && '+colour.green)
  message = message_see + message_rest + '\n' * 3
                              + 'Message of XX House'
  mime_message = MIMEText(message)
  mime_message["From"] = origin
  mime_message["To"] = address
  mime_message["Subject"] = topic+' '+time.strftime("%X  ")
  smtp = SMTP("smtp.gmail.com", 587)
  smtp.ehlo()
  smtp.starttls()
  smtp.login(smtp_user, smtp_pass)
  smtp.sendmail(origin, address, mime_message.as_string())
  smtp.quit()
  print (Cursor.POS(10, 21) + Fore.GREEN + enlarge('Wrong
                                                message:'))
  print (Cursor.POS(10, 22) + Fore.GREEN + enlarge(topic+':
                                    '+message_see[:26]))
  if address==address_1:
    line(traceback.extract_stack())
    write_outfile(message_ver)
    write_outfile(separator)
  see_colour(colour.off)
except:
  line(traceback.extract_stack())
  see_colour(colour.on+' && '+colour.red)
  line(traceback.extract_stack())
  say('Attention: SMTP error')

#-------------------------------------------------------------
# MODULE SEND_DAILY(): daily send with p_logfile.txt summary
# INPUTS:  origin, address, file, day_1
# OUTPUTS: gmail message with topic, message, file
#-------------------------------------------------------------
def send_daily():
  global orig,y_on
  try:
    # mail build
    line(traceback.extract_stack())
    see_colour(colour.on+' && '+colour.green)
    msg = MIMEMultipart()
    msg['To'] = address_1
    msg['From'] = origin
    msg['Subject'] = 'HOME AUTOMATION SUMMARY'+time.strftime(
                                                "%X  ")

    #message body:
    msg.attach(MIMEText('Daily summary at '+day_1+' Home','plain'))
    fp = open(daily,'rb')
    attached = MIMEBase('multipart', 'encrypted')
    attached.set_payload(fp.read())
    fp.close()
    encoders.encode_base64(attached) #base64 encrypted
    attached.add_header('Content-Disposition', 'attachment',
```

```
                                            filename='p_logfile.txt')
    msg.attach(attached)
    #stmp start
    smtp = SMTP("smtp.gmail.com", 587)
    smtp.ehlo()
    smtp.starttls()
    smtp.ehlo()
    smtp.login(smtp_user,smtp_pass)
    smtp.sendmail(origin,address_1,msg.as_string())
    log_drop()  #p_logfile.txt to DROPBOX/lofile/
    orig='send_daily()'
    line(traceback.extract_stack())
    say('En of the day, send summary')
    line(traceback.extract_stack())
    see_colour(colour.off)
    y_on=False
  except:
    orig='sen_daily()'
    line(traceback.extract_stack())
    say('Attention: SMTP error')
    line(traceback.extract_stack())
    see_colour(colour.red)


#-------------------------------------------------------------------
# MODULE SEND_SUMMARY(): send daily summary
# INPUTS:  day1 & day2 for change of day & p_logfile.txt
# OUTPUTS: send the file p_logfile.txt
#-------------------------------------------------------------------
def send_summary():
  global day_1,day_2,t_2,orig
  try:
    if day_2!=day_1:                  #other day?
      orig='send_summary()'
      line(traceback.extract_stack())
      write_outfile('Send & delete summary at '+dia_1)
      print (Cursor.POS(10, 21) + Fore.GREEN + enlarge(
                           'Send & delete summary at '+dia_1))
      send_daily()                  #send mail with summary
      os.remove(daily)              #delete & create new summary file
      outfile=open(daily,'w')       #open p_logfile.txt
      outfile.write('DAY:      HOUR:     ALARM:'+' '*54+'ORIGIN:\n')
      outfile.write(separator)
      outfile.close()
      orig='send_summary()'
      write_outfile(jump)
      write_outfile(separator)
      line(traceback.extract_stack())
      write_outfile('HOME AUTOMATIO CONTROL START')
      write_outfile(separator)
      write_outfile(title)
      write_outfile(separator)
      day_1=day_2
    else:
      t_2=time.localtime()          #day of the week
      day_2=time.strftime('%A',t_2)
```

```python
  except:
    orig='send_summary()'
    line(traceback.extract_stack())
    say('Attention: LOGFILE error')
    line(traceback.extract_stack())
    see_colour(colour.red)

#---------------------------------------------------------------
# MODULE SOUND(): buzz sound & ck signal
# INPUTS:   program activated
# OUTPUTS: x seconds pulse en la base del NPN, direct logic
#---------------------------------------------------------------
def sound(x):                              # x seconds
  try:
    GPIO.output(pin_buzz, GPIO.HIGH)  # turn on buzz
    time.sleep(x)
    GPIO.output(pin_buzz, GPIO.LOW)   # turn off buzz
    if x!=ck:
      print (Cursor.POS(10, 16) + Fore.GREEN + enlarge('Beep
                                          '+str(x)+' seconds'))
  except:
    orig='sound()'
    line(traceback.extract_stack())
    say('Attention: GPIO error')
    line(traceback.extract_stack())
    see_colour(colour.red)

#---------------------------------------------------------------
# MODULE AC_RESET():push button RESET, to clear screen/total reset
# INPUTS:   reset button
# OUTPUTS: reset_long variable
#---------------------------------------------------------------
def ac_reset(ev=None):
  global reset_pressed,reset_long,orig
  time.sleep(1)
  if GPIO.input(button_reset)==0:
    reset_pressed=True
    time.sleep(pause_reset_long)
    if GPIO.input(button_reset)==0:  # reverse logic
      reset_long=True
      print (Cursor.POS(42, 13) + Fore.RED   + 'YES')
      orig='ac_reset()'
      line(traceback.extract_stack())
      write_outfile('LONG RESET button pressed')
    else:
      reset_long=False
      print (Cursor.POS(42, 13) + Fore.GREEN + 'YES')
      orig='ac_reset()'
      line(traceback.extract_stack())
      write_outfile('SHORT RESET button pressed')
  else:
    reset_pressed=reset_largo=False
    orig='ac_reset()'
    line(traceback.extract_stack())
```

```python
      write_outfile('False RESET detected')
#---------------------------------------------------------------------
# MODULE SEE_RESET(): reset button management
# INPUTS:  reset button
# OUTPUTS: devices management as long/short
#---------------------------------------------------------------------
def see_reset():
  global reset_pressed,orig
  if (reset_pressed and reset_long):      #long RESET pressed
    ae_LED('R','E',long)
    sound(long)
    line(traceback.extract_stack())
    see_colour(colour.on+' && '+colour.red)
    print (Cursor.POS(10,  18) + Fore.RED + enlarge('RESET button
                                        pressed, TOTAL reset'))
    orig='reset_long'
    line(traceback.extract_stack())
    say('RESET button pressed, TOTAL reset')
    for i in range(30,-1,-1):
      print (Cursor.POS(10,20) + Fore.GREEN + enlarge('RESET at:
                                        '+str(i)+' seconds'))
      print (Cursor.POS(10, 4) + Fore.GREEN + time.strftime("%X"))
      blink_green()
      time.sleep(1)
    line(traceback.extract_stack())
    write_outfile('Wait 30 seconds to RESET')
    line(traceback.extract_stack())
    message('SYSTEM ALARM','RESET PRESSED, resets:
                          nas,ont,router,raspberry. ','Check:\n'+
          '-Correct start of: NAS, ONT & ROUTER.\n-Start home
                                    automation program.',address_1)
    off_device('ONT',2)
    blink_green()
    on_device('ONT',2)
...
    print (Cursor.POS(10,20) + Fore.GREEN + enlarge('Device RESET
                                        completed'))
    line(traceback.extract_stack())
    write_outfile('Device RESET completed')
    write_outfile('Raspberry reset')
    os.system('clear')
    os.system("sudo reboot -f")
  if (reset_pressed and reset_long==False):  #short RESET
    line(traceback.extract_stack())
    see_colour(colour.on+' && '+colour.red)
    blink_green()
    ae_LED('R','A',short)
    ae_LED('Y','A',short)
    ae_LED('G','A',short)
    os.system('clear')
    see_titles()
    orig='reset_short'
    line(traceback.extract_stack())
    say('Short reset pressed, clear screen')
    reset_pressed=False
```

```python
        line(traceback.extract_stack())
        see_colour(colour.off)

#------------------------------------------------------------------
# MODULE SENSOR(): read temperature & humidity in DHT22 sensor
# INPUTS:   sensor DHT22 inputs
# OUTPUTS: tem (temperature) & hum (humidity)
#------------------------------------------------------------------
def sensor():
    global orig,tem,hum
    try:
        # this connects to pigpio daemon which must be started first
        # run: sudo pgpiod
        pigpio.exceptions = False    #pigpio errors ignored
        global pi
        s.trigger()
        tem = s.temperature() / 1.
        hum = s.humidity() / 1.
    except:
        line(traceback.extract_stack())
        say('Attention: TRIGGER error')
        line(traceback.extract_stack())
        see_colour(colour.on+' && '+colour.red)
    if tem>=tmax:
        print (Cursor.POS(40, 3) + Fore.RED + ('{:3.1f}'.format(tem)) +
                                ' °C  '+Fore.RED+'('+str(tmax)+')')
        orig='sensor()'
        line(traceback.extract_stack())
        say('Attention: NAS temperature excessive')
        line(traceback.extract_stack())
        see_colour(colour.on+' && '+colour.red)
    else:
        if tem<-100:                  #sensor error
            print (Cursor.POS(40, 3) + Fore.RED+ ('Sensor is missing  '))
            if not start:
                orig='sensor()'
                line(traceback.extract_stack())
                write_outfile('NAS tem & hum sensor is missing')
                line(traceback.extract_stack())
                see_colour(colour.on+' && '+colour.red)
        else:
            print (Cursor.POS(40, 3) + Fore.GREEN+('{:3.1f}'.format(tem))
                                + ' °C  '+Fore.RED+'('+str(tmax)+')')

    if hum>=hmax:
        print (Cursor.POS(40, 4) + Fore.RED + ('{:3.1f}'.format(hum))
                            + ' %HR '+Fore.RED+'('+str(hmax)+')')
        orig='sensor()'
        line(traceback.extract_stack())
        say('Attention: excessive NAS humidity')
        line(traceback.extract_stack())
        see_colour(colour.on+' && '+colour.red)
    else:
        if hum<-100:
            print (Cursor.POS(40, 4) + Fore.RED+ ('Sensor is missing'))
```

```
      if not start:
        orig='sensor()'
        line(traceback.extract_stack())
        see_colour(colour.on+' && '+colour.red)
        write_outfile('NAS sensor is missing')
    else:
      print (Cursor.POS(40, 4) + Fore.GREEN+('{:3.1f}'.format(hum))
                              + ' %HR '+Fore.RED+'('+str(hmax)+')')
  pigpio.exceptions = True    #pigpio errors
  return(tem,hum)

#--------------------------------------------------------------------
# MODULE SEE_SENSOR(): look & acts with tem & hum NAS sensor
# INPUTS:  yes_sensor, sensor() & maxims
# OUTPUTS: devices off & send messages
#--------------------------------------------------------------------
def see_sensor():
  global yes_sensor,a_sensor_bad,a_sensor_bien,orig
  if yes_sensor==0:
    sensor()
    if ((tem>=tmax or hum>=hmax) and a_sensor_bad==False):
      off_device('NAS', 2)
      ae_LED('Y', 'E',largo)
      print (Cursor.POS(10,23)+Fore.RED+enlarge('Excessive tem or
                             hum: '+str(tem)+'°C '+str(hum)+'%HR'))
      time.sleep(long)
      line(traceback.extract_stack())
      see_colour(colour.on+' && '+colour.red)
      line(traceback.extract_stack())
      message('TEMPERATURE ALARM','Excessive Temperature or
                 Humidity: '+str(tem)+'°C '+str(hum)+'%HR.','\n'+
               'Check: \n-Real Temperature & Humidity.\n-NAS
                                       status.',address_1)
      message('NAS','NAS is off, until RESET or correct
                                  parameters','',address_1)
      orig='sensor()'
      line(traceback.extract_stack())
      write_outfile('EXCESSIVE Temperature or Humidity: '+str(tem)
                                +'°C '+str(hum)+'%HR.')
      a_sensor_bad=True
      a_sensor_good=False

    if ((tem<=tmax-1 and hum<=hmax-5) and a_sensor_good==False):
      on_device('NAS', 2)
      ae_LED('Y', 'A',long)
      print (Cursor.POS(10,23)+Fore.GREEN+enlarge('CORRECT
          Temperature & Humidity: '+str(tem)+'°C '+str(hum)+'%HR'))
      time.sleep(long)
      line(traceback.extract_stack())
      say('Correct Temperature & Humidity')
      line(traceback.extract_stack())
      see_colour(colour.off)
      blink_green()
      message('TEMPERATURE ALARM','Temperature & Humidity are
              CORRECT: '+str(tem)+'°C '+str(hum)+'%HR','',address_1)
```

```
        message('NAS','NAS is on.',' Check:\n-Temperature & humidity
                                    are stable.',address_1)
        orig='sensor()'
        line(traceback.extract_stack())
        write_outfile('Temperature or Humidity are CORRECT:
                        '+str(tem)+'°C '+str(hum)+'%HR')
        a_sensor_good=True
    yes_sensor+=1
    if yes_sensor==cycles_sensor:
      yes_sensor=0

#-----------------------------------------------------------------
# MODULE ONOFF(): Check if Raspberry is online or offline
# INPUTS:   GMAIL server answer
# OUTPUTS: online ON or OFF variables
#-----------------------------------------------------------------
def onoff():
  global connected,orig
  try:
    smtpserver = smtplib.SMTP("smtp.gmail.com", 587) #look Gmail
    smtpserver.ehlo()
    smtpserver.starttls()
    smtpserver.ehlo()
    connected = 'ON'
  except (socket.gaierror, socket.error, socket.herror,
                                    smtplib.SMTPException):
    connected = 'OFF'
  return(connected)

#-----------------------------------------------------------------
# MODULE SEE_ONOFF(): acts with Internet connection status
# INPUTS:   connected or not to Internet by onoff()
# OUTPUTS: messages & variables fo Internet status
#-----------------------------------------------------------------
def see_onoff():
  global cut_internet,t_off,hour_cut,counter,to_wait,orig
  if (connected=='OFF' and t_off>t_off_max):
    cut_internet=True
    t_off=0
    hour_cut=time.strftime("%d-%m-%y ")+time.strftime("%X")
  elif (connected=='OFF' and t_off<=t_off_max):
    t_off+=1
    cut_internet=False
  if (connected=='ON' and cut_internet==True):
    print (Cursor.POS(10, 5) + Fore.GREEN + 'Internet: ON ')
    line(traceback.extract_stack())
    message('INTERNET','OK Internet after cut: '+hour_cut,
                            '. Check: \n'+'-ONT & ROUTER status.
                      \n-Internet access.\n-Decoder',address_1)
    orig='onoff()'
    line(traceback.extract_stack())
    say('Recovered from Internet cutting')
    line(traceback.extract_stack())
    write_outfile('INTERNET OK after cut at: '+hour_cut)
    cut_internet=False
```

```
        ae_LED('Y','A',largo)
    elif (connected=='OFF' and cut_internet==True
                                       and to_wait==False):
        print (Cursor.POS(10,  5) + Fore.RED + Style.BRIGHT
                                      + 'Internet: OFF')
        print (Cursor.POS(10, 23) + Fore.RED + enlarge('Internet
                                      connection is OFF'))
        hour_cut=time.strftime("%d-%m-%y ")+time.strftime("%X")
        orig='onoff()'
        line(traceback.extract_stack())
        write_outfile('Internet connection is OFF')
        line(traceback.extract_stack())
        see_colour(colour.on+' && '+colour.red)
        write_outfile(separator)
        off_device('ONT',2)
...
        cut_internet=True
    if (counter<600 and connected=='OFF'): #600 cycles wait
        counter+=1
        to_wait=True
    elif (counter>=600 and connected=='ON'):
        to_wait=False
        counter=0

#-----------------------------------------------------------
# MODULE HEATER(): Check if heater is ON/OFF
# INPUTS:  time, schedule, activated[]
# OUTPUTS: is_heater
#-----------------------------------------------------------
def heater():
    global is_heater,see_heater,fhome,error_edimax,tado_state,
                                 tado_temp,tado_hum,y_on
    if error_edimax==False:
        try:
            is_heater=str(edimax.state+' ')[:3]       #Edimax status
        except:
            orig='heater()'
            line(traceback.extract_stack())
            say('Attention: Edimax error')
            see_colour(colour.on+' && '+colour.red)
            error_edimax=True
            is_heater='OFF'
        if (is_heater!='ON ' and is_heater!='OFF'):
            now=time.localtime()
            day=time.strftime('%w',now)
            h1i=schedule[int(day)][0 : 8]              #on  morning
            h1f=schedule[int(day)][9 :17]              #off morning
            h2i=schedule[int(day)][18:26]              #on  afternoon
            h2f=schedule[int(day)][27:35]              #off afternoon
            t=time.strftime("%X")
            if ((t>=h1i and t<=h1f) or (t>=h2i and t<=h2f)):
                is_heater='ON '
            else:
                is_heater='OFF'
    else:
```

```
      is_heater='---'
      try:
        is_heater=str(edimax.state+' ')[:3]
        error_edimax=False
        orig='heater()'
        line(traceback.extract_stack())
        say('Edimax is OK')
        see_colour(colour.off)

    except:
        pass

#look at Tadoº status in p_devices.txt
  if 'tado home                    ' in activated:
    tado_state='home'
    if fhome==True:
      line(traceback.extract_stack())
      write_outfile('Tado goes to Home state')
      fhome=False

  if 'tado away                    ' in activated:
    tado_state='away'
    if fhome==False:
      ifttt('ambient_off')
...
      y_on=False
      line(traceback.extract_stack())
      write_outfile('Tado goes to Away state')
      fhome=True
  if 'tado <22\xc2\xbaC                ' in activated:
    tado_temp='<22°C'
...
  see_heater='Edi:'+is_heater+' Tadoº:'+tado_state+
                                    tado_temp+tado_hum
  return(is_heater,see_heater,fhome)

#------------------------------------------------------------
# MODULE SEE_HEATER(): look to heater status (Edimax) cyclically
# INPUTS:  yes_heater, cycles_heater
# OUTPUTS: heater(), yes_heater
#------------------------------------------------------------
def see_heater():
  global yes_heater

  if yes_heater==cycles_heater:
    print (Cursor.POS(10,5)+' '*27)
    if is_heater=='ON ':
      print (Cursor.POS(10,5) + Fore.RED  + see_heater)
    else:
      print (Cursor.POS(10,5) + Fore.CYAN + see_heater)
    heater()
    yes_heater=0
  else:
    yes_heater+=1
```

```python
#----------------------------------------------------------------
# MODULE SEE_START(): update KNX thermostat on start
# INPUTS: start, states[]
# OUTPUTS:KNX thermostat updating doing: absence/presence
#----------------------------------------------------------------
def see_start():
  global start,orig
  if start==True:
    line(traceback.extract_stack())
    see_colour(colour.on+' && '+colour.verde)
    if states[13]=='KNX thermostat:  ABSENCE':
      knx_onoff(4,2,1,'ON')
      for x in range(0,4):
        time.sleep(1)
      knx_onoff(4,2,1,'OFF')
    if states[13]=='KNX thermostat:  PRESENCE':
      knx_onoff(4,2,1,'OFF')
      for x in range(0,4):
        time.sleep(1)
      knx_onoff(4,2,1,'ON')
    orig='start=True'
    line(traceback.extract_stack())
    say('KNX Thermostat started')
    start=False
    see_colour(colour.off)

#----------------------------------------------------------------
# MODULE SEE_ORIGIN(): origin update with p_sensors.txt actions
# INPUTS:  p_sensors.txt
# OUTPUTS: ori
#----------------------------------------------------------------
def see_origin():
  global ori,orig
  try:
    xx=[]
    inter=open(fsensors,'r')             #xx[] with p_sensors.txt
    while True:
      xj=inter.readline()
      if xj!='':
        xx.append(xj[:len(xj)-1])        #watch out with \n
      else:
        break
    inter.close()
  except:
    orig='see_origin()'
    line(traceback.extract_stack())
    say('Attention: SENSORS error')
    see_colour(colour.red)
  if len(xx)<19:                         #p_sensors.txt corrupt?
    os.system('sudo cp /home/pi/home_auto/p_sensors.ok
                       /home/pi/home_auto/p_sensors.txt')
    xx=[]
    inter=open(fsensors,'r')             #xx[] with p_sensors.txt
    while True:
      xj=inter.readline()
```

```
        if xj!='':
          xx.append(xj[:len(xj)-1])
        else:
          break
    inter.close()
    try:
      if xx[16]  =='Origin:      GOOGLE':
        ori='GOOGLE'
...
    except:
      ori='Unknown'

#-------------------------------------------------------------------
# MODULE SEE_TRACE(): display alarms
# INPUTS:   GPIO
# OUTPUTS: GPIO alarms display
#-------------------------------------------------------------------
def see_trace():
  global orig
  try:
    trace(Cursor.BACK(11)+'P'+str(GPIO.input(pin_power))
        +'h'+str(GPIO.input(pin_smoke))+'g'+str(GPIO.input(pin_gas))
      +'a'+str(GPIO.input(pin_water))+'p'+str(GPIO.input(pin_garage))
      +'t'+str(GPIO.input(pin_doorbell))+'c'+str(GPIO.input(pin_co2))
                            +'R'+str(GPIO.input(button_reset)))
  except:
    orig='see_trace()'
    say('Attention: GPIO error')

#-------------------------------------------------------------------
# MODULE SEE_EFFECTORS(): acts with effectors[]
# INPUTS:   effectors[] with actions to do
# OUTPUTS: ifttt,knx,movie,lights,blinds,holiday,valves
# IMPORTANT: tex actions must be the same as p_actuators.txt
#-------------------------------------------------------------------
def see_effectors():
  global effectors,movie,holidays,states,switched_on,open,
                                  tele,orig,error_edimax
  try:
    actions=open(factuators,'r')
    effectors=[]
    while True:
      x=actions.readline()
      if (x!='' and x!='\n' and x!=' '):
        effectors.append(x)
      else:
        break
    acciones.close()
  except:
    orig='see_effectors()'
    line(traceback.extract_stack())
    say('Attention: ACTUATORS error')
    see_colour(colour.red)
  if len(effectors)>=22:          #effectors[] full?
```

```
#SWITCH OFF ALL LIGHTS-----------------------------------------------
    if effectors[0]=='Switch off all lights: YES\n':
      orig=ori
      line(traceback.extract_stack())
      ifttt('ambient_off')
...
      if 'hall                     ' in switched_on:
        switched_on='hall                 '
      else:
        switched_on=[]
      delete_lights()
      line(traceback.extract_stack())
      say('All lights are switched off')

#SWITCH ON LIVING ROOM SOFA------------------------------------------
    if effectors[1]=='Switch on living room sofa: YES\n':
      pelicula=False
      states[12]='Movie:    OFF'
      orig=ori
      knx_onoff(2,3,0,'ON')
...
#WATCH MOVIE---------------------------------------------------------
    if (effectors[2]=='Watch movie: YES\n' and movie==False):
      movie=True
      close_high=True
      states[12]='Movie:    ON'
      orig=ori
      line(traceback.extract_stack())
      write_outfile('Activates movie ambient')
      ifttt('tv_on')
      t=time.strftime("%X")         #in night?
      if ((t>=day2 or t<=day1) and 'hall                      '
                                               in switched_on):
        ifttt('colours_auto')
      knx_onoff(1,11,0,'OFF')
      if 'wall living room sofa        ' in switched_on:
        switched_on.remove('wall living room sofa           ')
...
#CLOSE BLINDS--------------------------------------------------------
    if effectors[3]=='Close blinds : YES\n':
      movie=False
      close_high=True
      states[12]='Movie:    OFF'
      for j in blinds_without_alarm:
        knx_onoff(3,j,0,'ON')
        time.sleep(.5)
      orig=ori
      line(traceback.extract_stack())
      for x in blinds_without_alarm:
        if blind[x] in open:
          open.remove(blind[x])
      line(traceback.extract_stack())
      see_colour(colour.on+' && '+colour.green)
      say('Blinds closed, except the big ones')
```

```
#CLOSE ALL BLINDS------------------------------------------------
    if effectors[4]=='Close all blinds: YES\n':
        movie=False
        close_high=True
        states[12]='Movie:    OFF'
        knx_onoff(3,29,0,'ON')
        orig=ori
        line(traceback.extract_stack())
        open=[]
        see_colour(colour.on+' && '+colour.green)
        say('All blinds are closed')

#OPEN ALL BLINDS EXCEPT BIG ONES---------------------------------
    if effectors[5]=='Open blinds: YES\n':
        movie=False
        close_high=False
        states[12]='Movie:    OFF'
        orig=ori
        line(traceback.extract_stack())
        ifttt('ambient_off')
...
        say('Blinds open, except the big ones')

#OPEN ALL BLINDS-------------------------------------------------
    if effectors[6]=='Open all blinds: YES\n':
        movie=False
        states[12]='Movie:    OFF'
        orig=ori
        line(traceback.extract_stack())
        ifttt('ambient_off')
...
        say('All blinds are open')

#HOLIDAYS ON----------------------------------------------------
    if effectors[7]=='Holidays ON: YES\n':
        holidays=True
        states[11]='Holidays:  ON'
        orig=ori
        line(traceback.extract_stack())
        write_outfile('Holidays status ON')
        message('TELEGRAM ALARM','Holidays status ON. ',
                                  'Check:\n-All is ok.',address_1)
        movie=False
        line(traceback.extract_stack())
        write_outfile('Movie ambient is OFF')
        states[12]='Movie:    OFF'
        ifttt('ambient_off')
...
        say('Holidays status is ON')

#HOLIDAYS OFF---------------------------------------------------
    if effectors[8]=='Holidays OFF: YES\n':
        holidays=False
        states[11]='Holidays:  OFF'
        orig=ori
```

```
        ifttt('tado_auto')
        ifttt('deco_4k_on')
...
        say('Holidays status is OFF')

#WATER VALVE ON------------------------------------------------------
    if effectors[9]=='Water ON: YES\n':
      line(traceback.extract_stack())
      see_colour(colour.on+' && '+colour.green)
      knx_onoff(5,10,0,'OFF')              #off open
      states[14]='Water valve: OPEN'
      ifttt('tado_auto')
      say('Set Tado in auto mode')
      time.sleep(4)
      orig=ori
      line(traceback.extract_stack())
      message('TELEGRAM ALARM','Water valve is open',
              'Check:\n-All is ok.\n-Rust in the water.',address_1)
      say('Water valve is open')

#WATER VALVE OFF-----------------------------------------------------
    if effectors[10]=='Water OFF: YES\n':
      line(traceback.extract_stack())
      see_colour(colour.on+' && '+colour.red)
      knx_onoff(5,10,0,'ON')               #on closes valve
      states[14]='Water valve: CLOSE'
      orig=ori
      line(traceback.extract_stack())
      write_outfile('Water valve is close')
      message('TELEGRAM ALARM','Water valve is close. ',
                             'Check:\n-All is ok.',address_1)
      ifttt('tado_off')
...
      say('Water valve is close')

#GAS VALVE ON--------------------------------------------------------
    if effectors[11]=='Gas ON: YES\n':
      line(traceback.extract_stack())
      see_colour(colour.on+' && '+colour.green)
      knx_onoff(5,9,0,'OFF')               #off opens valve
      states[15]='Gas valve: OPEN'
      ifttt('tado_auto')
      orig=ori
      line(traceback.extract_stack())
      message('TELEGRAM ALARM','Gas valve is open. '
                       ,'Check:\n-Also open manually.',address_1)
...
      say('Gas valve is open')

#GAS VALVE OFF-------------------------------------------------------
    if effectors[12]=='Gas OFF: YES\n':
      line(traceback.extract_stack())
      see_colour(colour.on+' && '+colour.red)
      knx_onoff(5,9,0,'ON')                #on closes valve
      states[15]='Gas valve: CLOSE'
      orig=ori
```

```
      write_outfile('Gas valve is close')
      message('TELEGRAM ALARM','Gas valve is close . ',
                              'Check:\n-Heater is OFF.',address_1)
...
      say('Gas valve is close')

#HEATER ON--------------------------------------------------------
    if effectors[13]=='Heater ON: YES\n':
      line(traceback.extract_stack())
      see_colour(colour.on+' && '+colour.red)
      knx_onoff(4,2,1,'ON')
      orig=ori
      line(traceback.extract_stack())
      states[13]='Thermostat:  PRESENCE'
...
      say('KNX thermostat in presence')

#HEATER OFF-------------------------------------------------------
    if effectors[14]=='Heater OFF: YES\n':
      line(traceback.extract_stack())
      see_colour(colour.on+' && '+colour.blue)
      knx_onoff(4,2,1,'OFF')
      orig=ori
      states[13]='KNX thermostat: ABSENCE'
...
      say('KNX thermostat in absence')

#CLEAR SCREEN-----------------------------------------------------
    if effectors[15]=='Clear screen: YES\n':
      line(traceback.extract_stack())
      see_colour(colour.on+' && '+colour.green)
      print (Cursor.POS(44, 7) + Fore.WHITE + Back.GREEN
                                        + 'CLEAR (C)')
      sound(short)
      ae_LED('R','E',short)
...
      orig=ori
      line(traceback.extract_stack())
      write_outfile('Crear screen & exchange files')
      os.system('clear')
      see_titles()
      if 'hall                    ' in switched_on:
        switched_on='hall           '
      else:
        switched_on=[]
      clear_lights()
      clear_blinds()
      record_states()
      print (Cursor.POS(10,5) + Fore.RED  + see_heater)
      tele=save_tele
      see_thermostat()
      print (Cursor.POS(44, 7) + Fore.GREEN + Back.WHITE
                                        + 'CLEAR (C)')
      line(traceback.extract_stack())
      see_colour(colour.off)
      say('System screen is clear')
```

```
#NAS RESET---------------------------------------------------------------
    if effectors[16]=='Reset NAS: YES\n':
      line(traceback.extract_stack())
      see_colour(colour.on+' && '+colour.green)
      ae_LED('R','E',short)
      off_device('NAS',2)
      on_device('NAS',2)
      ae_LED('R','A',short)
      orig=ori
      write_outfile('Switch off & on the NAS')
      message('TELEGRAM','NAS reset. ',
                                        'Check:\n-NAS OK.',address_1)
...
      say('NAS reset')

#ONT RESET---------------------------------------------------------------
    if effectors[17]=='Reset ONT: YES\n':
      line(traceback.extract_stack())
      see_colour(colour.on+' && '+colour.green)
      ae_LED('R','E',short)
      off_device('ONT',2)
      on_device('ONT',2)
      ae_LED('R','A',short)
      orig=ori
      write_outfile('Switch off/on ONT')
      message('TELEGRAM ALARM','ONT reset. ',
                              'Check:\n-Internet access ok.',address_1)
...
      say('ONT reset')

#ROUTER RESET------------------------------------------------------------
    if effectors[18]=='Reset ROUTER: YES\n':
      line(traceback.extract_stack())
      see_colour(colour.on+' && '+colour.green)
      ae_LED('R','E',short)
      off_device('ROUTER',2)
      on_device('ROUTER',2)
...
      message('TELEGRAM ALARM','ROUTER reset.',
                                  'Check:\n-Internet access ok.'+
                                  '\n-Routers in 1st & 2nd are ok.'
                              +'\n-Tadoº Bridge is ok',address_1)
...
      say('Router reset')

#RESET RASPBERRY---------------------------------------------------------
    if effectors[19]=='RASPBERRY Reset: YES\n':
      line(traceback.extract_stack())
      see_colour(colour.on+' && '+colour.red)
      ae_LED('R','E',short)
      orig=ori
      message('TELEGRAM ALARM','RASPBERRY reset. ',
                              'Check:\n-Sistema is OK.',address_1)
      acciones.close()
      clear_actuators()
      ae_LED('R','A',short)
```

```
        say('The Raspberry is reset')
        os.system("sudo reboot -f")
#OPEN LIVING ROOM BLINDS------------------------------------------------
    if effectors[20]=='Open living room blinds: YES\n':
        movie=False
        close_high=False
        states[12]='Movie:    OFF'
        orig=ori
        line(traceback.extract_stack())
        write_outfile('Open living room blinds')
        ifttt('ambient_off')
...
        say('Living room blinds are open')

#SWITCH OFF LIVING ROOM SOFA--------------------------------------------
    if effectors[21]=='Switch living room sofa: YES\n':
        orig=ori
        line(traceback.extract_stack())
        knx_onoff(2,3,0,'OFF')
...
        say('Living room sofa lamp is off')
    clear_actuators()


#----------------------------------------------------------------------
# MODULE SEE_THERMOSTAT(): Display KNX thermostat data
# INPUTS:  telegram sent by KNX thermostat
# OUTPUTS: display t_s variable & states[] to
#          p_sensors.txt transfer
#----------------------------------------------------------------------
def see_thermostat():
  global t_s,t_sa,t_sp,t_r,states,open,orig,
                          is_heater,close_high,error_edimax
  offset=-7.4                 #KNX thermostat adjust
  orig='see_thermostat()'
  if j4==1:                   #on/off KNX relay
    if error_edimax==False:
      try:
        ss=edimax.state
      except:
        error_edimax=True
        orig='see_thermostat()'
        line(traceback.extract_stack())
        say('Attention: Edimax error')
        ss='OFF'
      if (j7==129 and ss=='ON'):   #heater is on
        is_heater='ON '
      if (j7==128 or  ss=='OFF'):  #heater is off
        is_heater='OFF'
    else:
      is_heater='---'
      line(traceback.extract_stack())
      write_outfile('Heater status unknown')
      error_edimax=False
  elif j4==2:                   #absence/presence status
    if j7==128:          #absence KNX
```

```
            states[13]=    'Thermostat:  ABSENCE'
            print (Cursor.POS(40,5) + Fore.CYAN+ str(t_sa) + ' °C  Abs ')
            line(traceback.extract_stack())
            write_outfile('KNX thermostat: set in ABSENCE,
                                        setpoint: '+str(t_sa)+' C')
            states[17]=    'Setpoint:  '+str(t_sa)+' °C'
         if j7==129:             #presence KNX
            states[13]=    'Thermostat:  PRESENCE'
            print (Cursor.POS(40,5) + Fore.RED + str(t_sp) + ' °C  Pre ')
            write_outfile('KNX thermostat: set in PRESENCE,
                                        setpoint: '+str(t_sp)+' C')
            states[17]=    'Setpoint:  '+str(t_sp)+' °C'

      elif (j4==3 and len(tele)>9): #data ok?
         t_r=float(ord(tele[8]))+float(ord(tele[9]))/10+offset
         if t_r>=40:
            t_r=t_r-24.5
...
         write_outfile('KNX Thermostat: Real temperature:'+str(t_r)+'C')
         states[18]=    'Real T.:        '+str(t_r)+' °C'

         if (t_r>25 and t_r<40 and not close_high):   #close blinds
            close=[19,21]         #living room small
            close_high=True
            for j in close:
               knx_onoff(3,j,0,'ON')
               time.sleep(.5)
               blink_green()
...
         say('Blinds closed by high temperature')
         t=time.strftime("%X")    #hour?
         if (t_r>=20 and t_r<=23 and t>=dia1 and t<=dia2 and 'hall
                      ' \ not in switched_on and close_high==True):
            open=[19,21]           #living room small
            close_high=False
            for j in open:
               knx_onoff(3,j,0,'OFF')
               time.sleep(.5)
               blink_green()
...
         say('Blinds open by low temperature')

      elif (j4==4 and len(tele)>9): #setpoint temperature
         if states[13]=='Thermostat:  ABSENCE':
            t_s=t_sa=float(ord(tele[9])/10)
            print (Cursor.POS(40,5) + Fore.CYAN+ str(t_s) + ' °C  Abs  ')
            line(traceback.extract_stack())
            write_outfile('KNX Thermostat: ABSENCE,
                                        setpoint: '+str(t_s)+' C')
            states[17]=    'Setpoint T:  '+str(t_s)+' °C'
         else:
            t_s=t_sp=float(ord(tele[8]))+float(ord(tele[9]))/10+offset
            print (Cursor.POS(40,5) + Fore.RED + str(t_s) + ' °C  Pre  ')
            write_outfile('KNX Thermostat: PRESENCE,
                                        setpoint: '+str(t_s)+' C')
            line(traceback.extract_stack())
```

```
          states[17]=     'Setpoint T:  '+str(t_s)+' °C'
      else:
        line(traceback.extract_stack())
        write_outfile('KNX Thermostat unknown state (j4='+str(j4)+')')

#------------------------------------------------------------------
# MODULE TELEGRAM(): KNX telegram reader
# INPUTS:   bus KNX
# OUTPUTS: tele[] with KNX telegram
#------------------------------------------------------------------
def telegram():
  global tele,received
  while ser.inWaiting()>0:          #something on the bus?
    received+=str(ser.readline())
  if len(received)>9:
    x=0
    for j in received:              #telegram structure
      if ord(j)==188:               #start telegram=188
        tele=received[x:]
        break
      else:
        x+=1
    if len(tele)>4:
      lon=ord(tele[5:6])-225+9      #telegram length
      tele=tele[:lon]               #length=9+octet LSB from [5]
      received=received[lon:]       #exclude part one
    crc=255                         #check crc=0
    for i in tele:                  #XOR must be 0
      crc=crc^ord(i)
    if crc!=0:
      ser.flushInput()              #with error empty buffer

#------------------------------------------------------------------
# MODULE SEE_TELEGRAM(): acts with devices according KNX
# INPUTS:   KNX telegram
# OUTPUTS: actuations
#------------------------------------------------------------------
def see_telegram():
  global save_tele,j1,j2,j3,j4,j7,tele,light,per,open,
                             switched_on,is_heater,text_tele,orig
  if len(tele[2:3])>0:
    for x in tele:
      text_tele+=str(ord(x))+'-'
    j=ord(tele[2:3])                #telegram origin direction
    if (j not in button and (tele[0:1]==128 and tele[1:2]==17)):
      print (Cursor.POS(9,23)+Fore.RED+'['+str(j)+']
                                              does not exists')
      line(traceback.extract_stack())
      message('KNX SENSOR','['+text_tele+'] does not exists.
                 ','Check:\n-New sensor or error.',address_1)
      orig='telegram()'
      line(traceback.extract_stack())
      write_outfile('KNX SENSOR ['+text_tele+'] does not exists. ')
...
    elif j in button:
```

```
      print (Cursor.POS(9,22) + Fore.BLACK +' '*44)
      print (Cursor.POS(9,22) + Fore.RED + button[j])

#---------------------------------------------------------------------
# KNX THERMOSTAT DISPLAY
#---------------------------------------------------------------------
      if button[j]=='thermostat              ':
        save_tele=tele
        j4=ord(tele[4:5]) #destination
        j7=ord(tele[7:8]) #presence/absence
        see_thermostat()
        record_sensors(states) #states[] to p_sensors.txt transfer

#---------------------------------------------------------------------
# RECORD TO FILES
#---------------------------------------------------------------------
      if len(tele[0:8])==8:
        j1=ord(tele[1:2]) #origin
        j2=ord(tele[2:3]) #origin
        j3=ord(tele[3:4]) #destination
        j4=ord(tele[4:5]) #destination
        j7=ord(tele[7:8]) #light on/off or blind open/close
        tele=light=per=''

        #look for a bulb
        #add to switched on file if are switched_on
        #remove from switched on file if are switched
        if (j3 in [8,48,16]) and (j4 in bulb_A or j4 in bulb_B
                                   or j4 in bulb_C):
          if (j3==8 and j4 in bulb_A):
            light=bulb_A[j4]
          elif (j3==48 and j4 in bulb_B):
            light=bulb_B[j4]
          elif (j3==16 and j4 in bulb_C):
            light=bulb_C[j4]

          if j7==129:                #light on
            if light not in switched_on:
              print (Cursor.POS(9,23) + Fore.RED + light + '    ')
              switched_on.append(light)
...
          if j7==128:                #light off
            if light=='all             ':
              if 'hall                  ' in switched_on:
                switched_on='hall                  '
              else:
                switched_on=[]
              clear_lights()
...
        #look for a blind
        #add to opened file if are open (total or partial)
        #remove from opened file if are total close
        if (j3==24 and j4 in blind):
          per=blind[j4]
          if (j7==128 and j4 not in [29,30]):
            if j4 in [31,32]:
```

```
                        movie=False
                    if per not in open:
                      print (Cursor.POS(9,23) + Fore.RED + per)
                      if ('stop' in per and blind[j4-1] in open):
                        open.remove(blind[j4-1])
                      else:
                        open.append(per)
                    if ((j7==128 and j4==29) or (j7==129 and j4==30)):
                      clear_blinds()
                      movie=False
                    if (j7==129 and j4 not in [29,30]):
...
                      blinds.close()

                    #look for heater relay on/off
                  if (j3==32 and j4==1):
                    print (Cursor.POS(10,5)+' '*27)
                    heater()
                    if (j7==128 or is_heater=='OFF'):
                      is_heater='OFF'
                      print (Cursor.POS(10,5) + Fore.CYAN + see_heater)
                    if (j7==129 and is_heater=='ON '):
                      is_heater='ON '
                      print (Cursor.POS(10,5) + Fore.RED  + see_heater)
        tele=''

#----------------------------------------------------------------
# MODULE SEE_GARAGE(): acts with con lights according garage
# INPUTS:  off_garage, switched_on[]
# OUTPUTS: off_garage, switched_on[]
#----------------------------------------------------------------
def see_garage():
  global switched_on,off_garage,orig
  if off_garage:
    loff=[20,25]                    #cellar & gym lights
    for j in loff:
      knx_onoff(1,j,0,'OFF')
      time.sleep(.5)
...
    orig='ac_alarm_porton()'
    line(traceback.extract_stack())
    say('Garage lights off')
    off_garage=False

#----------------------------------------------------------------
# MODULE AC_ALARM_POWER(): 0->1 power off, 1->0 power on
# INPUTS:  GPIO
# OUTPUTS: LED,ck,message,variables
#----------------------------------------------------------------
def ac_alarm_power(Ev=None):
  global a_power_yes,a_power_no,orig
  if (GPIO.input(pin_power)==1 and a_power_no==True):
    line(traceback.extract_stack())
    see_colour(colour.on+' && '+colour.red)
    ae_LED('R', 'E',largo)
```

```
    ae_LED('G', 'A',largo)
    sound(long)
    print (Cursor.POS(42, 10) + Fore.RED + 'NO')
    print (Cursor.POS(10, 15) + Fore.RED + enlarge('Power is off'))
    line(traceback.extract_stack())
    message('POWER ALARM','Power is off. ','Check:\n
        -Distribution panel.\n'+'-Refrigerators status.',address_1)
    orig='ac_alarm_power()'
    a_power_yes=True
    a_power_no=False
    line(traceback.extract_stack())
    write_outfile('Saves [*].txt on /home/pi/home_auto/safe/')
    try:
      os.mkdir('/home/pi/home_auto/safe')
    except:
      os.system('sudo cp /home/pi/home_auto/*.txt
                                    /home/pi/home_auto/safe')

  if (GPIO.input(pin_power)==0 and a_power_yes==True):    #power?
    line(traceback.extract_stack())
    see_colour(colour.off)
    ae_LED('R', 'A',largo)
    ae_LED('G', 'E',largo)
    sound(long)
    print (Cursor.POS(42, 10) + Fore.GREEN + 'OK')
    print (Cursor.POS(10, 15) + Fore.GREEN + enlarge('Power ok'))
    line(traceback.extract_stack())
    message('POWER ALARM','Power ok. ','Check:\n'+
            '-Absence/presence KNX & Tadoº thermostats.\n-Electric
                            clocks.\n-Blinds',address_1)
    orig='ac_alarm_power()'
    line(traceback.extract_stack())
...
    a_power_yes=False
    a_power_no=True
    say('Power ok')

#------------------------------------------------------------
# MODULE AC_ALARM_GARAGE(): 1->0 garage open, 0->1 garage close
# INPUTS:  GPIO
# OUTPUTS: LED,ck,message,variables
#------------------------------------------------------------
def ac_alarm_porton(Ev=None):
  global still_open,f_open,garage_open,garage_close,
                            state_garage,orig,off_garage
  if GPIO.input(pin_porton)==0 and GPIO.input(pin_power)==0:#open?
    if still_a==False and f_open==True:
...
      print (Cursor.POS(10, 15) + Fore.GREEN + enlarge('Alarm:
                            GARAGE STILL OPEN'))
      still_open=True
      orig='ac_alarm_porton()'
      f_open=False
      state_garage='Garage:      Still open\n'
      say('Attention: garage still open')
```

336

```
      if still_open==False and f_open==False:
...
          print (Cursor.POS(10, 15) + Fore.YELLOW + enlarge('Alarm:
                                                   GARAGE open'))
          message('GARAGE ALARM','Garage OPEN ','Check:\n
                            -Closing message must be exists.',address_1)
          porton_open=time.time()
          still_open=False
          orig='ac_alarm_porton()'
          f_open=True
          state_garage='Garage:       Open\n'
          say('Garage is open')
      else:                                #closed?
        garage_close=time.time()
        if garage_close-garage_open>(3*60+10) and (f_open==
                True or still_open==True) and GPIO.input(pin_power)==0:
...
            print (Cursor.POS(10, 15) + Fore.GREEN +
                                    enlarge('Alarm GARAGE closed'))
            message('GARAGE ALARM','Garage is CLOSED','Check:\n
                            -This message is informative.',address_1)
            porton_close=time.time()
            still_open=False
...
            say('Garage is close')

        if porton_cerrado-porton_open<=(3*60+10) and
        still_open==False and f_open==True and GPIO.input(pin_power)==0:
...
            print (Cursor.POS(23, 10) + Fore.RED + 'AB')
            print (Cursor.POS(10, 15) + Fore.GREEN +
                                    enlarge('Alarm GARAGE STILL OPEN'))
            message('GARAGE ALARM','Garage STILL OPEN. ','Check: \n'
                            +'-Garage open or close.\n-Power.',address_1)
...
            say('Attention: garage still open')

#------------------------------------------------------------------
# MODULE AC_ALARM_SMOKE(): 1->0 smoke alarm, 0->1 no smoke
# INPUTS:  GPIO
# OUTPUTS: LED,ck,message,variables
#------------------------------------------------------------------
def ac_alarm_smoke(Ev=None):
  global a_smoke_yes,a_smoke_no,orig
  if (GPIO.input(pin_smoke)==0 and a_smoke_no==True and
                                 GPIO.input(pin_power)==0):
...
    message('SMOKE ALARM', 'Smoke alarm in Kitchen or Roof. ',
                'Check:\n'+'-Real alarm?.\n-Gas valve.',address_1)
...
    say('Attention: smoke alarm')

  if (GPIO.input(pin_smoke)==1 and a_smoke_yes==True and
                                 GPIO.input(pin_power)==0):
...
    message('SMOKE ALARM','There isn't smoke alarm. ','Check:\n'+
```

337

```
                                            '-Gas valve.',address_1)
...
    say('There isn't smoke alarm')
#------------------------------------------------------------------
# MODULE AC_ALARM_WATER(): 1->0 flood alarm, 0->1 no flood
# INPUTS:  GPIO
# OUTPUTS: LED,ck,message,variables
#------------------------------------------------------------------
def ac_alarm_water(Ev=None):
  global a_water_yes,a_water_no,orig
  if (GPIO.input(pin_water)==0 and a_water_no==True and
                                GPIO.input(pin_power)==0):
...
    message('WATER ALARM', 'Flood alarm in Kitchen, Garage or Bath.
 ','Check:\n'+'-Where is the flood.',address_1)
...
    say('Attention: flood alarm')

  if (GPIO.input(pin_water)==1 and a_water_yes==True and
                                GPIO.input(pin_power)==0):
...
    message('WATER ALARM','There isn't flood alarm. ','Check:\n
        -If there is water flow.\n'+'-Main water valve.',address_1)
...
    say('There isn't flood alarm')

#------------------------------------------------------------------
# MODULE AC_ALARM_GAS(): 1->0 gas leakage, 0->1 no leakage
# INPUTS:  GPIO
# OUTPUTS: LED,ck,message,variables
#------------------------------------------------------------------
def ac_alarm_gas(Ev=None):
  global a_gas_yes,a_gas_no,orig
  if (GPIO.input(pin_gas)==0 and a_gas_no==True and
                                GPIO.input(pin_power)==0):
...
    message('GAS ALARM', 'Gas leakage in Kitchen. ','Check:\n
            -If the alarm is real.\n'+'-Open doors and windows to
                                ventilate.',address_1)
...
    say('Attention: gas leakage alarm')

  if (GPIO.input(pin_gas)==1 and a_gas_yes==True and
                                GPIO.input(pin_power)==0):
...
    message('GAS ALARM','There isn't gas alarm. ','Check:\n
                                -Gas valve.',address_1)
...
    say('There isn't gas alarm')

#------------------------------------------------------------------
# MODULE AC_ALARM_DOORBELL(): direct logic, bouncetime=2s
# INPUTS:  GPIO
# OUTPUTS: LED,ck,message,variables
#------------------------------------------------------------------
def ac_alarm_doorbell(Ev=None):
```

```python
    global a_doorbell_yes,a_doorbell_no,orig
    if (GPIO.input(pin_doorbell)==1 and a_doorbell_no==True and
                a_doorbell_yes==False and GPIO.input(pin_power)==0):
      say('*dog')                        #dog barking simulation
...
      print (Cursor.POS(10, 15) + Fore.RED + enlarge('Doorbell has
                                                           rang'))
      message('DOORBELL ALARM', 'Doorbell has rang. ','Check:\n
                    -Mobile calls.\n'+'-Delivery notices.',address_1)
...
      say('Attention: Doorbell has rang')

    if (GPIO.input(pin_doorbell)==0 and a_doorbell_yes==True and
                a_doorbell_no==False and GPIO.input(pin_power)==0):
...
      write_outfile('Doorbell no longer rings')
      a_doorbell_yes=False
      a_doorbell_no=True
...

#------------------------------------------------------------------
# MODULE AC_ALARM_CO2(): L alarm, H no alarm, reverse logic
# INPUTS:  GPIO
# OUTPUTS: LED,ck,message,variables
#------------------------------------------------------------------
def ac_alarm_co2(Ev=None):
  global a_co2_yes,a_co2_no,orig
  if (GPIO.input(pin_co2)==0 and a_co2_no==True and
                            GPIO.input(pin_power)==0):
...
      message('Co2 ALARM', 'HIGH level Co2. ','Check:\n
                    -If there is people or car in the garage.\n'+
                '-Open garage gate util alarm goes off.',address_1)
...
      say('Attention: toxic gas in the garage')

    if (GPIO.input(pin_co2)==1 and a_co2_yes==True and
                            GPIO.input(pin_power)==0):
...
      message('Co2 ALARM','NORMAL Co2 level. ','Check:\n
                        -That garage gate is close.',address_1)
...
      say('There's no longer any toxic gas in the garage')

#------------------------------------------------------------------
# MODULE WRITE_OUTFILE(): record messages to en [daily] file
# INPUTS:  program messages and origin of the action
# OUTPUTS: p_logfile.txt with program messages
#------------------------------------------------------------------
def write_outfile(men):
  time.sleep(.2)                        #wait for event viewer
  outfile=open(daily,'a')
  if men==title or men==separator or men==jump:
    outfile.write(men)
  else:
    changes=(('á','a'),('é','e'),('í','i'),('ó','o'),('ú','u')
```

```
                                                     ,('º',''))
    for a,b in changes:
      men=men.replace(a,b).replace(a,b) #delete invalid characters
    men=num_line+men
    outfile.write(time.strftime("%d-%m-%y ")+time.strftime("%X  ")
                                    +enlarge(men)+' '+orig+'\n')
  outfile.close()

#------------------------------------------------------------------
# MODULE SEE_TITLES(): write main titles of program
# INPUTS:  any
# OUTPUTS: titles on screen
#------------------------------------------------------------------
def see_titulos():
  global orig
  os.system('clear')
  print (Cursor.POS(10, 2) + Style.BRIGHT + Fore.RED + 'RASPBERRY
                                      -HOME AUTOMATION CONTROL')

  print (Cursor.POS(10, 6) + Fore.GREEN + 'Internet: ON ')
  print (Cursor.POS(27, 3) + Fore.GREEN + 'Temperature:     ')
  print (Cursor.POS(27, 4) + Fore.GREEN + 'Humidity:        ')
  print (Cursor.POS(10,5)+' '*27)
  print (Cursor.POS(10, 5) + Fore.CYAN  + see_heater)
  print (Cursor.POS(38, 5) + Fore.CYAN  + 'T:')

  print (Cursor.POS(25, 6) + Fore.RED +   'SERIOUS Alarm:  NO')
  print (Cursor.POS(44, 6) + Fore.RED   + Back.WHITE + 'RESET (R)')
  print (Cursor.POS(44, 7) + Fore.GREEN + Back.WHITE + 'CLEAR (C)')
  print (Cursor.POS(44, 8) + Fore.BLUE  + Back.WHITE + 'SEND  (S)')

  print (Cursor.POS(25, 7) + Fore.YELLOW+'SLIGHT Alarm:   NO')
  print (Cursor.POS(25, 8) + Fore.GREEN +'Clock:          x')
  print (Cursor.POS(10, 9) + Fore.GREEN +'-'*43)

  print (Cursor.POS(10,10) + Fore.CYAN  + 'Garage:       CL|')
  print (Cursor.POS(10,11) + Fore.CYAN  + 'Smoke:        NO|')
  print (Cursor.POS(10,12) + Fore.CYAN  + 'Flood:        NO|')
  print (Cursor.POS(10,13) + Fore.CYAN  + 'Gas Leakage: NO|')

  print (Cursor.POS(27,10) + Fore.CYAN  + 'Power        :  OK|')
  print (Cursor.POS(27,11) + Fore.CYAN  + 'Doorbell:       NO|')
  print (Cursor.POS(27,12) + Fore.CYAN  + 'CO2:            NO|')
  print (Cursor.POS(27,13) + Fore.CYAN  + 'RESET pressed: NO|')
  print (Cursor.POS(46,10) + Fore.CYAN  + 'NAS: ON')
  print (Cursor.POS(46,11) + Fore.CYAN  + 'ONT: ON')
  print (Cursor.POS(46,12) + Fore.CYAN  + 'ROU: ON')
  print (Cursor.POS(46,13) + Fore.CYAN  + 'HUB: ON')
  print (Cursor.POS(9,23)  + Fore.GREEN + 'KNX bus empty')
  print (Cursor.POS(10,14) + Fore.GREEN + '-'*43)

  for i in range(15,23):
    print (Cursor.POS(8,i) + Fore.WHITE +  enlarge('->'))
  orig='see_titulos()'
  line(traceback.extract_stack())
  write_outfile('Start Titles')
```

```
#------------------------------------------------------------------
# MODULE KESY(): red pressed keys
# INPUTS:   keyboard
# OUTPUTS: tec: pressed key
#------------------------------------------------------------------
def keys():
  global tec,orig
  keys=['R','r','B','b','E','e']
  try:
    tec=sys.stdin.read(1)   #key pressed?
  except IOError: pass
  if tec in keys:
    orig='keys()'
    line(traceback.extract_stack())
    write_outfile('Key '+tec+' pressed')
    line(traceback.extract_stack())
    see_colour(colour.on+' && '+colour.greed)
  elif tec!='':
    ae_LED('R','E',short)
    sound(ck)
    ae_LED('R','A',short)
  return(tec)


#------------------------------------------------------------------
# MODULE SEE_KEYS(): keys pressed management
# INPUTS:   tec, pressed key
# OUTPUTS: action with devices & variables
#------------------------------------------------------------------
def see_keys():
  global reset_pressed,reset_largo,tele,
                        t_tec,day_tec,tec,orig,switched_on
  if (tec=='r' or tec=='R'):     #RESET key
    line(traceback.extract_stack())
    see_colour(colour.on+' && '+colour.lilac)
    print (Cursor.POS(44, 6) + Fore.WHITE + Back.RED
                                           + 'RESET (R)')
    sound(short)
    reset_pressed=True
    reset_long  =True
    orig='keys()'
    say('Reset key pressed')
...

  elif (tec=='c' or tec=='C'):  #CLEAR key
    line(traceback.extract_stack())
    see_colour(colour.on+' && '+colour.lilac)
    print (Cursor.POS(44, 7) + Fore.WHITE + Back.GREEN
                                           + 'CLEAR (C)')
    sound(short)
    os.system('clear')
    line(traceback.extract_stack())
    see_titles()
...
    say('Clear key pressed')
...
```

```
  elif (tec=='s' or tec=='S'):  #SEND key
    line(traceback.extract_stack())
    see_colour(colour.on+' && '+colour.lilac)
...
    t_tec=time.localtime()
    day_tec=time.strftime('%A',t_tec)
    orig='keys()'
    write_outfile('Send summary at '+day_tec)
    say('Send key pressed')
...
    send_daily()
...
  tec=''

#---------------------------------------------------------------
# MODULE blink_green(): ck del watchdog & date/time refresh
# INPUTS:   any
# OUTPUTS: ae_LED green,ck & date/time refresh
#---------------------------------------------------------------
def blink_green():
  ae_LED('G','E',0)
  sound(ck)
  ae_LED('G','A',0)
  print (Cursor.POS(10, 3) + Fore.GREEN + time.strftime("%d-%m-%y")
                            +' ['+day_1[0:2]+']')
  print (Cursor.POS(10, 4) + Fore.GREEN + time.strftime("%X"))

#---------------------------------------------------------------
# MODULE DISKSPACE(): hard disk (USB)
# INPUTS:   USB hard disk status
# OUTPUTS: total, used & free diskSpace
#---------------------------------------------------------------
def diskSpace():
  global orig
  try:
    p = os.popen("df -h /")
    i = 0
    while 1:
      i += 1
      line = p.readline()
      if i == 2:
        return(line.split()[1:5])
  except:
    orig='diskSpace()'
    line(traceback.extract_stack())
    say('Attention: POPEN error')
    see_colour(colour.red)

#---------------------------------------------------------------
# MODULE VAR_CPU(): CPU temperature & HD free space
# INPUTS:   any
# OUTPUTS: cpu_temp & cpu_hd variables
#---------------------------------------------------------------
def var_cpu():
  global cpu_temp,cpu_hd,orig
```

```python
  try:
    tempFile = open( "/sys/class/thermal/thermal_zone0/temp" )
    cpu_temp = tempFile.read()
    tempFile.close()
    cpu_temp = round(float(cpu_temp)/1000)
    cpu_hd=diskSpace()[2]
  except:
    orig='var_cpu()'
    line(traceback.extract_stack())
    say('Attention: TEMPFILE error')
    see_colour(colour.red)

#-----------------------------------------------------------------
# MODULE SEE_VAR_CPU(): cpu & temperature alarm
# INPUTS:   cpu_temp,cpu_temp_max
# OUTPUTS: a_cpu_yes, messages
#-----------------------------------------------------------------
def see_var_cpu():
  global a_cpu_yes,orig
  print (Cursor.POS(10, 8) +    Fore.GREEN + 'HD free:'+str(cpu_hd))
  if cpu_temp<cpu_temp_max:
    print (Cursor.POS(10, 7) + Fore.GREEN +
                                'CPU(°C):'+str(cpu_temp))
    a_cpu_yes=False
  else:
    print (Cursor.POS(10, 7) + Fore.RED    +
                                'CPU(°C):'+str(cpu_temp))
    if a_cpu_yes==False:
      line(traceback.extract_stack())
      message('CPU ALARM', 'excessive CPU temperature
                  ('+str(cpu_temp)+'/'+str(cpu_temp_max)+'°C). ',
             'Check:\n'+'-General system status.\n-Software updated on
                  Raspberry\n'+'-Correct system start.',address_1)
      orig='var_cpu()'
      line(traceback.extract_stack())
      write_outfile('CPU ALARM: excessive CPU temperature
                  ('+str(cpu_temp)+'/'+str(cpu_temp_max)+'°C)')
      a_cpu_yes=True
      say('Alarm: excessive CPU temperature')

#-----------------------------------------------------------------
# MODULE DESTROY(): stops program
# INPUTS:   <ctrl>+<c> on keyboard or vnc
# OUTPUTS: GPIO start, display on screen, send message
#-----------------------------------------------------------------
def destroy():
  global error,orig
  orig='destroy()'
  if error == False:
    xx = 'Program completed by the user'
  else:
    xx = 'Program completed by parameters error'
  line(traceback.extract_stack())
  write_outfile(xx)
  print (Cursor.POS(10, 24) + Fore.RED + enlarge(xx))
```

343

```
    message('PROGRAM ALARM ',xx,'. Check:\n -If the program has
                started.\n'+'-There is no runtime error.',address_1)
    blink_green()
    os.system('setterm -cursor on') #show Terminal
    see_colour(colour.on+' && '+colour.red)

#-----------------------------------------------------------------
# Do not delete the following instructions, avoid temperature
# sensor errors
#-----------------------------------------------------------------
  try:
    pi=pigpio.pi()
    s = DHT22.sensor(pi, pin_sensor)
    s.cancel()
  except:
    orig='destroy()'
    line(traceback.extract_stack())
    say('Attention: DHT22 error')
    see_colour(colour.red)

#-----------------------------------------------------------------
# close key capture
#-----------------------------------------------------------------
  try:
    termios.tcsetattr(fd, termios.TCSAFLUSH, oldterm)
    fcntl.fcntl(fd, fcntl.F_SETFL, oldflags)
    GPIO.cleanup()                  # release resource
    outfile.close()
    sys.exit(0)
  except:
    orig='destroy()'
    line(traceback.extract_stack())
    say('Attention: KEYS error')
    line(traceback.extract_stack())
    see_colour(colour.red)

#-----------------------------------------------------------------
# START OF MAIN PROGRAM EXECUTION
#-----------------------------------------------------------------
if __name__ == '__main__':       #Program start from here
  os.system('clear')
  print '-'*50
  print 'Starting Home Automation Control Program....'
  print 'Version: '+version
  print '-'*50
  say('Starting Home Automation Control Program')
  orig='__main__'
  num_line=''
  write_outfile(jump)
  write_outfile(separator)
  write_outfile('Starting Home Automation Control Program')
  write_outfile(separator)
  write_outfile(title)
  write_outfile(separator)
  see_colour(colour.on+' && '+colour.red)
```

```
  say('Performing setup')
  print 'General setup...'
  setup_gral()
  print 'Setup LED...'
  setup_led()
  print 'Setup relays...'
  setup_relays()
  print 'Setup alarms...'
  setup_alarms()
  print 'Start alarms...'
  start_alarms()
  print 'Start Edimax...'
  start_edimax()
  print 'Start Sonoff...'
  start_sonoff()
  print 'Start Switched_on[]...'
  record_switched_on()            #switched_on[] with p_lights.txt
  print 'Start Open[]...'
  record_open()                   #switched_on[] with p_blinds.txt
  print 'Start States[]...'
  record_states()                 #states[] with p_sensors.txt
  print 'Start Pigpio...'
  orig='__main__'
  write_outfile('Start el GPIO & DHT22')
  try:
    pi=pigpio.pi()
  except:
    say('Attention: GPIO error')
    see_colour(colour.red)
  try:
    print 'Start DHT22...'
    s=DHT22.sensor(pi,pin_sensor)
  except:
    say('Attention: DHT22 error')
    see_colour(colour.red)
  say('Performing the initial test')
  test_initial()
  os.system('clear')
  try:
    GPIO.add_event_detect(boton_reset, GPIO.FALLING,
                          callback=ac_reset, bouncetime=bounce*500)
  except:
    say('Attention: GPIO error')
    see_colour(colour.red)
  see_titles()

#---------------------------------------------------------------
# MAIN PROGRAM LOOP
#---------------------------------------------------------------
  try:
    orig='try:'
    write_outfile(jump)
    write_outfile(separator)
    num_line=''
    write_outfile('MAIN PROGRAM LOOP START')
```

345

```
      write_outfile(separator)
      say('Program started successfully')
      see_colour(colour.verde)
      while True:                        #main loop

#------------------------------------------------------------------
# Alarms jumps falling or rising interruption
# Prioritised processes with yes_polling
#------------------------------------------------------------------
        if yes_polling==0:              #telegram actions
          see_mes()                     #summer or winter
          see_trace()                   #GPIO trace
          record_states()               #p_sensors.txt to states[]
          record_activated()            #p_devices.txt to activated[]
          see_heater()                  #heater status
          see_sensor()                  #sensor status
        telegram()                      #read KNX telegram to tele[]
        see_telegram()                  #acts with devices
        if yes_polling==0:
          record_lights(switched_on)    #p_lights.txt with switched_on[]
          record_blinds(open)           #p_blinds.txt with open[]
          onoff()                       #Internet connection
          see_onoff()                   #Internet management
          var_cpu()                     #cpu status
          see_var_cpu()                 #cpu status management
          update_states()              #states[] with real data
          record_sensors(states)        #p_sensors.txt with states[]
          record_switched_on()          #switched_on[] with p_lights.txt
          automatic()                   #automatic tasks
          see_garage()                  #garage lights actions
          see_origin()                  #origin with p_sensors.txt
          see_effectors()               #actions with effectors[]
          record_sensors(states)        #p_sensors.txt with states[]
          record_lights(switched_on)    #p_lights.txt with switched_on[]
          record_blinds(open)           #p_blinds.txt with open[]
          key()                         #key pressed
          see_keys()                    #action with key pressed
          see_start()                   #update thermostat status
          see_reset()                   #reset button
          send_summary()                #daily activity summary
          blink_green()                 #acoustic/visual/ck traces
        if yes_polling==cycles_polling:  #not essential tasks
          yes_polling=0
        else:
          yes_polling+=1
#------------------------------------------------------------------
# Here ends main program try loop
#------------------------------------------------------------------


#------------------------------------------------------------------
# Program interruptions, exceptions & errors management
#------------------------------------------------------------------
      except KeyboardInterrupt:         #ctrl+c stops program
        orig='keyboard'
        line(traceback.extract_stack())
```

346

```
      say('User terminated program')
      destroy()
  except OSError:                    #system error display
    orig='oserror'
    line(traceback.extract_stack())
    say('Attention: SYSTEM error')
  except IOError:                    #input/output error
    orig='ioerror'
    if str(sys.esc_info()[0])=="<class
                        'requests.exceptions.ConnectionError'>":
      err='Edimax is not connected, review its IP'
    else:
      line(traceback.extract_stack())
      say('Attention: I/O error')
  except Exception:                  #other exception
    orig='exception'
    if str(sys.esc_info()[0])=="<class
                        'requests.exceptions.ConnectionError'>":
      err='Edimax error terminated program...'
    else:
      err='Unknown exception terminated program'
    line(traceback.extract_stack())
    write_outfile(err)
  except:
    os.system('setterm -cursor on') #shows Terminal cursor
    err='Unknown error terminated program...'
  finally:
    line(traceback.extract_stack())
    see_colour(colour.on+' && '+colour.blue)
    record_lights(switched_on)      #switched_on[] to p_lights.txt
    record_blinds(open)             #open[] to p_blinds.txt
    record_sensors(states)          #states[] to p_sensors.txt
    line(traceback.extract_stack())
    write_outfile(str(sys.exc_info()[:2]))
    logging.exception('\n'+time.strftime("%d-%m-%y ")
                        +time.strftime("%X  ")+'\n'+'-'*40+'\n')
    raise
#----------------------------------------------------------------
```

*P_telegram.py

```python
#------------------------------------------------------------------
# P_TELEGRAM.PY: Telegram BOT to Home Automation Control
# Uses two exchange data files with p_global.py to act with sensors
# and effectors. This version acts with lamps, window blinds, gas &
# water valve, heater, holidays status, etc.
# Files:
#  p_sensors.txt:    sensors status: temperature, humidity, etc.
#  p_actuators.txt:  actuators, relays, etc.
#  commands: /start, /help & /exec
# Botfather Telegram Configuration
# BOT uses polling & can't be included in another program
# and must be run in parallel and share information through files
#------------------------------------------------------------------
#!/usr/bin/env python
# -*- coding: utf-8 -*-
import telebot
from    telebot import types
import time,os,sys
import urllib2
import psutil    #RAM management
import socket    #IP local management
from smartplug import SmartPlug    #Edimax status
from subprocess import Popen,PIPE #IP vs MAC mana
import re
import logging  #program errors log
try:
    logging.basicConfig(filename='/home/pi/home_auto/p_telegram.log'
                                      ,level=logging.ERROR)
except:
    os.system('sudo rm /home/pi/home_auto/p_telegram.log')
    logging.basicConfig(filename='/home/pi/home_auto/p_telegram.log'
                                      ,level=logging.ERROR)
url_ip="http://miip.es" #URL to read public IP
#others URL:
#http://miip.es en [4832:4854]
#http://www.mypublicip.com en [144:160]
#http://checkip.dyndns.org en [:]

mac_device={
'86:16:f9:xx:xx:xx':'Edimax','e0:41:36:yy:yy:yy':'Router Fiber',
'7c:2e:bd:zz:zz:zz':'Google','82:16:f9:aa:aa:aa':'TP-Link Exte',
...,
3c:5c:c4:cc:cc:cc':'Alexa   ','d0:7f:a0:bb:bb:bb':'Smart Watch'}

dispo={x:'router living room', y:'edimax',...,z:'Tadoº'}
```

```
#-------------------------------------------------------------
# MODULO ERROR(): displays error x
# INPUTS:  error x to display
# OUTPUTS: send message with error x
#-------------------------------------------------------------
def error(x):
  print(colour.RED + 'Error in: '+x+ colour.ENDC)
  exit


#-------------------------------------------------------------
# MODULE START_ACTIONS(): starts actions
# INPUTS:  actions[] to blank
# OUTPUTS: actions[] with blank actions (NO)
#-------------------------------------------------------------
def start_actions():
  global actions
  actions=[]
  actions.append('Switch off lights: NO\n')
...
  actions.append('Switch off living room sofa: NO\n')


#-------------------------------------------------------------
# MODULE READ(): reads data[] from p_sensors.txt
# INPUTS:  p_sensors.txt, exchange file p_global.py & data[]
# OUTPUTS: data[]
#-------------------------------------------------------------
def read():
  global data,v_thermostat,v_water,v_gas
  exchange_sensors='/home/pi/home_auto/p_sensors.txt'
  inter_sensors=open(exchange_sensors,'r')
  data=[]
  while True:
    x=inter_sensors.readline()
    if x!='':
      datos.append(x[:len(x)-1]) #watch out: \n
    else:
      break
  inter_sensors.close()

  if len(data)<19:                  #p_sensors corrupt?
    os.system('cp /home/pi/home_auto/p_sensors.ok
                              /home/pi/home_auto/p_sensors.txt')
    exchange_sensors='/home/pi/home_auto/p_sensors.txt'
    inter_sensors=open(exchange_sensors,'r')
    data=[]
    while True:
      x=inter_sensors.readline()
      if x!='':
        datos.append(x[:len(x)-1])
      else:
        break
    inter_sensors.close()
  if data[13]=='Thermostat:  ABSENCE':
    v_thermostat='absence'
...
```

```python
#-------------------------------------------------------------------
# MODULE WRITE(): update actions in p_actuators.txt
# INPUTS:  actions[]
# OUTPUTS: p_actuators.txt & p_sensors.txt
#-------------------------------------------------------------------
def write():
  try:
    exchange_actuators='/home/pi/home_auto/p_actuators.txt'
    inter_actuators=open(exchange_actuators,'w')
    for i in actions:
      inter_actuators.write(i)
    inter_actuators.close()
    leer()              #read sensor status in data[]
    data[16]='Origin:      TELEGRAM'
    exchange_sensors='/home/pi/home_auto/p_sensors.txt'
    inter_sensors=open(exchange_sensors,'w')
    for i in data:
      inter_sensors.write(i+'\n') #transfer to p_sensors.txt
    inter_sensors.close()
  except:
    error('p_actuators.txt open')
TOKEN = "token_token_token"        #see TOKEN on Telegram
idi   = 1234567890                 #user code on Telegram
userStep = {}
knownUsers = []
commands = {  'start': 'Starts bot',
              'help' : 'Available commands',
              'exec' : 'Executes one command'}
menu = types.ReplyKeyboardMarkup()
menu.add("Raspberry", 'Home_Auto')
menu.add('System', 'Info')
raspberry_menu = types.ReplyKeyboardMarkup()
raspberry_menu.add('Temperatures', 'HD')
raspberry_menu.add('RAM', 'CPU')
raspberry_menu.add('Back')
home_automation_menu = types.ReplyKeyboardMarkup()
home_automation_menu.add('Status', 'Action')
home_automation_menu.add('Lights/Others', 'Blinds')
home_automation_menu.add('Heater','Devices')
home_automation_menu.add('Holidays','Movie')
home_automation_menu.add('Back')
system_menu = types.ReplyKeyboardMarkup()
system_menu.add('IP','Clear')
system_menu.add('NAS reset','ONT reset')
system_menu.add('ROUTER reset','RASPBERRY reset')
system_menu.add('Back')
state_menu = types.ReplyKeyboardMarkup()
state_menu.add('Temperatures', 'Humidity')
state_menu.add('Power', 'Internet', 'Edimax')
state_menu.add('Garage', 'Doorbell', 'Smoke')
state_menu.add('Water', 'Gas', 'CO2')
state_menu.add('Back')
action_menu = types.ReplyKeyboardMarkup()
action_menu.add('Switch off lights','Back')
action_menu.add('Close blinds', 'Open blinds')
```

```
action_menu.add('Heater ON', 'Heater OFF')
action_menu.add('Water ON', 'Water OFF')
action_menu.add('Gas ON', 'Gas OFF')
action_menu.add('Holidays ON', 'Holidays OFF')

# TEXT COLOUR
class colour:
  RED       = '\033[91m'
  BLUE      = '\033[94m'
  GREEN     = '\033[32m'
  ENDC      = '\033[0m'      #end colour
  BOLD      = '\033[1m'
  UNDERLINE = '\033[4m'

#-----------------------------------------------------------------
# MODULE: WIFI_BULB(): ON/OFF status of WIFI_bulb
# INPUTS:  WIFI bulb details /home/pi/home_auto/p_WIFI_bulb.txt
# OUTPUTS: state='ON/OFF'
#-----------------------------------------------------------------
def WIFI_bulb():
  global state
  try:
    fWIFI_bulb='/home/pi/home_auto/p_WIFI_bulb.txt'
  except:
    os.system('sudo cp /home/pi/home_auto/p_WIFI_bulb.ok
                         /home/pi/home_auto/p_WIFI_bulb.txt')
    error('p_WIFI_bulb.txt opening')

  try: #WIFI_bulb available?
    response = os.system("ping -w 1 192.168.1.xx") #1s ping
  except:
    error('WIFI bulb no available')
    state='WIFI_bulb ???'
    response=1
  if response == 0:
    os.system('tplight details 192.168.1.xx > '+fWIFI_bulb)
    os.system('sudo cp /home/pi/home_auto/p_WIFI_bulb.txt
                         /home/pi/home_auto/p_WIFI_bulb.ok')
    ffile=open(fWIFI_bulb,'r')
    text=ffile.readlines()[19][14]
    if text=='0':
      state='WIFI_bulb OFF'
    elif text=='1':
      state='WIFI_bulb ON'
    else:
      state='WIFI_bulb ???'
    ffile.close()
  else:
    state='WIFI_bulb ???'

#-----------------------------------------------------------------
# MODULE GET_USER_SETP: gets pulsation movement
# INPUTS:  uid
# OUTPUTS: userStep
#-----------------------------------------------------------------
```

```
def get_user_step(uid):
  if uid in userStep:
    return userStep[uid]
  else:
    knownUsers.append(uid)
    userStep[uid] = 0
    print(colour.RED + "¡¡New user!!" + colour.ENDC)

#------------------------------------------------------------
# MODULE LISTENER(): receives info from telebot
# INPUTS:  bootpolling() of telebot
# OUTPUTS: messages
#------------------------------------------------------------
def listener(messages):
  for m in messages:
    if m.content_type == 'text':
      print("[" + str(m.chat.id) + "] " +
                        str(m.chat.first_name) + ": " + m.text)
bot = telebot.TeleBot(TOKEN)
bot.set_update_listener(listener)

#------------------------------------------------------------
# MODULE START: starts basic menu of bot
# INPUTS:  message of bootpolling()
# OUTPUTS: access to main menu
#------------------------------------------------------------
@bot.message_handler(commands=['start'])
def command_start(m):
  cid = m.chat.id
  if cid==idi: #user code
    userStep[cid] = 0
    bot.send_message(cid, "*Home Automation System of " +
str(m.chat.first_name)+'-Other*',parse_mode='Markdown')
    time.sleep(1)
    bot.send_message(cid, "*Available Commands:*"
                              ,parse_mode='Markdown')
    time.sleep(1)
    bot.send_message(cid, "/start, /help, /exec, \n"
                              , reply_markup=menu)
  else:
    permission_denied()

#------------------------------------------------------------
# MODULE HELP: displays commands of help
# INPUTS:  message of bootpolling()
# OUTPUTS: available commands on help
#------------------------------------------------------------
@bot.message_handler(commands=['help'])
def command_help(m):
  cid = m.chat.id
  if cid==idi:
    help_text = "*Available Commands: \n*"
    for key in commands:
      help_text += "/" + key + ": "
      help_text += commands[key] + "\n"
```

```
      bot.send_message(cid, help_text,parse_mode='Markdown')
    else:
      permission_denied()

#-------------------------------------------------------------------
# MODULE COMMAND_EXEC(): runs basic Linux commands
# INPUTS:   message of bootpolling()
# OUTPUTS: runs these Linux commands
#-------------------------------------------------------------------
@bot.message_handler(commands=['exec'])
def command_exec(m):
  cid = m.chat.id
  if cid == idi:
    bot.send_message(cid, "Running: " + m.text[len("/exec"):])
    bot.send_chat_action(cid, 'typing')
    time.sleep(2)
    f = os.popen(m.text[len("/exec"):])
    result = f.read()
    bot.send_message(cid, "Result: " + result)
  else:
    permission_denied()

#-------------------------------------------------------------------
# MODULE: MAIN_MENU(): main program menu
# INPUTS:   bootpolling() options
# OUTPUTS: main menu options
#-------------------------------------------------------------------
@bot.message_handler(func=lambda message:
                                get_user_step(message.chat.id) == 0)
def main_menu(m):
  cid = m.chat.id
  text = m.text
  if cid==idi:
    if text == "Raspberry":
      bot.send_message(cid, '*Available Information:*'
                  ,parse_mode='Markdown',reply_markup=raspberry_menu)
      userStep[cid] = 1
    elif text == "Home Automation":
      bot.send_message(cid, '*Home Automation options:*'
            ,        parse_mode='Markdown',reply_markup=home_auto_menu)
      userStep[cid] = 2
    elif text == 'System':
      bot.send_message(cid, '*System Options:*',
                    parse_mode='Markdown',reply_markup=system_menu)
      userStep[cid] = 3
    elif text == 'Info':
      command_start(m)
      userStep[cid]=0
    else:
      command_text(m)
  else:
    permission_denied()

#-------------------------------------------------------------------
# MODULE RASP_OPT(): basic status of Raspberry_home automation
```

```python
# INPUTS:  bootpolling() options
# OUTPUTS: displays Raspberry_home automation status
#-----------------------------------------------------------------
@bot.message_handler(func=lambda message:
                          get_user_step(message.chat.id) == 1)
def rasp_opt(m):
  cid = m.chat.id
  txt = m.text
  if cid==idi:
    if txt == "Temperatures":
      bot.send_message(cid,"*Raspberry Temperatures*"
                            ,parse_mode='Markdown')
      print(colour.BLUE +   "Raspberry Temperatures" + colour.ENDC)
      tempFile = open( "/sys/class/thermal/thermal_zone0/temp" )
      cpu_temp = tempFile.read()
      tempFile.close()
      cpu_temp = round(float(cpu_temp)/1000)
      bot.send_message(cid,"CPU: %s °C" % cpu_temp)
      print(colour.GREEN +  "CPU: %s °C" % cpu_temp + colour.ENDC)
      gpu_temp = os.popen('/opt/vc/bin/vcgencmd
                      measure_temp').read().split("=")[1][:-3]
      bot.send_message(cid, "GPU: %s °C" % gpu_temp)
      print(colour.GREEN +   "GPU: %s °C" % gpu_temp + colour.ENDC)
    elif txt == "HD":
...
    elif txt == "RAM":
...
    elif txt == "CPU":
...
    elif txt == "Back":   # ATRAS
      userStep[cid] = 0
      bot.send_message(cid, "*Main Menu:*"
                          ,parse_mode='Markdown',reply_markup=menu)
    else:
      command_text(m)
  else:
    permission_denied()


#-----------------------------------------------------------------
# MODULE DOMO_OPT(): main options
# INPUTS:  bootpolling() options
# OUTPUTS: main options
#-----------------------------------------------------------------
@bot.message_handler(func=lambda message:
                          get_user_step(message.chat.id) == 2)
def home_auto_opt(m):
  global cid
  cid = m.chat.id
  text = m.text
  if cid == idi :
    if text == "State":
      bot.send_message(cid, "*State Menu:*",parse_mode='Markdown')
      print(colour.BLUE +    "State Menu: " + colour.ENDC)
      bot.send_message(cid, "*Available Options*"
                      ,parse_mode='Markdown',reply_markup=state_menu)
```

```
      userStep[cid] = 4
    elif text == "Action":
...
      #-------------------------------------------
      #LIGHTS
      #-------------------------------------------
    elif text == "Lights/Others":
      cid = m.chat.id
      text=m.text
      if cid==idi:
        print(colour.BLUE + "LIGHTS ON: " + colour.ENDC)
        bot.send_message(cid, "*LIGHTS ON:*",parse_mode='Markdown')
        try:
          fluces='/home/pi/home_auto/p_lights.txt'
          lights=open(flights,'r')
          x=lights.readline()
          if len(x)==0 or x=='\n':
            bot.send_message(cid,'*[24/24] All off*',
                                          parse_mode='Markdown')
            print(colour.RED + '[24/24] All off...\n'
                                          + colour.ENDC)
          else:
            t=0
            while len(x)!=0 and x!='\n' and x[0:1]!=' ':
              bot.send_message(cid,x)
              print(colour.RED + x + colour.ENDC)
              x=lights.readline()
              t+=1
            bot.send_message(cid,'*['+str(t)
                        +'/24]...end...*',parse_mode='Markdown')
            print(colour.RED+'['+str(t)
                                  +'/24]...end...'+colour.ENDC)
          lights.close()
        except:
          error('Opening p_lights.txt')
        print(colour.BLUE + "OTHERS:" + colour.ENDC)
...
        userStep[cid] = 2
      else:
        permission_denied()

      #-------------------------------------------
      #WINDOW BLINDS
      #-------------------------------------------
    elif text == "Blinds":
      print(colour.BLUE + "Open blinds: " + colour.ENDC)
      bot.send_message(cid, "*Open blinds:*",parse_mode='Markdown')
      cid = m.chat.id
      text=m.text
      if cid==idi:
        try:
          fblinds='/home/pi/home_auto/p_blinds.txt'
          blinds=open(fblinds,'r')
          x=blinds.readline()
          blinds.close()
```

```python
            if len(x)==0 or x=='\n':
                bot.send_message(cid,'*[7/7] All close...*'
                                        ,parse_mode='Markdown')
                print(colour.RED + '[7/7] All close...' + colour.ENDC)
            else:
                blinds=open(fblinds,'r')
                x=blinds.readline()
                t=0
                while len(x)!=0 and x!='\n':
                    x=blinds.readline()
                    t+=1
                blinds.close()
                if t==7:
                    bot.send_message(cid,'*[7/7] All open...*'
                                        ,parse_mode='Markdown')
                else:
                    blinds=open(fblinds,'r')
                    x=blinds.readline()
                    t=0
                    while len(x)!=0 and x!='\n':
                        bot.send_message(cid,x)
                        print(colour.RED + x + colour.ENDC)
                        x=blinds.readline()
                        t+=1
                    blinds.close()
                    if t==0:
                        bot.send_message(cid,'*[7/7] All close...*'
                                        ,parse_mode='Markdown')
                    else:
                        bot.send_message(cid,'*['+str(t)
                                +'/7]...end...*',parse_mode='Markdown')

        except:
            error('opening of p_blinds.txt')
        userStep[cid] = 2
    else:
        permission_denied()

    #-----------------------------------------------
    #HEATER
    #-----------------------------------------------
elif text == "Heater":
...
    permission_denied()

    #-----------------------------------------------
    #CONNECTED DEVICES
    #-----------------------------------------------
elif text == "Devices":
    print(colour.BLUE + "Connected devices: " + colour.ENDC)
    bot.send_message(cid, "*Connected devices:*"
                                ,parse_mode='Markdown')
    cid = m.chat.id
    text=m.text
    if cid==idi:
```

```python
#------------------------------------------------------------
# Connected devices identified in ARP
#------------------------------------------------------------
        bot.send_message(cid,'*...According IP-MAC...*'
                                        ,parse_mode='Markdown')
        print(colour.RED + '...According IP-MAC...' + colour.ENDC)
        bot.send_message(cid,'*...updating arp-scan...*'
                                        ,parse_mode='Markdown')
        print(colour.RED + '...updating arp-scan...' + colour.ENDC)
        bot.send_message(cid,'*...wait 2 seconds...*'
                                        ,parse_mode='Markdown')
        print(colour.RED + '...wait 2 seconds...' + colour.ENDC)
        mac_file='/home/pi/home_auto/p_ip_mac.txt'
        try:
          os.system('sudo arp-scan -r 1 -I eth0 -localnet
                                        -t 1000 > '+mac_file)
        except:
          error('arp-scan')
        ffile=open(mac_file,'r')
        names={}
        hostname = '192.168.1.'
        while True:
          x=ffile.readline()
          if x!='':
            t=x.find('\t')
            host=x[:t]
            mac=  x[t+1:t+18]
            if mac in mac_device:
              names[mac_device[mac]]=host
            else:
              if host.find(hostname)==0:
                names['Unknown']=host[:13]
          else:
            break
        list=[]
        for j in names:    #add device names to sort them
          list.append(j)
        list.sort()
        c=0
        for j in list:
          jj='['+names[j]+']:\t'+j
          bot.send_message(cid,jj)
          print(colour.RED+jj+colour.ENDC)
          time.sleep(.1)    #waiting for bot
          c+=1
        bot.send_message(cid,'*['+str(c)+'/'+str(len(mac_device))
                                +']*',parse_mode='Markdown')
        print(colour.RED +     '['+str(c)+'/'+str(len(mac_device))
                                +']'+colour.ENDC)


#------------------------------------------------------------
# Devices that are not connected or are not in ARP list
#------------------------------------------------------------
        missing=[]
        ff=0
```

```
      bot.send_message(cid,'*...Missing devices...*',
                                      parse_mode='Markdown')
      print(colour.RED + '...Missing devices...' + colour.ENDC)
      for x in mac_device:
        if mac_device[x] not in names:
          missing.append(mac_device[x])
      missing.sort()
      for x in missing:
        bot.send_message(cid,x)
        print(colour.RED+x+colour.ENDC)
        ff+=1
      bot.send_message(cid,'*...Missing: *'
                          +str(ff),parse_mode='Markdown')
      print(colour.RED +     '...Missing: ' +str(ff)
                                        + colour.ENDC)


#-----------------------------------------------------------------
# Main devices identified by its IP
#-----------------------------------------------------------------
      any=False
      n_device=[]
      bot.send_message(cid,'*...According to PING...*',
                  parse_mode='Markdown')
      print(colour.RED + '...According to PING...' + colour.ENDC)
      bot.send_message(cid,'*...wait 10 seconds...*'
                                    ,parse_mode='Markdown')
      print(colour.RED + '...wait 10 seconds...' + colour.ENDC)
      for x in device:
        print(colour.RED + str(x) + colour.ENDC),
        host=hostname+str(x)
        try:
          response = os.system("ping -w 1 "+host)
        except:
          error('ping'+host)
        if response == 0:
          n_device.append(dispo[x])
          any=True
      n_device.sort()        #sort by connected name
      for x in n_device:
        bot.send_message(cid,x)
        print(colour.RED + x + colour.ENDC)
      if any==False:
        bot.send_message(cid,'*None*',parse_mode='Markdown')
        print(colour.RED + 'None' + colour.ENDC)
      else:
        bot.send_message(cid,'*['+str(len(n_device))+'/'
            +str(len(device))+']...end...*',parse_mode='Markdown')
        print(colour.RED + '...end...' + colour.ENDC)
      userStep[cid] = 2
    else:
      permission_denied()
  elif text == 'Holidays':
    read()                   #read p_sensors.txt to data[]
    if len(data)>13:         #data[] full?
      bot.send_message(cid,data[11])
```

```
            if 'OFF' in data[11]:
                print(colour.GREEN+data[11]+colour.ENDC)
            else:
                print(colour.RED  +data[11]+colour.ENDC)
        elif text == 'Movie':
            leer()                        #read p_sensors.txt to data[]
            if len(data)>13:              #data[] full
                bot.send_message(cid,data[12])
                if 'OFF' in data[12]:
                    print(colour.GREEN+data[12]+colour.ENDC)
                else:
                    print(colour.RED  +data[12]+colour.ENDC)
        elif text == "Back":
            userStep[cid] = 0
            bot.send_message(cid, "*Main Menu:*",parse_mode='Markdown',
reply_markup=menu)
        else:
            command_text(m)
    else:
      permission_denied()


#-----------------------------------------------------------------
# MODULE SAY(): announces text by Google Home
# INPUTS:   text
# OUTPUTS: verbally announce by Google Home
#-----------------------------------------------------------------
def say(text):
    ip_google='192.168.1.xx'
    location='/home/pi/home_auto/gTTS/'
    try:
        os.system(location+'./p_ghome_say.py '+ip_google+' "'
                                      +text+'" > /dev/null 2>&1')
        time.sleep(5)
    except:
        pass


#-----------------------------------------------------------------
# MODULE SIST_MENU(): system status options
# INPUTS:   options captured by bootpolling()
# OUTPUTS: system status Raspberry_home automation options
#-----------------------------------------------------------------
@bot.message_handler(func=lambda message:
                            get_user_step(message.chat.id) == 3)
def sist_menu(m):
    cid = m.chat.id
    text=m.text
    start_actions()
    if cid==idi:
        if text == 'IP':
            try:
                x=[l for l in ([ip for ip in
                        socket.gethostbyname_ex(socket.gethostname())[2]
                                if not ip.startswith("127.")][:1],
                                    [[(s.connect(('8.8.8.8', 53)),
                                s.getsockname()[0], s.close()) for s in
```

```
                                  [socket.socket(socket.AF_INET,
                          socket.SOCK_DGRAM)]][0][1]]) if l][0][0]
        except:
          error('getting local IP')
        if x!='' and len(x)<15: #to avoid bot errors
          bot.send_message(cid,'*local IP:      *'
                              +x,parse_mode='Markdown')
          print(colour.BLUE+x+colour.ENDC)
        ip=urllib2.urlopen(url_ip).read()[4832:4854]
        ip_ok=''
        ip_val=['1','2','3','4','5','6','7','8','9','0','.']
        for x in ip:               #estrange characters filter
          if x in ip_val:
            ip_ok=ip_ok+x
        bot.send_message(cid, '*public IP: *'
                              +ip_ok,parse_mode='Markdown')
        print(colour.BLUE +ip + colour.ENDC)
      elif text == "Clear":
...
      elif text == "NAS Reset":
...
      elif text == "ONT Reset":
...
      elif text == "ROUTER Reset":
...
      elif text == "RASPBERRY Reset":
...
      elif text == "Back":
        userStep[cid]=0
        bot.send_message(cid, "*Main Menu:*",parse_mode='Markdown'
                              , reply_markup=menu)
      else:
        command_text(m)
    else:
      permission_denied()
    write() #saves actions to exchange files

#----------------------------------------------------------------
# MODULE STATE_OPT(): main menu
# INPUTS:  bootpolling() options
# OUTPUTS: main menu options to perform
#----------------------------------------------------------------
@bot.message_handler(func=lambda message:
                          get_user_step(message.chat.id) == 4)
def state_opt(m):
  cid = m.chat.id
  text = m.text
  if cid == idi :
    read()
    if len(data)>=18:               #to avoid error
      if text == "Temperatures":
        bot.send_message(cid, '*NAS Temp:              *'+
                  data[0][len(data[0])  -9:],parse_mode='Markdown')
        print(colour.BLUE  +data[0] +colour.ENDC)
...
```

```
      elif text == "Humidity":
...
      elif text == "Power":
...
      elif text == "Internet":
...
      elif text == 'Edimax':
        try:
          edimax=SmartPlug('192.168.1.xx',('[user]','[password]'))
          edi=edimax.state
          bot.send_message(cid, '*Edimax*'
                                      +edi,parse_mode='Markdown')
          print(colour.BLUE  +edi+colour.ENDC)
          if edi=='OFF':
            edi='switched off'
          else:
            edi='switched on'
          say('Edimax state: '+edi)

        except:
          bot.send_message(cid, '*Edimax
                                   ---*',parse_mode='Markdown')
          print(colour.BLUE  +'---'+colour.ENDC)
      elif text == "Garage":
...
      elif text == "Back":
        userStep[cid] = 2
        bot.send_message(cid, "*Options:*"
          ,parse_mode='Markdown',reply_markup=home_automation_menu)
      else:
        command_text(m)
  else:
    permission_denied()

#------------------------------------------------------------------
# MODULE ACCION_OPT(): home automation actions
# INPUTS:  options captured by bootpolling()
# OUTPUTS: home automation actions to perform
#------------------------------------------------------------------
@bot.message_handler(func=lambda message:
                              get_user_step(message.chat.id) == 5)
def accion_opt(m):
  global actions,v_water,v_gas,v_thermostat,data
  cid = m.chat.id
  text = m.text
  start_actions()
  if cid == idi :
    if text == "Lights off":
      bot.send_message(cid, "*Switching off lights...*"
                                  ,parse_mode='Markdown')
      print(colour.BLUE +    "Switching off lights..."
                                          + colour.ENDC)
      actions[0]='Switch off lights: YES\n'

    elif text =='Switch on living room sofa':
...
```

```
    elif text =='Watch movie':
...
    elif text == "Back":
      userStep[cid] = 2
      bot.send_message(cid, "*Options:*",parse_mode='Markdown'
                          , reply_markup=home_automation_menu)
    else:
      command_text(m)
  else:
    permission_denied()
  write() #saves actions to exchange file

#---------------------------------------------------------------
# MODULE PERMISSION_DENIED(): denies permission for token error
# INPUTS:  bot identification & token
# OUTPUTS: permission denied if identity errors
#---------------------------------------------------------------
def permission_denied():
  bot.send_message(cid, "*¡¡Permission denied!!*",
                                      parse_mode='Markdown')
  print(colour.RED + " ¡¡Permission denied!! " + colour.ENDC)

#---------------------------------------------------------------
# MODULE DISKSPACE(): gets disk space
# INPUTS:  Raspbian system on Raspberry_home automation
# OUTPUTS: total and free disk space in float format
#---------------------------------------------------------------
def diskSpace():
  global disk
  disk=[]

  try:
    p = os.popen("df -h /")
    i = 0
    while 1:
      i += 1
      line = p.readline()
      if i == 2:
        x=line.split()[1:5]
        total=x[0]
        available=x[2]
        total=total[:total.find('G')]
        if ',' in total:
          total=total[:total.find(',')]+'.'
                                  +total[total.find(',')+1:]
        disk.append(float(total))
        available=available[:available.find('G')]
        if ',' in available:
          available=available[:available.find(',')]
                          +'.'+available[available.find(',')+1:]
        disk.append(float(available))
        return

  except:
    error('popen error')
```

```
#--------------------------------------------------------------
# MODULE COMMAND_TEXT(): quality bootpolling() messages
# INPUTS:   bootpolling() messages
# OUTPUTS: captured messages validation
#--------------------------------------------------------------
@bot.message_handler(func=lambda message: True,
                                        content_types=['text'])
def command_text(m):
  cid = m.chat.id
  if cid==idi:
    if (m.text.lower() in ['hello', 'hi', 'good morning']):
      bot.send_message(cid, 'Hi, '
                 + str(m.from_user.first_name) + '. How are you?.')
    elif (m.text.lower() in ['bye', 'see you', 'end']):
      bot.send_message(cid, 'See you, ' +
                      str(m.from_user.first_name) + '. Bye')
    else:
      bot.send_message(cid, 'I don't understand, use /start')
  else:
    permission_denied()


#--------------------------------------------------------------
# MODULE TELEGRAM_POLLING(): to avoid errors in bot.polling
# INPUTS:   bootpolling()
# OUTPUTS: received messages from Telegram
#--------------------------------------------------------------
def telegram_polling():
  try:
    global err
    err='Program stopped by '
    bot.infinity_polling(True, timeout=500)
    bot.stop_polling()      #to ensure a single instance
    time.sleep(3)
  except KeyboardInterrupt: #ctrl+c stops program
    err='Program stopped by the user...'
  except Exception:
    if str(sys.esc_info()[0])=="<class 'requests
                              .exceptions.ConnectionError'>":
      err=err+'Edimax error...'
    else:
      err=err+'other exception'
  except IOError:
    err=err+'input/output error'
  except TeleBot:
    err=err+'Telebot error'
  except:
    err=traceback.format_exc()
  finally:
    if err!='' and err!='None\n':
      logging.exception('\r\n'+time.strftime("%d-%m-%y ")
                    +time.strftime("%X ")+'\r\n'+'-'*40+'\n'+err)
    bot.stop_polling()      #to avoid polling errors
    time.sleep(10)
    telegram_polling()      #start again
```

```
#------------------------------------------------------------------------
# MAIN BODY OF BOOTPOLLING() PROGRAM
#------------------------------------------------------------------------
if __name__ == '__main__':
    os.system('clear')
    star_actions()
    write()
    print (colour.RED+'Running Bot...'+colour.ENDC)
    telegram_polling()
```

*P_screen.py

```python
# -*- coding: utf-8 -*- #special characters management
#------------------------------------------------------------------
# MODULE: P_PANTALLA.PY button interface, home automation control
#         Running on Raspberry_screen
# INPUTS:  buttons in tactile screen to get actions
# OUTPUTS: p_actuators.txt in Raspberry_home automation
#------------------------------------------------------------------
from Tkinter import *        #button management
import time
import os
import logging               #error handling
logging.basicConfig(filename='/home/pi/home_auto/p_pantalla.log'
                                        ,level=logging.ERROR)
from pygame import mixer  #sound play
sound='/home/pi/home_auto/conga.wav'
os.system('setterm -cursor off') #hide Terminal cursor
os.system("xte 'mousemove 0 0'") #cursor out screen
ven=Tk()
delay=15                             #Chromium needs >10s to start
font=tkFont.Font(family='Helvetic',size=20,) #in lines
ven.geometry('800x600+100+0') #wide, tall & rights offset
ven.resizable(width=False, height=False) #avoid screen changes
ven.config(cursor="none") #avoid cursor display with buttons
ven.config(background='cyan') #background colour

#Actions exchange files
file= '/home/pi/DISCOS/home_auto/p_actuators.txt'
file2='/home/pi/DISCOS/home_auto/p_sensors.txt'

#Main window title
ven.title('Home Automation Control')

#Background colours
red  ='#F50743'
green='#38EB5C'

#Buttons size
width_short   =300 #small buttons
height_short  =65  #small buttons
width_large   =620 #big buttons
height_large  =100 #big buttons
left          =60  #position x for left buttons
right         =460 #position x for right buttons
height        =35  #position height buttons separation
offset        =30  #up or down all buttons
type_cur      ='none' #cursor type over button
```

```
#------------------------------------------------------------
# MODULE BEEP(): beep sound by analog output
# INPUTS:   file [*].wav in /home/pi/home_auto/
# OUTPUTS: audio by analog jack output
#------------------------------------------------------------
def beep():
  mixer.init()
  sounds=mixer.Sound(sound)
  sounds.play()


#------------------------------------------------------------
# MODULE START_ACTIONS(): starts actions list
# INPUTS:   actions[]
# OUTPUTS: actions[] filled with initial state NO
#------------------------------------------------------------
def start_actions():
  global actions
  actions=[]
  actions.append('Switched off lights: NO\n')
...
  actions.append('Switched off living room sofa: NO\n')


#------------------------------------------------------------
# MODULE WRITE(): starts p_actuators with actions[]
# INPUTS:   actions[] & p_actuators.txt
# OUTPUTS: p_actuators.txt with con actions
#------------------------------------------------------------
def write():
  global file,actions
  inter_actuators=open(file,'w')
  for i in actions:
    inter_actuators.write(i)
  inter_actuators.close()
  start_actions()
  inter_sensors=open(file2,'r')
  a=[]
  while True:
    x=inter_sensors.readline()
    if x!='':
      a.append(x[:len(x)-1])
    else:
      break
  inter_sensors.close()
  a[16]='Origin:      SCREEN'
  inter_sensors=open(file2,'w')
  for x in a:
    inter_sensors.write(x+'\n')
  inter_sensors.close()


#------------------------------------------------------------
# MODULE BLOCK(): blocks/unlocks buttons use
# INPUTS:   locked=True/False variable
# OUTPUTS: runs ok() or nook() & updates locked like a flip-flop
#------------------------------------------------------------
def block():
```

366

```
    global locked
    if locked:
      ok()
      locked=False
    else:
      nook()
      locked=True

#----------------------------------------------------------------
# MODULE OK(): shows ok button
# INPUTS:   button call
# OUTPUTS: shows ok button, sound & pause
#----------------------------------------------------------------
def ok():
    global button_ok
    button_ok=Button(ven,borderwidth=5,background=green)
    button_ok.pack()
    button_ok.place(x=left+width_short+17,y=height*7+offset+10
                      ,width=height_short,height=height_short*4)
    image0=PhotoImage(file='/home/pi/home_auto/photos/ok.gif')
    button_ok.config(image=image0)
    beep()
    time.sleep(.3)

#----------------------------------------------------------------
# MODULE NOOK(): shows nook button
# INPUTS:   button call
# OUTPUTS: shows nook button, sound & pause
#----------------------------------------------------------------
def nook():
    global button_nook
    button_nook=Button(ven,borderwidth=5,background=red)
    button_nook.pack()
    button_nook.place(x=left+width_short+17,y=height*7+offset+10
                      ,width=height_short,height=height_short*4)
    image0=PhotoImage(file='/home/pi/home_auto/photos/nook.gif')
    button_nook.config(image=image0)
    beep()
    time.sleep(.3)

#----------------------------------------------------------------
# MODULE OPEN(): shows open button
# INPUTS:   button call
# OUTPUTS: shows open button & updates actions[]
#----------------------------------------------------------------
def open():
    actions[6]='Open all window blinds: YES\n'
    write()
    ok()

#----------------------------------------------------------------
# MODULE CLOSE(): shows close button
# INPUTS:   button call
# OUTPUTS: shows close button & updates actions[]
#----------------------------------------------------------------
```

```
def close():
  actions[4]='Close all window blinds: YES\n'
  write()
  nook()

#-----------------------------------------------------------------
# MODULE OFF(): shows off button
# INPUTS:  button call
# OUTPUTS: shows off button & updates actions[]
#-----------------------------------------------------------------
def off():
  actions[0]='Switch off lights: YES\n'
  write()
  ok()

#-----------------------------------------------------------------
# MODULE AMBIENT(): shows ambient button
#-----------------------------------------------------------------
# MODULE HOLIDAYS_ON/OFF(): shows holidays_on/off button
#-----------------------------------------------------------------
# MODULE GAS_ON/OFF(): shows gas_on/off button
#-----------------------------------------------------------------
# MODULE WATER_ON/OFF(): shows water_on/off button
#-----------------------------------------------------------------
# MODULE RESET_ROUTER/NAS(): shows reset_router/nas button
#-----------------------------------------------------------------

#-----------------------------------------------------------------
# MODULE EXIT(): show exit button
# INPUTS:  button call
# OUTPUTS: show exit button & updates actions[]
#-----------------------------------------------------------------
def exit():
  ven.quit()

#-----------------------------------------------------------------
# Button definition: 2 instructions with location & content, image
# compound position, relief or overrelief, achor text position,
# run command, activebackground colour, left and upper offset
#-----------------------------------------------------------------
button_ok_ini=Label(ven,compound=BOTTOM,relief="raised"
                                           ,borderwidth=5)
button_ok_ini.pack()
button_ok_ini.place(x=left+width_short+17,y=height*7+offset+10
                      ,width=height_short,height=height_short*4)

image0=PhotoImage(file='/home/pi/home_auto/photos/ok.gif')
button_ok_ini.config(image=image0)

#-----------------------------------------------------------------
# OPEN BUTTON
#-----------------------------------------------------------------
button_open=Button(ven,text='Open
Blinds',anchor='w',compound=LEFT,font=font,relief="raised"
                      ,overrelief='sunken',borderwidth=5,command=open
```

```
                                    ,activebackground=green,cursor=type_cur)
button_open.pack()
button_open.place(x=left,y=height+offset,width=width_short
                                        ,height=height_short)

image1=PhotoImage(file='/home/pi/home_auto/photos/open blinds.gif')
button_open.config(image=image1)

#---------------------------------------------------------------
# CLOSE BUTTON
#---------------------------------------------------------------
button_close=Button(ven,text='Close blinds',anchor='w'
        ,compound=LEFT,font=font,relief="raised",overrelief='sunken'
                ,borderwidth=5,command=close,activebackground=red
                                        ,cursor=type_cur)

button_close.pack()
button_close.place(x=right,y=height+offset,width=width_short
                                        ,height=height_short)

image2=PhotoImage(file='/home/pi/home_auto/photos
                                        /close blinds.gif')
button_close.config(image=image2)

#---------------------------------------------------------------
# OFF BUTTON
#---------------------------------------------------------------
button_off=Button(ven,text='Switch off All
Lights',anchor='c',compound=LEFT,font=font,relief="raised",
                    overrelief='sunken',borderwidth=5,command=off
                        ,activebackground=green,cursor=type_cur)

button_off.pack()
button_off.place(x=left+40,y=height*3+offset,width=ancho_largo,heig
ht=height_short)
I
mage3=PhotoImage(file='/home/pi/home_auto/photos/off all.gif')
button_off.config(image=image3)

#---------------------------------------------------------------
# AMBIENT BUTTON
#---------------------------------------------------------------
button_ambient=Button(ven,text='Movie Ambient',anchor='c'
        ,compound=LEFT,font=font,relief="raised",overrelief='sunken'
                ,borderwidth=5,command=ambient,activebackground=green
                                        ,cursor=type_cur)

button_ambient.pack()
button_ambient.place(x=left+40,y=height*5+offset,width=ancho_largo
                                        ,height=height_short)

image4=PhotoImage(file='/home/pi/home_auto/photos
                                        /movie ambient.gif')
button_ambient.config(image=image4)
```

```
#------------------------------------------------------------------
# HOLIDAYS BUTTON
#------------------------------------------------------------------
button_holidays_on/off=Button(ven,text='Holidays ON/OFF',anchor='w'
        ,compound=LEFT,font=font,relief="raised",overrelief='sunken'
         ,borderwidth=5,command=holidays_on/off,activebackground=red
                                              ,cursor=type_cur)

button_holidays_on/off.pack()
button_holidays_on/off.place(x=left,y=height*7+offset
                         ,width=width_short,height=height_short)
I
mage5=PhotoImage(file='/home/pi/home auto/photos/holidays
                                              on/off.gif')

button_holidays_on/off.config(image=image5)

#------------------------------------------------------------------
#GAS ON/OFF BUTTONS
#------------------------------------------------------------------
button_gas_on/off=Button(ven,text='Gas ON/OFF',anchor='w'
        ,compound=LEFT,font=font,relief="raised",overrelief='sunken'
           ,borderwidth=5,command=gas_on/off,activebackground=green
                                              ,cursor=type_cur)

button_gas_on/off.pack()
button_gas_on/off.place(x=left,y=height*9+offset,width=width_short
                                         ,height=height_short)

image7=PhotoImage(file='/home/pi/home_auto/photos/gas on/off.gif')
button_gas_on/off.config(image=image7)

#------------------------------------------------------------------
# WATER ON/OFF BUTTONS
#------------------------------------------------------------------
button_water_on/off=Button(ven,text='Water ON/OFF',anchor='w'
        ,compound=LEFT,font=font,relief="raised",overrelief='sunken'
          ,borderwidth=5,command=water_on/off,activebackground=green
                                              ,cursor=type_cur)

button_water_on/off.pack()
button_water_on/off.place(x=left,y=height*11+offset
                         ,width=width_short,height=height_short)

image9=PhotoImage(file='/home/pi/home_auto/photos
                                      /water on/off.gif')
button_water_on/off.config(image=image9)

#------------------------------------------------------------------
# RESET ROUTER/NAS BUTTONS
#------------------------------------------------------------------
button_reset_router/nas=Button(ven,text='Router/NAS Reset'
              ,anchor='w',compound=LEFT,font=font,relief="raised"
        ,overrelief='sunken',borderwidth=5,command=reset_router/nas
                       ,activebackground=green,cursor=type_cur)
```

```
button_reset_router/nas.pack()
button_reset_router/nas.place(x=left,y=height*13+offset
                              ,width=width_short,height=height_short)

image11=PhotoImage(file='/home/pi/home_auto/photos
                                    /reset router/nas.gif')
button_reset_router.config(image=image11)

#----------------------------------------------------------------
# MAIN BODY OF THE PROGRAM
#----------------------------------------------------------------
try:
    start_actions()
    lock=True                #if it can acts control
    print 'Waiting '+str(delay)+' seconds to Chrome starts'
    time.sleep(delay)
    mainloop()               #to star buttons actions

except Exception:
    logging.exception('\n'+time.strftime("%d-%m-%y ")
                            +time.strftime("%X ")+'\n'+'-'*40+'\n')

    os.system('python /home/pi/domotica/p_pantalla.py')
```

*P_logfile.py

```python
# -*- coding: utf-8 -*-
#-------------------------------------------------------------
# MODULE: P_LOGFILE.PY Displays the last line in execution of the
# home automation program located in p_logfile.txt
# INPUTS:  p_logfile.txt
# OUTPUTS: display of the last line in execution
#-------------------------------------------------------------
import time,os
log='/home/pi/home_auto/p_logfile.txt'
old_line=''
try:   #if p_logfile.txt does not exist, it is created
  fic=open(log,'r')
except Exception:
  os.system('sudo cp /home/pi/home_auto/p_logfile.ok
                              /home/pi/home_auto/p_logfile.txt')

# TEXT COLOUR
class colour:
  RED       = '\033[91m'
  BLUE      = '\033[94m'
  GREEN     = '\033[32m'
  YELLOW    = '\033[33m'
  PURPLE    = '\033[35m'
  CYAN      = '\033[36m'
  SIN       = '\033[0m'    #without effect
  BOLD      = '\033[1m'
  UNDERLINE = '\033[4m'
  CURSIVA   = '\033[3m'

while True:
  time.sleep(.05)                    #reduces CPU consumption <10%
  fic=open(log,'r')
  lines=fic.readlines()
  fic.close()
  last_line=lines[len(lines)-1]      #without character \n
  if last_line<>old_line:
    date =last_line[:19]             #main fields
    topic=last_line[19:80]
    origin=last_line[80:len(last_line)-1]
    print
colour.RED+date+colour.GREEN+topic+colour.BLUE+colour.CYAN+origin
                                               +colour.SIN

    old_line=last_line
```

☺☺☺

31.–SCHEMES

In this section several simulations made with **iCircuit*** are attached to test the designs made before creating the project prototype.In these schemes it can see a project module, adapted to the simulation and temporal evolution of some critical variables (voltage, current, frequency, etc.) to ensure that the circuit works as expected.

With this useful application it can simulate virtually any circuit, both analog and digital and adjust the parameters of the components: resistors, capacitors, transistors, diodes, etc. and several electrical variables: voltages, frequencies, etc., to obtain the best performance and reduce the error proof binomial.

The circuits that have been simulated are the following:

1. General 220v interface.

2. Power alarm interface.

3. Buzzer and CK circuit.

4. Garage gate circuit.

5. Watchdog circuit.

6. Logic levels converter.

*General 220v
Interface

This scheme represents the interface between 220v power supply and **Raspberry*_home automation** system with optical coupler.

The **iCircuit*** application does not have optical couplers, here it is simulated with a relay that performs a similar function.

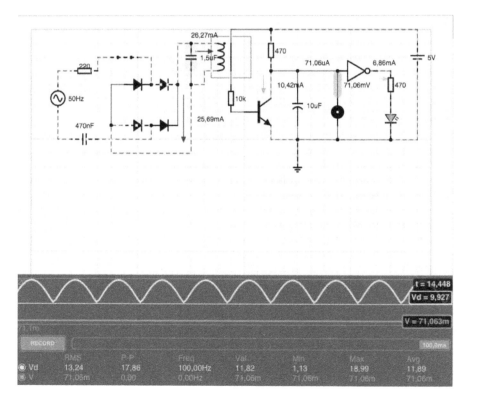

*Power Alarm Interface

As a detail of the 220v power supply interface, here we can see the specific interface for **POWER alarm** (the others interfaces for alarms are similar). When the power supply fails, the signal at the output of the optical coupler is deactivated (represented here with a relay) and this activates the input signal of the **Raspberry*_home automation** pin that detects the lack of power supply, generating the corresponding alarm by an e-mail (there is a small UPS that feeds the system for such an operation).

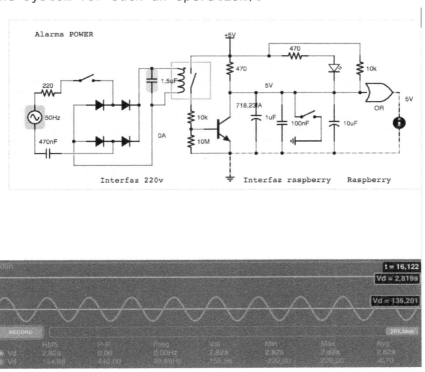

*Buzz an CK
Circuit

In this simple circuit it simulates the parameters of the resistances and frequencies necessary for the **Watchdog** and **CK** signal to generate a useful acoustic signal that indicates the correct operation of the **p_global.py** module that runs on the **Raspberry*_home automation** and resets and starts the system if the program, for various reasons, does not run properly.

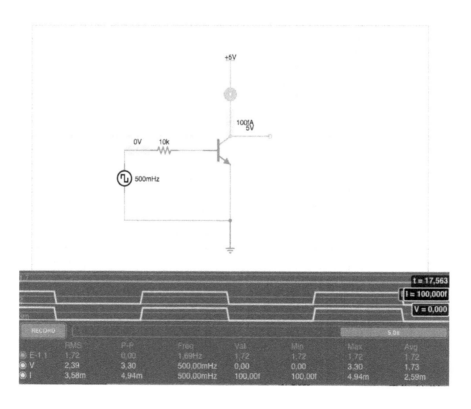

*Doorbell
Circuit

In the following circuit we can see the interface with the signal generator of the house bell.

When the bell is pressed, the integrated circuit **NE555***, configured in monostable mode, starts a square pulse that attacks the corresponding pin of the **Raspberry*_home automation,** generating the corresponding alarm that is sent by e-mail.

The function of the monostable is to filter the high frequency of the signal generated by the bell, obtaining a pulse of 2 seconds controlled by a pair: resistance vs capacitor of 8k2Ω and 270uF respectively.

With this filtering it prevents the bell signal from jumping constantly generating dummy alarms, in this way it will jump every time someone presses the doorbell of the house door in a time greater than those 2 seconds.

It is convenient to make the monostable retriggerable, for that a **PNP 8550*** transistor is connected to the input.

The pulse, of +18v generated by the bell, activates, by falling edge, the monostable and this creates the pulse of 2 seconds and +5v.

This pulse is converted to +3.3v by the logic level converter **SODIAL*** or equivalent, which can be treated by a **GPIO*** pin of the **Raspberry*_home automation** and processed by the **Python*** module **p_global.py**.

On the other hand, when the signal generated at the doorbell is detected, a *.mp3 file that simulates the barking of a **guard dog,** that is used as an additional element to the security of the house, is automatically sent to **Google Home***.

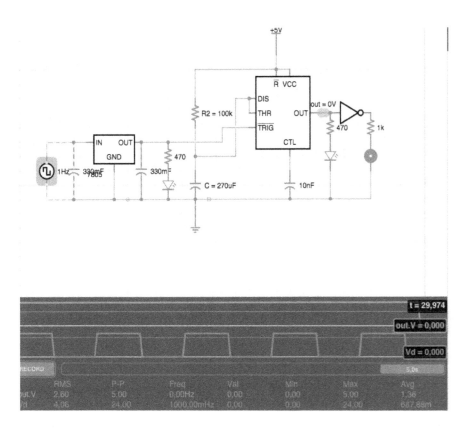

*Watchdog Circuit

Here we see the **Watchdog** circuit that protects t h e **Raspberry*_home automation** that **p_global.py** leaving the program execution or taking actions not contemplated.

For this, there are two **NE555*** timer circuits that, when they do not detect the appropriate **CK** signal (generates by software), generate the timing pulses necessary to attack a relay that acts on the reset of this **Raspberry***.

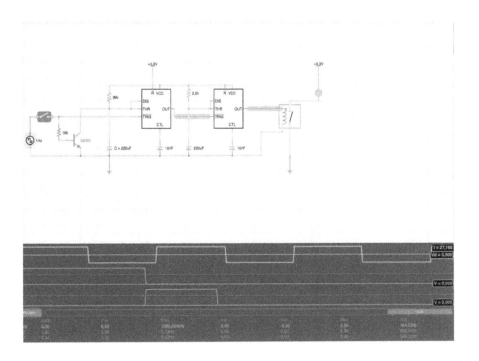

*Logic Levels Converter

Here the logic level converter is tested, equivalent to the **SODIAL***, which allows adapting signals of levels 0/+5v to inputs and outputs of the **Raspberry*_home automation** operating at 0/+3.3v. This converter is very important to avoid damaging **Raspberry***.

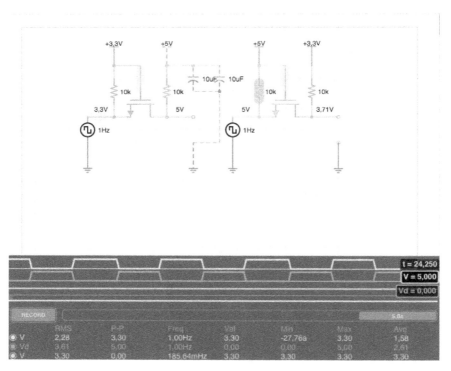

*Other Schemes

In this section are attached schemes and diagrams with the general operation of the system and that provide a clear idea of its main elements, both in the hardware and software. All of them can be seen in detail in my blog:

gregochenlo.blogspot.com

The schemes described are:

- Home Automation with **Raspberry***, **Google*** and **Python***, taken from my English presentation of this book.
- General elements.
- Hardware elements.
- Software elements.
- **eWelink*** switches.
- **KNX*** vs **Raspberry*** diagram.
- Global home automation circuit.

In each of the schemes a brief description is attached that allows to capture a general idea of the project.

*Home Automation with Raspberry, Google & Python: "A useful and fun home automation project"
(Book Presentation)

The goal of this project is to achieve optimal communication between sensors (the devices from which the information flows to the system) and actuators (vice-versa), sensors like: light switches, water detectors, smoke detectors, devices that measure temperature, humidity, air toxicity, garage gate status, doorbell detectors, thermostat, and so on) and actuators are things like: lights, window blinds, gas & water valves, infrared controls, email, etc.)

*At the heart of this project is a **Raspberry*** CPU with the **Linux*** operating system and **Python*** software, where both of them working together, give total control of the system.*

The system has three main channels of user-interaction:

1. ***Voice control:*** *using a **Google*** **Home Mini** speaker (**Alexa*** would also be valid).*

2. ***Message control:*** *using the personal communicator **Telegram****

3. ***A tactile screen:*** *using another **Raspberry*** CPU, running a special software, written in **Python*** language too, which offers:*

   a) Several tactile buttons on the screen to control home automation tasks.

b) A **PLEX*** server to play home multimedia (movies, pictures, series, etc.) from a hard disk or a laptop, to the TV of the home, with a lot of additional information including the title, year, director, cast, contents, genre and so on.

This server can be accessed outside the home, for example it can even watches movies from the home multimedia system when it is at the beach.

c) Pictures frame to see, for example, pictures of the family album from the laptop.

The system is based on **IFTTT*** (if this then that) technology which permits an easy integration between sensors and actuators of many brands.

In the main **Raspberry*** is running another **Python*** module is running at the same time to provide the user with a list of main tasks, alarms and a daily update. Both of them are sending this information, via **Gmail***, to the main user of the home automation control.

Additionally, this **Raspberry*** has an exclusive interface to adapt the different electric signals of the sensors and the actuators at the heart of the system.

Moreover all the system can be supervised, check and modified in remote mode, using **VNC*** free software, from a laptop or a mobile.

This home automation system offers three kinds of services to the user, first of all, via Voice Control:

1. **Outbound/Inbound voice messages,** for example:

If the user says '**OK Google***.... good morning', the system: replies "good morning John", for example, it also provides:

383

*A summary of the weather forecast of the day.
*A summary of the main news (which the user can previously programme the news channel source).
*A summary of main user's daily schedule.
*An approximate time of a journey (the user can previously insert Point A to Point B trip).
*Open specific window blinds (user can choose them).
*Turn off specific lights.
*Turn on the TV, and the audio amplifier, and put on a specific channel.

To sum up, if the user says 'OK **Google***.... I want to watch Vikings* series at TV', the system can accordingly:

*Close the window blinds of the living room to 50%.
*Switch on the preselected soft lighting.
*Switch on the TV.
*Switch on the audio amplifier and adjust to the preselected volume.
*Via **Chromecast***, open the **Netflix*** account.
Starts the Vikings series where you previously ended.

2. **Automatic tasks,** for example:

By day time, the system can open a few window blinds and vice-versa, by night time: close the blinds.

Additionally, if the temperature of the living room goes above than 26°C (78,8°F), the system can automatically close a set of blinds.

If you are on holiday, the system can open and close a set of blinds and switch on and off another set of lights to simulate that people are at home. If fire alarm is activated, the system can switch off the gas valve.

In the same way, if water alarm is

384

activated, the system can switch off the water valve. With these tasks, **Google Home*** announces voice messages.

3. **Geolocation tasks,** for example:

The system has a **Tadoº*** intelligent thermostat, which controls the heater and, via the user's mobile, it will know if anyone is at home.

On the other hand, if nobody is at home, **IFTTT*** and **Raspberry*** acts and switch off the lights, the tactile screen, the TV, down the thermostat temperature, etc.

This explanation and more are available in my book (paper or ebook) "Home Automation with Raspberry, Google & Python": "An useful and fun home automation project" (English or Spanish versions) at Amazon.

Thanks so much.

*Scheme: General

In the general scheme of this home automation project described in the present book "Home automation with **Raspberry***, **Google*** and **Python***: "An useful and fun home automation project", basically the following areas can be observed:

1. Inputs/outputs to the system with voice commands or messages (**Google Home***), messages (with the **Telegram*** Bot) or directly with the touch screen connected by HDMI and USB to a **Raspberry***.
2. Sensors: flood, smoke, temperature, humidity, air toxicity, garage status, twilight sensor, thermostat, sensor of presence switches, buttons, garage gate status, doorbell, power failure, connectivity, etc.
3. Actuators: lights & window blinds relays, water & gas valves, thermostat, buzzer, LED, WIFI bulbs, switches & plugs, etc.
4. Additional functions of the touch screen: input of home automation commands using buttons created with **Tkinter*** in **Python***, **PLEX*** multi-media server and photo frame.
5. Interface with traditional devices with infrared controls: TV, decoder, audio amplifier, ambient colour lights, **Apple*** TV, etc.
6. Acting with the **IFTTT*** integrator on the switches: lights, entertainment systems, home appliances, etc.
7. **Raspberry*** interface with **KNX*** to control **KNX*** devices: switches, lamps, window blinds relays, valves, LCD display, presence sensors, etc.
8. Support in **IFTTT*** for automatic actions and simple device integration.
9. Support over **NO-IP*** for access from outside when the IP of the main Router changes.
10. Remote system management from **VNC***

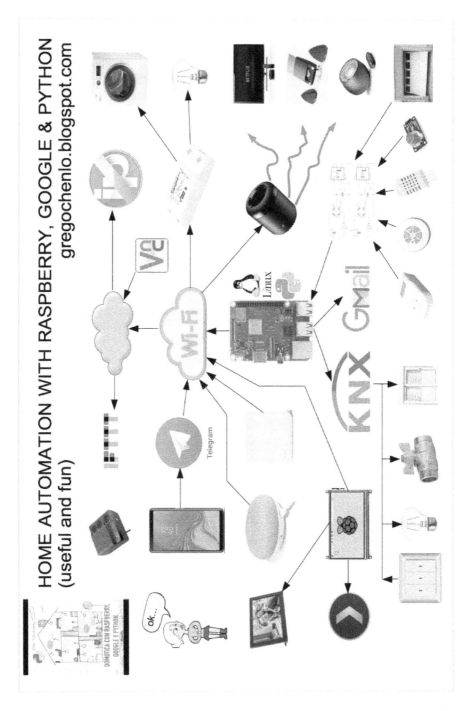

*Scheme: Hardware

In the Hardware scheme of the home automation project described in this book, basically the following areas can be observed:

1. Internet connection, in this case with optical fiber (it could be another type of connection like **DSL***, cable, **3G/4G***, etc.) through an **ONT*** and a specific fiber communications Router.

2. The structure of the home network: Main Router, Switches, other Routers configured in Bridge mode and WIFI extender (not essential), which extend the coverage of the WIFI signal from the home to the different floors and rooms.

3. **Raspberry*** main with **KNX*** bus interface, for actuator control and sensor status.

4. Connection of various devices to the corresponding WIFI, both 2.4GHz and 5GHz. Highlights the **Google Home*** Mini that allows bidirectional *.mp3 sounds (bark of the guard dog simulation, etc.) & voice command management of the entire system.

5. Connection of the Bridge, Thermostat and **Tadoº*** Extension Kit for intelligent heating control and with extra user geolocation function for intelligent management of other devices (absence or presence of any household component).

6. WIFI to infrared converter interface for operation with devices with traditional remote control: TV, IR lamps, air conditioning, audio amplifiers, decoders, **Apple*** TV, etc.

7. Secondary **Raspberry*** with the 3 functions described in the general scheme: touch screen control for home automation buttons, multimedia server management with **PLEX***, a photo frame simulator and automatic transition algorithm between these three functions.

8. NAS and HD extension as a multimedia centre, controlled by **PLEX*** from the secondary **Raspberry*** and with **DLNA*** from home TV.

9. WIFI switches to restart critical devices: secondary **Raspberry*** (because it is embedded in the wall), Bridge **Tadoº***, main **Raspberry*** (to perform a remote reset), some general switches and ambient lamps (Christmas Tree, movie scene mode, little home appliances, laundry dehumidifier...), etc.

10. UPS to power, briefly, the **Raspberry***_**home automation** and the structure of the main network, to allow the orderly closure of the processes of this **Raspberry*** and sending alarms by **Gmail***.

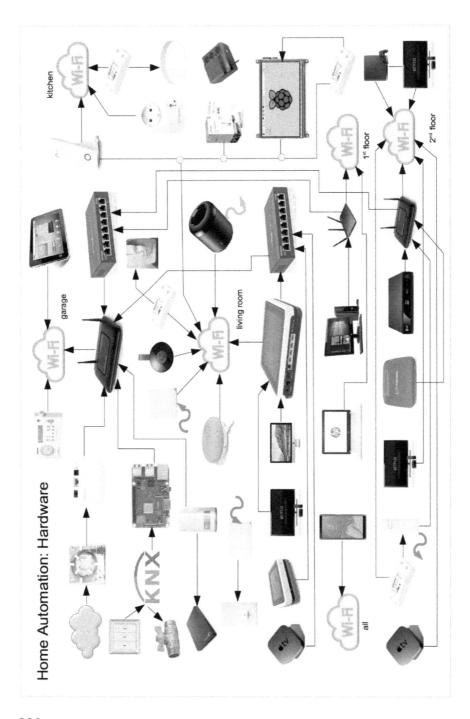

Home Automation: Hardware

*Scheme: Software

In the software scheme of the home automation project described in this book, it can basically observes the following areas:

1. The system uses three operating systems: **Linux*** on **Raspberry*** (**Raspbian***), various APP on mobile systems, both **Android*** and **iOS*** and applications on **PC*** or **MAC*** with **Windows*** or **Mac OS***.

2. In **Linux*** **Raspbian*** **Stretch** is used, which is a specific and easy to get and install **Debian*** variant for **Raspberry*** very easy to use, configurable and very powerful.

3. In **Raspbian*** they are used: **VNC*** for the remote control of the whole system (from a computer, tablet or mobile), **Samba*** to share files between **Raspberry*** and computers, **Plex*** as a multimedia server over **Chrome*** and **Apache*** as a file hosting web server [*].php

4. Home automation control is based on programs written in **Python*** (mostly in version 2.7 and very few in 3.5 version) with **Tkinte**r* modules (to control the buttons), **Colorama*** (semi graphic presentation), **Dropbox*** (cloud storage of summary daily files), **Gmail*** (main alarms communication program) and **Telegram*** (personal to machine messaging program).

5. **Python*** modules manage: home automation control, **Telegram*** Bot, event viewer and access buttons on the **Tkinter*** application. In addition, **LXTerminal*** is used as a generic interface with the system.

6. On **Android*** or **iOS*** **Telegram*** (sending, receiving control messages and knowledge states) and the proprietary applications of the devices are used: **Edimax*** (heater switch and programming schedule), **eWelink*** (general switch with on/off schedule), **Tadoº*** (smart thermostat with geolocation and reporting), **ihc*** (infrared traditional devices control), **Home*** (**Google*** **Home Mini** configuration and management), **Kasa*** (WIFI bulb pairing and management) and **Tether*** (WIFI extender control), for access to various actions.

7. In **MacOs*** use: **Pycharm*** (advanced **Python*** editor and programming environment), **Eagle*** (schematic, auto routing and PCB generator), **iCircuit*** (electronic analog & digital circuit simulation), **Apple-Pi Baker*** (uSD backup and recording with the operating system, **ETS*** (interface with **KNX*** bus and device parameters and addresses management) , **Virtualbox*** (access to other operating systems), **IP Scanner*** (IP management and network monitoring), **NO-IP*** (remote access control by IP change) and **IFTTT*** (as main devices and applications integrator).

8. The scheme represents the information exchange files between both **Raspberry***.

9. Finally the **Python*** modules are listed: **p_global.py** (global home automation control), **p_telegram.py** (**Telegram*** bot manager), **p_pantalla.py** (home automation access buttons, **PLEX*** manager, photo frame simulator and automatic transition algorithm) and **p_logfile.py** (system event viewer).

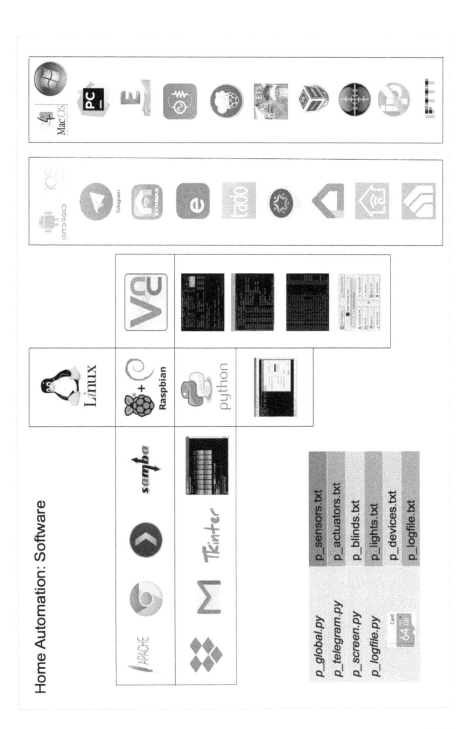

Scheme: Switches eWelink

In the detailed scheme of the connection of the **eWelink*** **Sonoff*** switches of **Itead*** (which are used as general purpose WIFI switches), of the home automation project described in this book, basically it can observes the following areas:

1. **Itead*** **Sonoff*** switches are paired with the WIFI, of the 2.4GHz type (remember that the 5Ghz connection cannot be used), corresponding and with the **eWelink*** APP of the same manufacturer that allows its control with every detail: time control, programming, routines, etc.

2. They can be used to control actuators in general up to a fairly wide load limit. For example: ambient light, kitchen light, some small home appliances, fan, small stove, dehumidifier, Christmas Tree etc.

3. They can be used as a reset control (by on/off) of certain critical devices: Display of the secondary **Raspberry***, because it is embedded in the wall and cannot access its power button, Bridge **Tadoº*** or main **Raspberry***,to remotely restart and reset them, etc.

4. Ensure that the system connected to the **Sonoff*** meets the maximum power specifications supported by the switch: 90v–250v AC and 2,200w/10A. If necessary, in the market there are other WIFI switches with greater switching power.

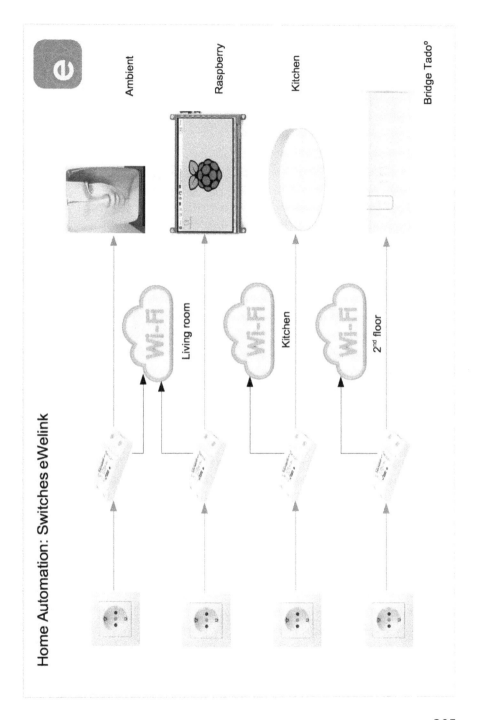

Scheme: KNX vs Raspberry*

In the detail scheme of the **KNX*** (not essential but it is advisable to know how to integrate it in our project) and **Raspberry*** connection of the home automation project described in this book, it can basically observes the following areas:

1. The **KNX*** bus is connected, in addition to the power supply, as inputs: lighting switches, binary inputs for 220v alarms, general sensors, thermostat, twilight, presence sensor switches, LCD control display, etc., and as outputs: **KNX*** switches that supply 220v to the actuators: lights, valves, window blinds, etc.

2. In turn, several sensors: smoke, fire, flood, gas, temperature, humidity, doorbell, power, connectivity, toxic air, watchdog, etc., are connected to a specific interface, which adapts the signals of each of these elements (with various voltages and intensities), to the **GPIO*** of the **Raspberry*** (which only supports +3.3v signals).

3. The **Raspberry*** home automation control is connected to the **KNX*** bus with the corresponding adapter type **PEI-10***, which allows the adaptation of levels between the **KNX*** and the **UART***

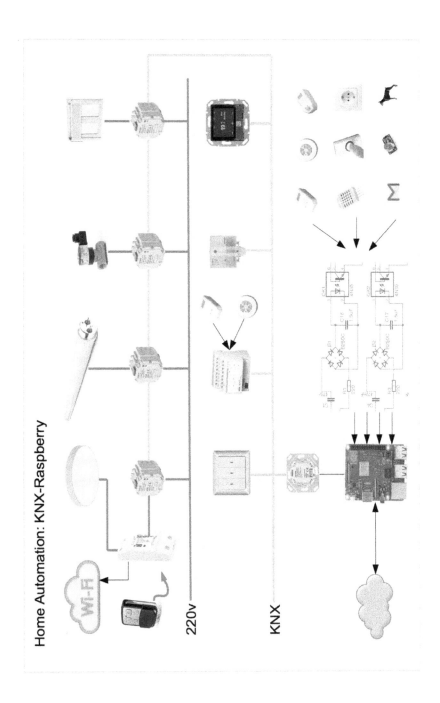

Scheme: Complete Circuit

The entire circuit of the home automation interface that includes the following sub circuits and interfaces and which we have seen in detail in the first chapters of the book is contemplated in the complete circuit scheme (generated with **Eagle*** and tested with **iCircuit***):

- 220v interface with alarms: smoke, flood, gas, power, etc.
- Garage gate status sensor circuit.
- Interface with the doorbell.
- Reset buttons (short and total Reset) and alarms simulation.
- Interface with the temperature & humidity sensor.
- Interface with the air quality sensor.
- Buzzer and CK control circuit.
- Drivers for status display LED.
- Relays module, control circuit, drivers and input stabilisers.
- Module of adaptation of logical levels and electrical isolation of systems.
- Watchdog safety circuit.
- Reset circuit of the **Raspberry***.
- Interface with RS232 (optional).
- Dual power supply.

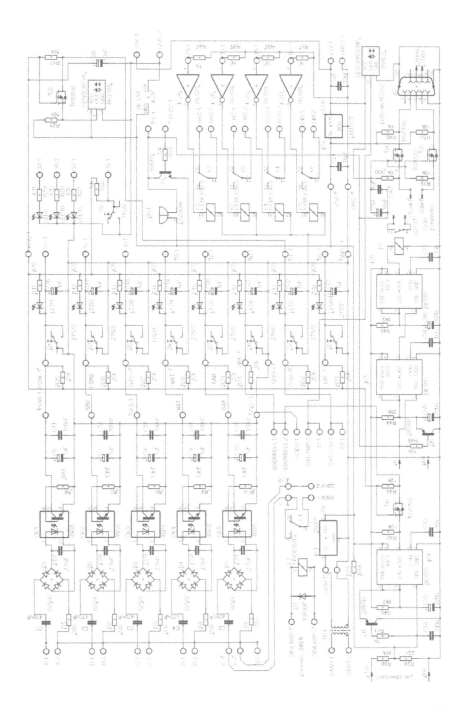

32.—MINIMUM AND
SCALED SOLUTIONS

I n this section are attached minimum and scaled proposals schemes (from simpler to more complex), without the need to implement all the sensors, actuators, devices and software described in this book.

This allows each reader to better adapt the content of this book to the needs of home automation.

As it commented at the beginning of it, this book includes a very global proposal for a home automation control of a concrete and large house, with many communication needs, various devices, various home automation standards, etc., but to start in this exciting world of Home Automation, it can starts with some simpler solutions, which are proposed below and in which it can takes advantage of what is described in the complete solution.

The possibilities are virtually endless:

*OPTION 1:
The Minimum Necessary

The minimum would be a sensor and an actuator, as a sensor it proposes the **Google Home*** **Mini** (or other speaker with an artificial intelligence system) itself that directly captures the user's orders and executes them on the actuators and also includes the control system that can be managed by voice and with the APP **Home***.

An interesting actuator can be a **Sonoff*** basic switch, to which it can connects a lamp or a home appliance, but if it wants to make it even easier, it can replaces this switch with a WIFI lamp, for example the **TP-Link***, which it can turns off, on or, change its brightness or colour directly with the **Google Home*** **Mini.**

With the proprietary APP of the switch or **TP-Link*** lamp (or other brand) it can even acts with these devices when it is away from home.

Google Home* incorporates routines that can be configured to perform several actions with just one voice command: "good morning ...", "good night ...", "I'm leaving ....", "already I'm at home ... ", etc.

Logically it will not have supervision by **VNC*** (remote control) or automatic actions, except those that **IFTTT*** can provide depending on the brand of the sensors and actuators.

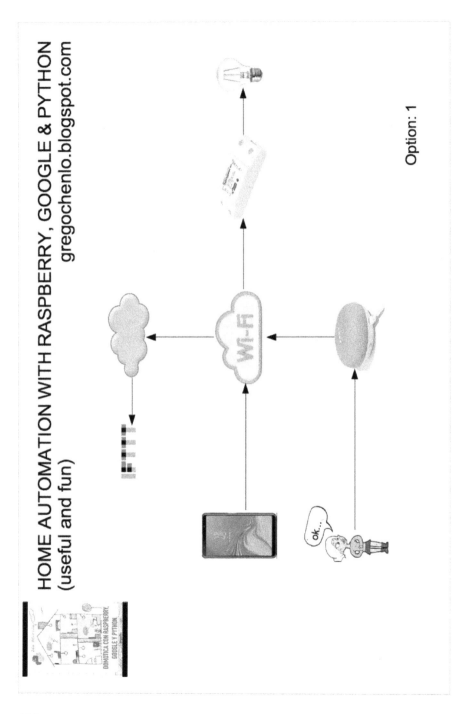

*OPTION 2:
With Some Control

This solution is like the previous one but it has included some more element.

Specifically, it is proposed to ensure that the brand of the sensors, but above all that the actuators (lamps or WIFI switches) support the management by **IFTTT*** to include certain routines.

A **Google Chromecast*** is added that allows it to act with multimedia on the TV from **Google Home***, for example: it can indicates by voice that photos from **Google Photos*** of some year, of some person, of an album, of some subject, etc. It can asks to play **Spotify*** songs on TV or watch chapters of a series on **Netflix*** etc.

With this device it can also requests by voice to turn on or off the TV, and even includes in a routine of **Google Home*** or **IFTTT*** several of the previous actions.

It will not has supervision with **VNC*** or many **IFTTT*** options or reporting by **Gmail***, but this option has many possibilities and is quite cheap.

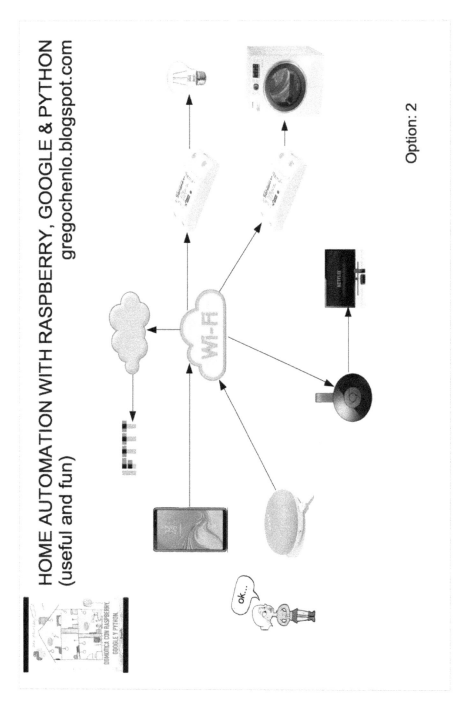

*OPTION 2a:
With More Control

This solution is the same as the previous one but it includes an additional element that is very interesting and highly recommended: a **Tadoº*** smart thermostat (it could be another, such as the **Google Nest***, **Netatmo***, **Honeywell Home***,etc.), which not only provides temperature and humidity sensor functions, it also provides geolocation of home users (through its mobile APP) and system energy reporting.

With the user geolocation function, the system knows when someone is at home or close to it (in an area previously defined by the user) and therefore can perform functions that drastically affect energy savings, activation of certain functions, etc. For example:

- I f **Tadoº*** "away" mode is activated, devices connected to **Sonoff*** (lights, home appliances, etc.), TV with **Chromecast***, etc. are turned off. If the temperature or humidity exceeds a certain level, additional home automation orders are generated.
- Add the temperature and humidity control with assignment (manual, automatic, face-to-face or remote), by hourly sections of the setpoint temperature.
- Daily graphs of monitoring of temperature, humidity, on and off of the heater, detection of window opening, monthly energy saving report (geolocation, adaptation to the meteorology of the place, automatic or manual control), etc. And all this perfectly integrated by **IFTTT*** with the rest of sensors and actuators.

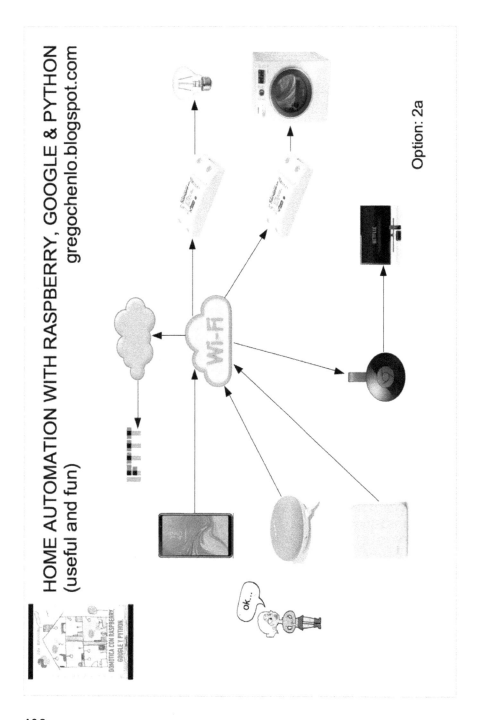

*OPTION 3:
Advanced Option

Here the sensors are: the basic voice with **Google Home***, for capturing home automation commands, and a **DHT22*** sensor as a temperature and humidity sensor, which can be located in any room (laundry, to know if the clothes are already dry, bedroom if it is necessary to raise or lower window blinds, next to the NAS, etc.) The **Tadoº*** thermostat could also be added.

As actuators we have: two **Sonoff*** basic switch for controlling lights and home appliances (dehumidifier, fan, air conditioner, etc.) and a **Google Chromecast*** to manage multimedia playback on TV.

Additionally it will has a hard disk or NAS as a storage centre for home multimedia files. **Chromecast*** is optional, multimedia can be controlled by **DLNA*** directly from home TV (but with less features).

The control systems are two: the **Google Home*** **Mini**, which controls the system by voice and its own **Home*** APP and additionally a **Raspberry***, which with a brief **Python*** script manages the entire system, collects temperature and humidity data, manages multimedia via **PLEX*** and reports alarms and important information, via **Gmail*** and voice via **Google Home***.

The entire system is directly integrated by the **Google Home*** proprietary software, **IFTTT*** applets and global monitoring can be performed with **VNC***, accessible from any Internet connection (mobile, tablet, computer, etc.).

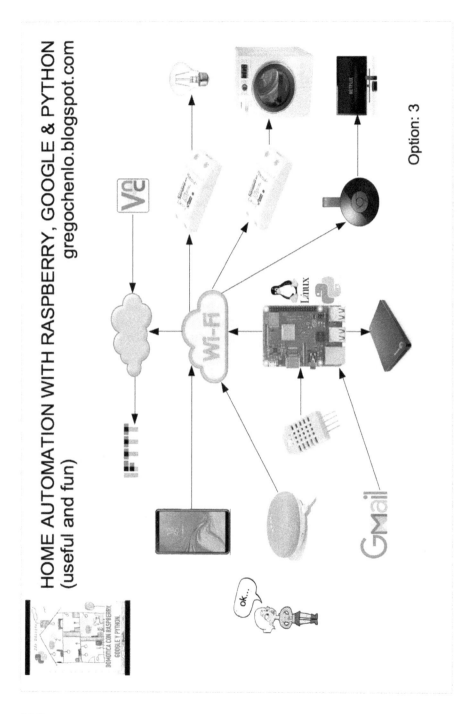

33.-WEB BIBLIOGRAPHY

A series of web pages that have helped to build this project are summarised below. In them there is the solution to 100% of the problems sought, perhaps the learning process is based precisely on the path of information search, rather than on the information itself, but in them there is a lot of useful information and a lot of work for part of many enthusiasts of Home Automation, Software, Hardware, etc., to which I thank again their gesture of sharing with everyone, via the Internet, their experiences, their ideas and their efforts.

Finally, indicate that the possible rights that correspond to these websites are reaffirmed and any responsibility, guarantee, etc., as a consequence of the variation or disappearance of these sources of information is declined.

Raspberry

https://www.raspberrypi.org/
https://www.berryterminal.com/doku.php/berryboot
https://azure-samples.github.io/raspberry-pi-web-
simulator/
http://www.kami.es/2016/ejecutar-script-al-inicio-
raspberry-pi/
https://www.cnet.com/how-to/how-to-setup-bluetooth-on-
a-raspberry-pi-3/
https://raspberryparatorpes.net/sistemas-
operativos/nuevo-raspbian-stretch/
https://www.deacosta.com/instrucciones-para-
actualizar-raspbian-8-jessie-raspbian-9-stretch-en-
raspberry-pi/
https://raspberrypi.stackexchange.com/questions/10209/
how-to-disable-mouse-cursor-on-lxde
https://raspberrypi.stackexchange.com/questions/30056/
raspberry-pi-raspbian-multiple-desktops

Linux

http://www.raspbian.org
http://www.linux.org
http://ekiketa.es/crear-un-script-ejecutable-por-el-
shell-en-linux/
https://wiki.lxde.org/en/Talk:LXTerminal
https://www.luisllamas.es/tutoriales-de-raspberry-pi-
linux/
https://www.raspberrypi.org/blog/another-update-
raspbian/
https://www.raspberrypi.org/forums/viewtopic.php?
t=99646

*Hardware

https://www.cetronic.es
https://www.mouser.es/
https://www.kubii.fr/
https://mydevices.com/
http://kookye.com/category/tutorials/rapsberry-pi-projects/
http://www.electronicaestudio.com/
https://computers.tutsplus.com/articles/creating-a-speaker-for-your-raspberry-pi-using-a-piezo-element--mac-59336
https://www.eibmarkt.com/cgi-bin/eibmarkt.storefront/DE/Product/NS6512716?PID=DE_NS6512716
https://www.domotiga.nl/projects/domotiga/wiki/Hardware_RaspberryPi
http://www.eelectron.com/it/prodotto/interfaccia-raspberry-pi-knx/?lang=en
https://www.hqs.sbt.siemens.com/cps_product_data/data/produktdb_en.htm
http://www.ugreen.com.cn/product-681-en.html

Tkinter

https://github.com/eliluminado/Guia-Tkinter/blob/master/Interfaz%20grafica%20con%20Tkinter.wiki
https://guia-tkinter.readthedocs.io/es/develop/
https://python-para-impacientes.blogspot.com/2016/07/animaciones-con-pyapng.html

Python

http://www.python.org
https://www.codecademy.com/catalog/subject/all
https://drive.google.com/drive/folders/0B-
EjJI8oLlmdZDRyMkM0UTNmZ00
https://plot.ly/python/
https://inventwithpython.com/es/7.html
http://acodigo.blogspot.com/2013/11/python-gui-
ventanas.html
https://linuxconfig.org/how-to-change-default-python-
version-on-debian-9-stretch-linux
https://packages.debian.org/stretch/all/python-
pychromecast/download

Telegram

https://web.telegram.org/
https://geekytheory.com/tutorial-raspberry-pi-uso-de-
telegram-con-python
https://www.fwhibbit.es/controla-tu-raspberry-pi-
mediante-telegram
https://www.atareao.es/tutorial/crea-tu-propio-bot-
para-telegram/bot-en-python-para-telegram/

KNX & Serial*

https://my.knx.org/
https://raspberrypi.stackexchange.com/questions/45570/

how-do-i-make-serial-work-on-the-raspberry-pi3-pi3b-pizerow
http://jjmilburn.github.io/2016/04/04/ttyUSB-to-vagrant-virtualbox/
http://vendomotica.com/imgcsv/Guia%20de%20programacion%20KNX(ES)_MWS3AKNX.pdf
http://www.futurasmus-knxgroup.es/
https://support.industry.siemens.com/cs/products/5wg1117-2ab12/-?pid=354073&dtp=Certificate&mlfb=5WG1117-2AB12&mfn=ps&lc=es-ES
https://cursodidacticoknx.wordpress.com/2-12-acuse-de-recibo/
https://blog.openalfa.com/instalacion-y-uso-de-eibd
https://github.com/weinzierl-engineering/baos
http://perso.wanadoo.es/pictob/comserie.htm
https://www.dehof.de/eib/DE/raspi.htm
https://www.bauwas.eu/?tag=raspberry
http://www.peatonet.com/raspberry-pi-y-los-pinesgpio-controlando-raspberry-a-traves-del-puerto-serie-de-consola/
https://pyserial.readthedocs.io/en/latest/pyserial_api.html
http://es.tldp.org/COMO-INSFLUG/COMOs/Terminales-Como/Terminales-Como-3.html
http://trasteandounpoco.blogspot.com/2007/12/interfaz-serie-rs232-knx-ft12-con.html
https://www.mac-usb-serial.com/docs/tutorials/serial-port-access-virtualbox-machines-running-mac-os-x.html
https://forums.virtualbox.org/viewtopic.php?t=26860
https://www.virtualbox.org/manual/ch03.html#serialports

NO-IP

https://www.noip.com/
https://www.realdroid.es/2016/10/29/configurar-no-ip-para-raspberry-pi-y-de-paso-que-es-no-ip/

Samba

https://www.samba.org/
https://www.naguissa.com/foro/i601/configurar-fstab-para-montar-unidades-de-windows-o-samba-automaticamente
https://www.atareao.es/tutorial/raspberry-pi-primeros-pasos/compartir-archivos-en-red-con-samba/

VNC

http://www.vnc.com/
https://geekytheory.com/tutorial-raspberry-pi-7-escritorio-remoto-vnc-no-ip/
https://www.realvnc.com/es/connect/docs/server-parameter-ref.html
https://librebit.github.io/raspberry/raspbian/vnc/server/2016/09/14/habilitar-vnc-server-en-raspberry-pi.html

PLEX

https://www.plex.tv/
https://thepi.io/how-to-set-up-a-raspberry-pi-plex-server/
https://www.codedonut.com/raspberry-pi/raspberry-pi-plex-media-server/

Google Home

https://store.google.com/es/product/google_home
https://medium.com/google-cloud/building-your-first-
action-for-google-home-in-30-minutes-ec6c65b7bd32
https://www.instructables.com/id/Google-Home-
Raspberry-Pi-Power-Strip/
https://www.sistemasorp.es/2018/08/07/ordenar-
comandos-a-un-robot-con-tu-propia-voz-y-el-altavoz-de-
google-home/
https://github.com/greghesp/assistant-relay
https://github.com/harperreed/google-home-notifier-
python

IFTTT

http://www.ifttt.com
https://ifttt.com/applets/85059471d-if-you-say-
enciende-luz-sofa-then-make-a-web-request
https://ifttt.com/services/maker_webhooks/settings
https://www.xatakahome.com/trucos-y-bricolaje-
smart/the-maker-channel-es-lo-mejor-que-le-ha-pasado-
a-ifttt-y-a-la-internet-de-las-cosas

Edimax

http://www.edimax.com/
https://github.com/bablokb/ediplug
https://github.com/wendlers/ediplug-py

*Various

http://www.portchecktool.com/
http://www.intranet-of-things.com/smarthome/infrastructure/knx/arduino/
https://www.calculadoraconversor.com/conversor-binario/
https://image.online-convert.com/convert-to-gif
http://www.findsounds.com/ISAPI/search.dll
https://developer.microsoft.com/en-us/microsoft-edge/tools/vms/
http://codigodiario.me/proteger-autenticacion-una-ruta-apache2/
https://www.enmimaquinafunciona.com/pregunta/536/puedes-pasarpase-de-usuario-para-la-autenticacion-basica-http-en-parametros-de-url

☉☉☉

34.–NEWS OF THIS EDITION

In this new edition of this book, the following topics have been added and or corrected and some improvements have been introduced.

Correction of typographical errors, general formats, margins, data tables, etc. Expansion of information in some sections.

New intuitive schemes of the operation and description of the project have been added.

New electrical diagrams of the most important systems and detailed mathematical calculations of the electrical variables in some of them.

Description of the automatic management of **Itead*** switches, **Sonoff*** model, with **Python*** modules without using **IFTTT*** and without hacking its firmware.

Improvements in **Python*** modules: contemplate actions according to summer or winter. Performance improvements on **Sonoff*** basic switches when using **Python*** modules instead of **IFTTT***.

Support for **Google Cast*** with two-way messages to control home automation states, general messages, barking simulation of the guard dog, general *.mp3 playback, etc.

File management in power outages.

Higher level of detail in sensors and actuators with several features and options.

Proposals for minimum and scaled solutions, from simple options to more complex, without the need to implement only global solutions.

Inclusion of **Chromecast*** as a multimedia and TV smart switch control device.

Final review of the **Google Cast*** process, in this edition an effective and 100% operational solution is presented in detail to get two-way voice control and *.mp3 file transmission.

Use of **Google Home*** to capture and respond by voice to questions about system variable status.

Finally, I want to take advantage of the present edition of this book to thank all the readers of the 1st edition for suggestions and contributions to correct, improve and be able to create this 2nd edition.

⊖⊕⊖

35.-GLOSSARY
OF TERMS

Term	Description
868	Low power consumption transmission system
1-Wire*	Serial communications protocol
2-Wire*	Circuit supporting transmission in 2 directions
3G/4G	3rd & 4th generation of mobile technology transmission system
4K	High definition TV format
6LowPAN	Low power wireless Personal Area Network
A/D	Analog/Digital converter
AC/DC	Alternating Current to Direct Current converter
Actuator	A device that causes a machine o other device to operate
ADS	Audio Digital System Fermax* protocol
AI	Artificial Intelligence
Alexa*	Amazon* assistant
Android*	Google* mobile operative system
Apache*	WEB server with open source for several platforms
APCI	Aplication Protocol Control Information
APP	Application abbreviation
Apple* TV	Apple digital multimedia receiver
Arduino*	Development platform based on a free hardware board

Term	Description
ARP	Address Resolution Protocol
ARC	Audio Return Channel HDMI protocol
ARM*	Advanced RISC* Machine
Asynchronous	Synchronisation process between sender and receiver is performed in each word
Bluetooth*	Industrial specification for wireless personal area networks
BOT	Computer program that automatically performs repetitive tasks
BotFather*	Telegram keys, aliases & permissions management
Bridge	Procedure connects two networks or groups of clients in cable networks
Broadlink*	RM* mini manufacturer
BTI	Bus Transceiver Interface
Bus	Digital system that transfers data between components
Buzz	Audio generator
C–NC	Closed–Normally Closed
CEC*	Consumer Electronics Control
Chromecast*	Google* portable device synchroniser
Chromium*	Google* free & open source web browser
Clock	Binary signal to coordinate the actions of several circuits
CO_2	Carbon dioxide
Colorama*	Module for displaying colour texts in LXTerminal* Raspbian* windows
Converter	Electronic device to transform an analog signal into a digital signal
CSMA/CA*	Carrier Sense Multiple Access with Collision Avoidance
Daemon	Program running in the background
DAT	Software–managed bidirectional serial protocol
Decoder	Receiver device and TV signal converter

Term	Description
DHCP	Dynamic Host Configuration Protocol
Differential	Electro mechanical device for the electrical protection of people
DIN	Standardised format in electrical installations
DLNA*	Digital Living Network Alliance
DNS*	Domain Name System
DSL*	Digital Subscriber Line
DUC*	Dynamic DNS* Update Client
DVI*	Digital Visual Interface (only video)
DYN*	Dynamic DNS* or DDNS*
Eagle*	Electronic Design Automation software
Edilife*	APP to control Edimax* devices
EIB*	European Installation Bus (currently KNX*)
EIS*	EIB* Interworking Standard KNX* protocol
Etcher*	Free & open source APP used to write image files
Ethernet*	Standard of local area networks for computers
ETS*	Engineering Tool Software (software for KNX* installations)
ext3	Third Extended Filesystem format
FAT32*	File Allocation Table with 32 bits
Fermax*	Electronic intercoms manufacturer
Finder*	Relays manufacturer
Fing*	To quickly know all the equipment connected to a network APP
Flip-flop	Multivibrator capable of remaining in one of two possible states
FreeDyn*	Software to update dynamic DNS*
Gateway	Device that acts as a connection interface between devices or computers
GIF	Graphics Interchange Format
Gigabit	Ethernet* standard that achieves 1 gigabit per second

Term	Description
Gmail*	Google* email service
Google Home*	Google* smart speaker with Artificial Intelligence
GPIO*	General Purpose Input Output
Handshake	Communication establishment protocol
HDMI*	High Definition Multimedia Interface
HGU*	Home Gateway Unit
Home*	Google* APP to Google Home* Mini management
Home automation	Set of techniques aimed at automating a home
http://	Hypertext Transfer Protocol
https://	Hypertext Transfer Protocol Secure
HUB	Network element used to connect several Ethernet* devices
I2C*	Inter-Integrated Circuit Raspberry* interface
iCircuit*	Electronic circuit simulation software
IDLE*	Integrated Development Environment for Python*
IFTTT*	If This Then That integrator software
IGMP*	Internet Group Management Protocol
IHC*	Broadlink RM* mini APP
Impedance	Apparent resistance of a circuit equipped with capacity & self-induction
Integrator	Software that manages interactions between applications or devices
Interface	Connection between devices or systems
iOS*	Apple* mobile operating system
IP	Internet Protocol address
IPScanner*	Software to know the IP of the devices connected to the network
IR	Infrared device
ISO	Exact image or copy of a file
Itead*	Sonoff* switches manufacturer
Kasa*	APP to control WIFI bulbs of TP-Link*

422

Term	Description
KNX*	Standard open world for the control of houses and buildings (before EIB*)
LAN	Local Area Network
LB100*	TP-Link* WIFI bulb
LED	Light-Emitting Diode
LXTerminal*	Terminal software integrated in Raspbian*
MAC	Media Access Control address
McAfee*	Antivirus software
MD5*	Message-Digest Algorithm 5 encryption management
Mesh	Wireless network with a single SSID
MHL	Mobile High-definition Link
MOSFET	Metal Oxide Semiconductor Field Effect transistor
NAS	Network Attached Storage
NAT	Network Address Translation
Netflix*	Multimedia content provider
NFC*	Near Field Communication
NGROK*	Software to access to the local server from the internet with dynamic URL
NO-IP DUC*	Dynamic DNS* Update Client for NO-IP* environment
NOOBS*	New Out Of Box Software to Raspberry* software installation
NPCI	Network Protocol Control Information
NPM	Node Package Manager
NPN	Transistor with N, P & N layers
ONT*	Optical Network Termination
Optocoupler	Light activated switch device
OSX*	Apple Operating System for computers
PCB	Printed Circuit Board
PCM	Pulse Code Modulation
PEI-10*	Physical External Interface of the Bus Coupling Unit with 10 pin on KNX* systems
PHP	Hypertext Preprocessor general purpose programming language

Term	Description
Piezoelectric	Electroacoustic transducer with piezoelectric crystal
Ping	Network diagnostic program
PLEX*	Multimedia content server
PNP	Transistor with P, N & P layers
Port	Router channel in which the sending of information is organised
Pycharm*	Professional Python* script editor
Python*	Interpreted programming language
Raspberry*	Micro computer created by the Raspberry* Foundation & based on ARM* technology
Raspbian*	Distribution of the Debian-based Linux* operating system
Relay	Electromagnetic switch
Retriggerable	Allows to reset the pulse with a new shot before completing the timing
Ripples*	Screensaver in Raspbian*
RISC*	Reduced Instruction Set Computer
RJ11	Connector used in telephone networks
RJ45	Connector used in computer networks
Router	Device to connect computers within a network
Routine	Script that contains a series of independent activities or instructions
RS232	Serial binary data communication interface
RTS/CTS	Request to Send/Clear to Send flow control signals
RxD	Receive Data
Samba*	Microsoft* file sharing protocol
Schmitt* trigger	Special type of electronic comparator and trigger
Sensor	Device that captures physical quantities
Server	Running application capable of responding to customer requests
Sodial*	Manufacturer of the logical level converter device ADUM1201*

424

Term	Description
Sonoff*	Itead* basic switch
Speedtest	Network speed test software
SPI*	Serial Peripheral Interface in Raspberry* device
SQL*	Structured Query Language used in programming to manage databases
SSH*	Secure Shell for remote access to a server
SSID	Server Set Identifier
STB	Set Top Box connection
Stretch*	Raspbian* version operating system
Switch	Device that allows diverting or interrupting the course of an electric current
Tadoº*	Electronic thermostat with geolocation
Tao-Glow*	Infrared colours lamp
TCP/UDP	Transmission Control Protocol/User Datagram Protocol
TCPI	Transport Protocol Control Information
Telegram*	Personal communication software
Terminal	Entry text mode application to Raspbian* system
Timeout	Pre-established maximum time to execute a process
Tkinter*	To create and locate software buttons on the screen
TP-Link*	LB100* WIFI bulb & WIFI extender manufacturer
Transistor	Electronic device to switching or amplify electronic signals
TTL	Transistor Transistor Logic
TxD	Transmit Data
UART*	Universal Asynchronous Receiver-Transmitter
Ubuntu*	Distribution of the Linux* operating system
Ugreen*	USB to Serial interface manufacturer

Term	Description
UHD*	Ultra High Definition, similar to 4K
UPS	Uninterruptible Power Supply
URL	Uniform Resource Locator
uSD	Micro Security Digital memory
Valve	Fluid regulation and control instrument
VDS**	Video Digital System Fermax* protocol
VirtualBox*	Software for virtualisation several operating systems
VNC*	Virtual Network Computing
WAP*	Wireless Application Protocol
Watchdog	Electronic flow control circuit
WD*	Western Digital* manufacturer
Webhook*	Method of altering the operation of a web page
WIFI	Wireless Fidelity
Workgroup	Working group in a Microsoft* network protocol
x bauds	Symbol (1 or more bits) per second
x bps	Bits per second
x cm	Centimetres
x dB	Decibels
x fps	Frames per second
x Hz	Hertz
x mA	Mili amperes
x uF	Micro farads
x v	Volts
x w	Watts
x Ω	Ohm
Xscreensaver*	Screensaver on Raspbian*
ZIP	Lossless file compression format

⊖⊖⊖

Thank you very much for purchasing and especially for reading this book. My intention was always to help and share experiences with other people like you.

I hope you liked it and any suggestions I would appreciate if you indicated it on my blog.

gregochenlo.blogspot.com

Thank you very much again.

www.ingramcontent.com/pod-product-compliance
Lightning Source LLC
Chambersburg PA
CBHW051044050326
40690CB00006B/590